THE PROCESSING OF
INFORMATION AND STRUCTURE

THE EXPERIMENTAL PSYCHOLOGY SERIES

Arthur W. Melton · Consulting Editor

THE PROCESSING OF INFORMATION AND STRUCTURE

BY WENDELL R. GARNER

YALE UNIVERSITY

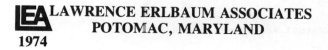 LAWRENCE ERLBAUM ASSOCIATES
POTOMAC, MARYLAND
1974

DISTRIBUTED BY THE HALSTED PRESS DIVISION OF

JOHN WILEY & SONS
New York   Toronto   London   Sydney

Lawrence Erlbaum Associates, Publishers
12736 Lincolnshire Drive
Potomac, Maryland 20854

Distributed solely by Halsted Press Division
John Wiley & Sons, Inc., New York.

Library of Congress Cataloging in Publication Data

Garner, Wendell R.
  The processing of information and structure.

  (The Experimental psychology series)
  1. Human information processing. I. Title.
II. Series. [DNLM: 1. Information theory.
2. Psychology. BF455 G234p 1974]
BF455.G18   153.7   73–22174
ISBN 0–470–29233–4

Printed in the United States of America

CONTENTS

THE PAUL M. FITTS
MEMORIAL LECTURES
DELIVERED AT
THE UNIVERSITY OF MICHIGAN
ANN ARBOR, MICHIGAN
MARCH, 1973

PREFACE

In April, 1971 I received a letter from Arthur W. Melton at the University of Michigan in which he invited me to give the second series of Paul M. Fitts Memorial Lectures. I was both flattered and pleased to do so for several reasons. First, and by far most important, I had known Paul Fitts and had greatly admired his work. We had, in fact, worked very much in the same tradition, both of us being concerned with performance aspects of perception, and with applications of our research outside the academic world. So I felt especially honored to give a series of lectures bearing his name, and I hope that this book, resulting from these lectures, will honor Paul Fitts in a way that he would have appreciated. His death was indeed tragically too soon.

Second, the first series of Fitts lectures had been given by Donald E. Broadbent, and they resulted in his book *Decision and Stress*. That book shares also the traditions of concern with performance aspects of perception and concern with the real world. So I felt pleased to be able to further an emphasis which Donald Broadbent had already established.

Third, the invitation gave me the impetus to do something I had been wanting to do anyway, namely, pull together the several threads of research I and my coworkers had been carrying out for the past decade or so. The year-by-year process of research often obscures the general themes and the longer-term goals, even though these themes and goals actually exist. It takes the format of a book to pull them together.

The Lectures are intended to be given every three years and mine were in fact delivered at Ann Arbor in March, 1973, two years after the invitation arrived. The intervening years were spent preparing them, and the time since then in modifying and expanding them. This book contains the lectures essentially as given, except that I was able, of course, to add material for the printed version. Even though I had time to change the style from the lecture form, I decided to keep that form. The material was in fact prepared for the lecture style, and I found that I appreciated the latitude of discourse which the less formal lecture style allowed me. So in this book I sound as though I am speaking the lectures, and that is intended. I hope that the freedom of expression this style gave me does not detract from its comprehension by those who read the material rather than listen to it. And I hope that having the chapters labeled Lectures, because each chapter does correspond to one lecture, will not confuse the reader unduly.

It is inevitable that I contrast this volume with my previous book *Uncertainty and Structure as Psychological Concepts,* published in 1962. In the Preface to that book, I disclaimed it as a book on information theory in psychology, even though I did make heavy use of some mathematical derivations which came from formal information theory. This book is even less directly related to information theory, and that fact represents, I think, a healthy advance. This book does use the basic idea of information as number of alternatives, and the concept of redundancy, but little else from formal information theory. We are now less concerned with the quantity of information, a concept that information theory did give us, and are more concerned with the specifics of information and structure. For example, the ideas of dimensional integrality, and the distinction between state and process, are concerned with the specific nature of psychological information and not with the amount of it.

Another change from 1962 can be noted by my expression of thanks for the help my research has received since 1965 from the National Institute of Mental Health, and from the Office of Naval Research before that. NIMH Grant 14229 to Yale University is titled *The Perception of Structure.* My earlier work was indeed more concerned with perception of structure, but much of my later work has been concerned with the processing of both information and structure; thus the title of this book. This emphasis on processing, the concern for what the organism does with information and structure, is especially strong in the second, fourth, sixth, and seventh lectures.

One last comment about changes in my research over the past ten years: The importance of the idea of converging operations has become much greater for me. I, along with Harold Hake and Charles Eriksen, expanded and illustrated in 1956 the concept of converging operations, which I had more briefly mentioned two years earlier. At that time I certainly felt that it was an important principle in my own metascience; in reviewing research both of my own and others for these lectures, I came to realize that I now consider it the major aspect of my own scientific methodology. This point is discussed at some length in the last lecture.

There are many people who are important in preparing a manuscript for publication. The typing was done by Maggie Davis, and by Elizabeth Poor before her; thanks are extended happily to both. But the other thanks go primarily to the many students and colleagues who have participated in the research reported here. Without their collaboration the research would not have been done, and I think it is almost needless to say that. But I shall not attempt to mention them all by name here. Rather, the reporting of their research in this book is my way of acknowledging my debt to them. The debt is real, as I hope they will all understand.

W. R. G.

November, 1973

THE PROCESSING OF
INFORMATION AND STRUCTURE

LECTURE 1
STIMULUS SETS, SUBSETS, AND PATTERN GOODNESS

INTRODUCTION

In this series of lectures I am going to describe research and ideas which have developed over the past decade on the general topic of the perception and processing of stimulus structure. Even though many laboratories have contributed to the research I shall describe, these lectures will be very much a personal statement, leaning most heavily on research done in my own laboratories, with the very active and valuable assistance of students and other collaborators. The main thrust of the research I shall describe was pretty well generated by my book, *Uncertainty and Structure as Psychological Concepts,* published just twelve years ago (1962). In that book the idea of structure as a key psychological concept evolved, primarily in the context of information theory and with the mathematics of multivariate uncertainty analysis. The idea of structure has remained a key concept in most of the research I shall describe, although its dependence on the specific mathematical formulations used in that book has lessened considerably.

Research on all aspects of perception and information processing has become increasingly complex in recent years, more complicated because today we psychologists make meaningful distinctions of a subtlety considered unnecessary, or even improper, just a few years ago. Perception, as Garner, Hake, and Eriksen argued in 1956, occurs in the head, somewhere between the stimulus and the response which are available for direct observation by the psychological experimenter. Furthermore, what goes on in the head is processing, of many different kinds; so the response is not to be considered as a simple representation of the stimulus. These processes that occur in the head need not be relegated to the territory of the unknown, however, since with sufficient ingenuity we psychologists can devise and carry out experiments which provide converging operations to tell us about the properties of that which cannot be observed directly.

Before getting more deeply into the specific subject of these lectures, I would like to comment a bit on three aspects of our research problem—first, the stimulus set which is used by the experimenter; second, the task specified by the experimenter for the subject, which ordinarily consists of the experimenter defining the set of possible responses and the mapping of these responses onto the stimulus set; and third, the processing mechanisms which the experimenter hypothesizes or imputes to the subject in trying to explain the empirical result obtained in an experiment.

Stimulus Structure

First, consider the stimulus; and for me the important concept is that of stimulus structure. Structure, according to one dictionary, is a complex system considered from the point of view of the whole rather than of any single part. That will serve us quite well as a very general definition. However, it is not a simple concept, and many different kinds of structure can and do exist and are important to the human organism's perception. Throughout these lectures we will be concerned with different kinds of structure: for example, dimensional structure, correlational structure, or structure based on similarities. To say that structure is a property of the whole rather than of the part is only a very crude beginning, because we need to determine exactly what properties of the whole are relevant to the perceiving organism.

There are some general points about structure which should be made early. Information and structure are to me essentially identical terms, and they refer to that property of a stimulus which is processed or perceived. In this matter I am agreeing with James Gibson (1966) in differentiating the informational properties of a stimulus from its energic properties. While this distinction between the stimulus as energy and the stimulus as information or structure is very general, in some of the research I shall report it assumes a very specific role, since it differentiates alternative ways in which stimulus redundancy can affect discrimination performance. Stimulus energy provides activation of the sense organ, but it is stimulus information or structure that provides meaning and is pertinent to what I would call perception.

However, this distinction between stimulus energy and stimulus information should not obscure a very important fact, namely, that structure and information are every bit as much properties of the stimulus as are energic variables. They can be defined entirely independently of the organism under study and can exist without an organism's existence. This is not to say that an organism will not impose structure on a stimulus if none exists in it, or at least none that an organism can perceive and use. What the Gestalt psychologists called autochthonous perceptual factors are real enough. For example, if a series of clicks with no variation in time, intensity, or any other measurable stimulus property is presented to a subject, it will nevertheless be heard as a series of clicks grouped in time. But the fact that the organism can impose structure does not mean that doing so is its usual or only mode of dealing with structure, or that structure is strictly an organismic property. Structure exists in the stimulus, and our experimental task is to determine when it can be perceived, used, cr processed, and which kinds of structure are in fact used. So our experiments often involve variations in type of stimulus structure as an important and critical aspect of research on the processing of structure.

Intrinsic and extrinsic structure. One distinction about structure, important for our purposes, needs to be made, and that is between intrinsic and extrinsic structure. Intrinsic structure is that inherent in the stimulus itself. It is the structure of stimulus properties, and these stimulus properties are those which can be defined independently of a user-organism. Extrinsic structure occurs when the stimulus denotes or signifies something other than itself, and these significations themselves have structure.

To illustrate, consider a set of printed letters. The optical and geometric properties of these letters form the intrinsic structure. However, each letter has a phonetic representation, one which is completely arbitrary, but thoroughly learned by the usual subject in our perceptual experiments. The phonetic representations can have a structure of their own, and this structure would clearly be extrinsic. Furthermore, the letters can be put together to form words, and these words refer to real objects, concepts, and actions. The structure of these significations would again constitute extrinsic structure, while the optical and geometric properties of the printed words would form the intrinsic structure.

In the main, the research to be reported here is concerned with intrinsic stimulus structure, which is to say that I will not be concerned to any great extent with extrinsic stimulus structure, nor with structure imposed by the organism. My primary interest in the perceiving organism is in its selection and utilization of structure inherent in the directly perceivable stimulus.

Task Demands

The experimenting psychologist decides what stimuli will be presented to the human subject. He then also instructs the subject what is to be done with the stimuli presented to him. In other words, the experimenter sets the task. He may ask the subject to discriminate the stimuli from each other, as fast or as accurately as possible; he may ask the subject to learn classifications of them, as in concept tasks; he may ask the subject to remember them for another day; or he may ask the subject to judge the apparent similarity of pairs of stimuli. What is the effect of different kinds of structure on performance when such very different tasks are required of the subject?

Well, structure is not just good or bad in general. Whether structure improves or degrades performance depends on what the particular structure is and what the subject is required to do with it. I have made this general point before (Garner, 1962) but can only emphasize it again. The psychologist's goal is to determine what kinds of structure are good for what kinds of task, and to be as analytic as possible about finding out why, but not to attempt a simplistic answer to an overly simplistic question. The question is not simple, nor can our answers be.

In recent years we (my collaborators and I) have come increasingly to use experimental tasks that are less constraining to the subject. Since we accept the position that structure is in the stimulus, but that the subject may use some kinds and not others, or may not even be able to perceive some kinds at all, then it is only natural that we should use techniques that allow the subject as much freedom as possible to tell us which structure he perceives. Thus we have used free classification, where the subject simply forms classes from a set of stimuli, in several experiments. And we have used simple stimulus description in much of our work on temporal pattern perception, since we want to know what structure is perceived by the subject from the many alternatives available to him.

By no means do we use such techniques exclusively. Frequently they are simply inappropriate. But we have discovered that such techniques often yield answers much more quickly than the indirect techniques so common to American psychology, wherein the task is completely constraining on the subject and we measure how difficult or how easy a given task is compared to another. For example, nearly all concept research has used such indirect techniques, with the result that much about dimensional salience or preference has not been discovered. As we have learned, it is always necessary to distinguish between what a subject can do and what he would do if given no constraint. Differentiations with the free-performance tasks are frequently much more sensitive and precise than with constrained tasks.

Processing Mechanisms

The experimenter, having used particular stimuli with their own properties, and having decided what task the subject must engage in, then tries to understand why the results come out as they do. We are not content to state that this task leads to a favorable use of this kind of structure, and that task to an inability to use a particular structure; we want to know why, and the why ordinarily requires that we understand, in addition to the properties of the stimuli and those of the task, different processing mechanisms which the subject can use in carrying out the task. If we are very ingenious in constructing our tasks, we might manage to have one task correspond to each possible processing mechanism. But we are rarely that ingenious, or the fates which decide such matters for us rarely make our scientific lives that simple. So we have to construct hypothetical mechanisms whose properties are understood from a series of pertinent experiments.

Some of the processing mechanisms which can be used are the selection of information, the integration of information, the holding of a set of stimuli in memory, the encoding of stimuli into a different form or even into a form appropriate to a different modality, and the numeric estimation of magnitudes of stimuli. In other words, the results of our experiments are not to be understood in terms of a single internal mechanism called perception or processing. The organism is complex, has many mechanisms available to it, and will ordinarily use those most appropriate to the stimuli and the task demands. It is our task to try to determine what these mechanisms are, and what their properties are. We do not hold to the idea of an empty organism. Our organism is perhaps still a black box, but it is a black box filled with many different and fascinating mechanisms.

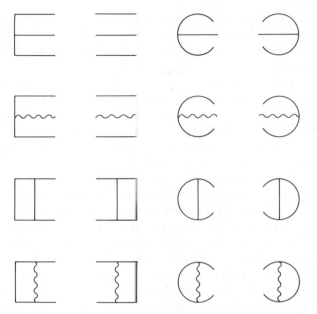

FIG. 1.1. A total set of 16 stimuli formed from four dichotomous dimensions: (circle or square) × (open on the left or right) × (vertical or horizontal center line) × (wavy or straight center line).

STRUCTURE, TOTAL SETS, AND SUBSETS

The first topic I shall discuss is that of pattern goodness and its relation to the idea of inferred subsets of stimuli. To introduce and develop the idea of inferred subsets, let me outline in a general fashion the ideas of dimensional structure and correlational structure (or redundancy) and their corollary ideas of total sets and subsets of stimuli. The connection I shall demonstrate between pattern goodness and inferred sets of stimuli comes about because pattern goodness is related to the informational concept of redundancy, but that concept itself can be seen as specified by the relative sizes of subset and total set of stimuli. What I shall be demonstrating is that the critical aspect of redundancy pertinent to pattern goodness (and to other aspects of pattern perception as well) is this idea of subset size, either real or inferred.

Dimensional Structure and Total Sets

Figure 1.1 will help to develop these relationships.[1] In this illustration there are 16 different visual stimuli constructed by producing all possible combinations of four stimulus dimensions, each dimension having two possible values or levels. These stimuli are either circles or squares, so form is one dimension; they are open on the left or on the right, so position of the opening is a second dimension; each has a center line which is either vertical or horizontal, so position of the

[1]Figures 1.1, 1.2, 1.3, 1.4, 1.7, 1.8, 1.9, 1.10, 1.11, and 1.14 are reproduced from Garner (1970) with permission from the *American Scientist*.

center line is a third dimension; and the center line is either wavy or straight, giving us a fourth dimension. Now with four two-leveled dimensions, 16 and only 16 stimuli can be formed, this number being the product of the number of levels of each dimension: $2 \times 2 \times 2 \times 2 = 16$.

This set of 16 stimuli constitutes a *total set* because it contains all the stimuli that can be generated with these particular dimensions and levels. If there were additional perceivable dimensions, or more than two levels on any of the dimensions, these 16 stimuli would not be a total set. The point is that to say a set of stimuli constitutes a total set assumes the contextual understanding that there are no other pertinent dimensions or levels of variation. Even a total set has only contextual or relational meaning, because as soon as another dimension of variation is introduced, the ground rules for defining the total set have changed.

But just as the existence of a number of dimensions and levels defines a total set, so also does the existence of a total set define a dimensional structure. In a very real sense the total set and the dimensional structure define each other.

This idea of stimuli being defined in terms of dimensional structure is now fairly common, certainly being a major consideration in the work of such psychologists as Eleanor Gibson (1969) and Ulric Neisser (1967), although they tend to talk about features rather than dimensions. Features are, in the present language, equivalent to the levels on a dimension. However, here I am trying to emphasize the interplay between the stimulus dimensions and the set of stimuli which they define. If organisms perceive features, or dimensions and their levels, then there is always the consequence of a defined *set* of stimuli, and this set enters into the perception of each stimulus within it.

Redundancy and Subsets

Let us now consider what happens when we select various subsets of stimuli from this total set. We might first consider the almost trivial case in which we select all eight stimuli which are squares. This case is trivial because such a selection simply defines a smaller total set and a new dimensional structure. That point is important enough, but does not develop the idea of redundancy.

Figure 1.2 shows a more meaningful subset of eight stimuli. In this subset, all four dimensions of variation are still represented, and furthermore, each level of each dimension occurs in exactly half of the stimuli. What has happened? The answer is that two of the dimensions are correlated. For these eight stimuli, the square is always open on the right and the circle on the left. Since the form and position of opening are correlated, clearly we can dispense with either of them and still have eight different stimuli. So we have a redundant dimension. It is not clear which of the two dimensions is the redundant one, since we could get along without either (but not both). But the important point is that the selection of a subset from a total set creates redundancy, and this redundancy exists in the form of a correlation between two dimensions. This correlation is itself a kind of structure, one

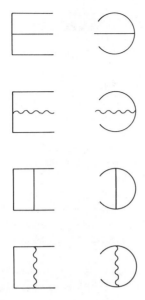

FIG. 1.2. A redundant subset of eight stimuli. In this subset, the redundancy is due to (or produces) a correlation between form and position of the opening: The square is always open on the right, and the circle is open on the left.

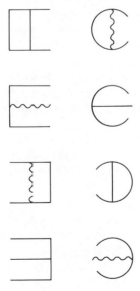

FIG. 1.3. Another redundant subset of eight stimuli. In this subset, no pair of dimensions is correlated, yet any single dimension of variation can be removed, and there will still be eight different stimuli.

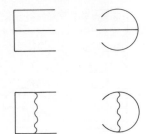

FIG. 1.4. A redundant subset of four stimuli. In this subset, two pairs of dimensions are correlated: Form is correlated with position of the opening, and the direction and nature of the center line are correlated. Thus two dimensions are redundant.

which exists definably in the subset of stimuli, and which may or may not be perceived by a human subject. So redundancy is correlational structure and exists in a set of stimuli whenever we can define that set of stimuli as a subset from a larger, total set of stimuli.

Whether this correlational structure can be perceived or used by a human organism is a proper experimental question. That it is so, and that redundancy can be defined as a stimulus property independently of the perceiving organism, can be seen in Fig. 1.3. This is another subset of eight stimuli, and once again each dimension from the total set is represented, and each level on each dimension occurs exactly half the time. In this case, however, no pair of dimensions is correlated. But inspection of the figures will reveal that redundancy does exist, since we can remove any one of the dimensions of variation and there will still be eight different stimuli in the set. For example, if all squares were made circles, the eight stimuli would still all be different. But if no pair of dimensions is correlated, does correlational structure exist? The answer is still yes, but the correlation is a partial one, and in this particular illustration it is a double partial correlation. To illustrate, if we hold form and position of the opening constant, then the nature and direction of the center line are correlated. Note the two upper squares, each with the opening on the right. Now the vertical line is straight and the horizontal line is wavy. This is the form of structure that I have previously (Garner, 1962) described as a four-term interaction uncertainty, but the existence of redundancy with a complicated form of correlational structure can be seen without recourse to the formal mathematical proof.

So correlational structure exists in this subset of stimuli. But, as we shall see later, such structure is not easily perceived or used in many perceptual tasks.

Now consider a smaller subset of stimuli, shown in Fig. 1.4. In this illustration there are just four stimuli in the subset. Each dimension of variation, and each level, are still represented equally often. The redundancy in this case consists of two different correlations between stimulus dimensions: The square is always open on the right, and the circle is open on the left, so these two dimensions are correlated and one is redundant; in addition, the vertical line is always wavy while the horizontal line is straight, so these two dimensions are also correlated and one can be considered redundant. Once again, we cannot say which is redundant, since either is. But for the subset of four stimuli, clearly two dimensions can be eliminated without making any two stimuli identical.

The point of this last illustration is to demonstrate that the *amount* of redundancy is greater the smaller the subset of stimuli from the same total set. If a subset exists at all, redundancy exists, although the correlational structure may be complicated. But the smaller the subset, the greater the amount of redundancy, regardless of the nature of the correlations that can be considered to be the locus of the redundancy.

The Nature of a Stimulus

These illustrations clearly demonstrate that structure is a specifiable and even measurable property of the stimulus, or more properly, of sets of stimuli. But what about the single stimulus in this picture? Does the stimulus have no intrinsic meaning of its own, or does it simply exist to provide structure (and thus intrinsic meaning) for the sets in which it exists? The answer to this question is that the properties of the single stimulus cannot be specified except in relation to the properties of the sets within which it exists. The properties of the total set and the subset in which a stimulus exists are at once the properties of each stimulus within the sets. Thus, if we want to understand how the single stimulus is perceived, we must understand how the set of stimuli is perceived. To illustrate, refer to the total set of stimuli in Fig. 1.1. It is impossible to describe any one of these figures without using the dimensional structure which only the total set can provide. For example, we would not ordinarily describe any of these figures in terms of its spatial location, since that is not a relevant dimension of variation for the total set. But then how can any single stimulus be defined in terms other than the structure of the total set, and the subset as well? Notice, for example, that as soon as two dimensions are correlated, the meaning of these dimensions in the stimulus has changed. So there is no real awkwardness here unless any of you thinks he can describe a single stimulus without a reference set. It cannot be done.

An excellent experimental illustration of some of these points concerning the nature of a stimulus is provided in recent research by Mavrides (1970). Her experimental task was a direct judgment of perceptual difference of pairs of stimuli on a 7-point rating scale. She used all possible pairs of 12 different stimuli for judgment. Her stimuli were star-like figures (pointed cones extending from an inner circle) varying in five ways: the radius of the smallest enclosing circle, the number of points, the depths of the points of the star, the exterior interpoint angle, and the interior point angle. (Each of these dimensions of variation was used with several degrees of differentiation.) She obtained correlations of these various physical measures of the stimulus with the psychological (i.e., judged) differences as her primary experimental measure.

The first result of interest is that not all of these physical dimensions were used equally by the subjects. The diameter of the smallest enclosing circle (as a measure of overall size) did not correlate at all with the judgments of differences. Of the other four measures, clearly two of them were most important in the judgments, namely, the number of points in the star, and the exterior interpoint angle (indicating the sharpness of the points). Thus over the entire set of judgments, the dimensional structure of this set of stimuli as used by the subjects was not identical to that provided by the experimenter. In effect, the size of the total set used by the subjects was smaller than that provided by the stimuli as seen from the point of view of the experimenter. So this experiment showed what aspects of the stimulus structure were in fact used by the subjects.

But the second result, of even greater interest, is this: For each pair of stimuli presented to the subject, one dimension provided the maximum differentiation. If a measure for this maximally differentiating dimension is correlated with the judged stimulus difference, it turns out to be as strong a predictor as either of the two best overall predictors. What this result shows is that the immediately presented subset of two stimuli determines the perceived properties of the stimuli in it, and the perceived properties of any single stimulus change as that stimulus is variously paired with other stimuli, since the dimension which maximally differentiates a pair of stimuli depends on the particular pair of stimuli involved.

Mavrides talks of this factor as involving selective attention. The subject presumably attends most to the most differentiating variable on a particular pair of stimuli. But the point for the moment is that the properties of a single stimulus are at once the properties of the perceived total set and also the subset within which the stimulus is immediately contained. Within this experimental context this point seems almost self-evident. Yet it needs emphasizing that information and structure are properties of sets of stimuli, and while the individual stimulus certainly has meaning, that meaning derives from its location in relevant sets and subsets.

It is worth finally remarking on this matter that herein lies the difference between informational and energic properties of stimuli. Some stimuli need have no such relevant reference group to be effective. If you are burned by picking up a hot coal, you need no reference group, no total set or subset, to respond appropriately. No change in the number or nature of alternative stimuli will affect your reaction to the pain of the burn, and that is as it should be. There really is a difference between the energic and informational properties of stimuli, and that difference is that the energic properties can be responded to as isolated stimuli, with no need of a reference set, while informational properties give no meaning to the individual stimulus until the reference group has been specified.

PATTERN GOODNESS

Now let us refer more specifically to the Gestalt concept of figural or pattern goodness and the structural property of redundancy, the idea to test being that pattern goodness is correlated with pattern redundancy. The information-theoretic concept of redundancy has long had an appeal to psychologists as an explanatory principle for the concept of goodness, since good figures seem to be those with regularities, with simplicity, with predictability, and all of these certainly are part of what one means by redundancy. With information theory at hand, we should be able to measure the actual amount of redundancy, but this amount pertains to sets of stimuli, not individual stimuli, so how do we relate the two concepts of goodness and redundancy?

The answer lies in understanding two points: First, as we have seen, redundancy is related to the *size* of a subset of stimuli. For a given size of total set, the smaller the subset, the more redundant the subset is. So if a given stimulus exists in a small subset, it is more redundant insofar as it has the properties of that subset. A stimulus in a larger subset would be less redundant, although such a comparison is valid only with the assumption of the same size of total set.

The second point is that any single stimulus can produce an *inferred subset* on the part of the perceiving human. This is not really a strained idea at all, nor is it discrepant with the notion that the properties of the single stimulus are at once the properties of the subset and total set within which it exists. Think once again of the stimuli I have been using as an illustration. Suppose that we present just one of them to you, the one that looks like an upper case E. You do not know the total set of stimuli, much less the particular subset. Nevertheless, you immediately perceive that E as a member of a set. Perhaps you assume that five straight lines are the components of the stimulus—the four outside lines plus the horizontal center line. If you also assume that each line can exist or not exist, then there are 31 positive stimuli (excluding the one with all lines missing) and you have an inferred set of stimuli, the inference being based on the single stimulus. Alternatively, you might have assumed that the set of possible stimuli consisted of all the letters of the alphabet, or just the subset of vowels. To illustrate how easily the single stimulus can lead to a different inferred subset, consider this same stimulus reversed so that it looks like the numeral 3. Now no inference of a set of letters would be made, but possibly an inference of a set of numerals would be made.

So a single stimulus can lead to an inferred set and subset of stimuli. This inference is clearly the consequence of the stimulus properties of the single stimulus, but remember that these stimulus properties are meaningful only insofar as they are perceived as the dimensions that define a set of stimuli. Our experimental problem in this case is to investigate the properties of stimuli that lead to different inferred sets of stimuli. Even better, we would like to understand how the same stimulus can lead to an inference of both a total set and a subset, because then we would have the complete tie-in between the goodness of a particular stimulus form or pattern and the concept of redundancy.

Does the fact that a stimulus is perceived as a member of a set of stimuli mean that only with experience can humans perceive single stimuli as meaningful objects, because only with experience can the organism know the nature and kinds of dimensions of variation which are possible? I do not presume to know fully the answer to this question. Certainly there are many cases where specific experience is important in determining the nature of a stimulus set, the set of alphanumeric symbols, for example. Yet it seems to me quite possible that some stimuli have properties which lead to inferred subsets with little need for, or effect of, prior experience. I think that the dot patterns we have used as research stimuli are of this sort.

Goodness of Dot Patterns and Size of Subset

The first research undertaken to test the notion of inferred subsets in relation to pattern goodness was done by Garner and Clement (1963). The stimuli used consisted of five dots placed in the imaginary cells of a 3 × 3 matrix, as illustrated by 17 prototypical patterns shown in Fig. 1.5. There are 120 such stimuli possible, although only 90 were used in this experiment. The patterns which were not used were those in which either a row or column was left vacant, since we felt that without the lines marking off the cells it might be difficult to perceive these patterns in correct spatial location. (Subsequent research showed this to have been an unfounded fear.) These patterns were drawn on white cards 3-inches square, with the dot pattern centered in the card, the dots themselves separated by 1/4 inch. These dimensions are not in fact very critical. Nor is the use of dots, since the entire experiment was replicated with patterns of X's and O's (the X's replacing the dots, and the O's replacing the vacant cells) with identical results.

Two groups of subjects were required to perform two separate tasks. One task was to make a goodness rating for each of the 90 patterns, and subjects rated the goodness on a scale from 1 to 7, with 1 being the best pattern and 7 being the poorest. The other task was a free classification in which each subject sorted all 90 patterns into groups according to a similarity criterion. Subjects were allowed

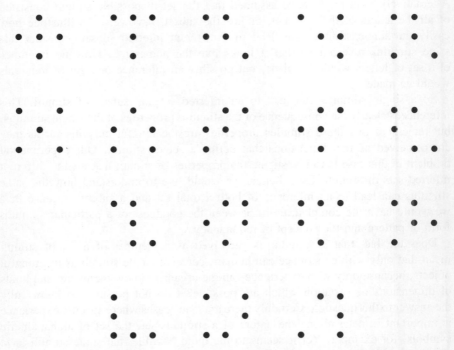

Fig. 1.5. Prototypical patterns used by Garner and Clement (1963). Subjects were required either to rate the goodness of such patterns or to sort them into groups according to a similarity criterion.

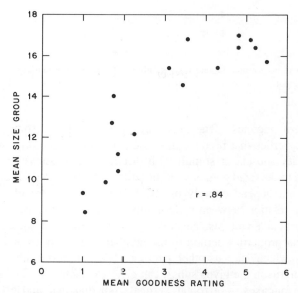

FIG. 1.6. The relation between rated goodness and size of group sorted, for the 17 prototypical patterns in Fig. 1.5. (Data from Garner and Clement, 1963.)

to use as many groups as they liked, but it was suggested that they use approximately eight. The groups did not have to be of equal size.

There were two measures of interest to us in this experiment: the mean goodness rating for each of the 90 patterns, and the mean size of the group that each pattern was placed in with the free classification. If in fact subjects used groups of equal size, this measure would have been useless, but they actually produced groups varying greatly in size. The hypothesis under test, of course, says that these two measures—both of them behavioral—should be correlated across all patterns.

Figure 1.6 shows that they are indeed correlated. The data given are for the prototypical patterns shown in Fig. 1.5, but they would look similar if data for all 90 patterns were shown. Mean goodness ratings ranged from about 8 to 17, a good spread on this measure as well. The overall correlation between these two measures was .84, the kind of correlation that left no doubt as to the initial validity of the idea being tested, namely, that good figures are perceived as being in small subsets and poor figures as being in large subsets. Thus pattern goodness and redundancy (measured indirectly as subset size) are indeed related, and in a way that is logically sensible.

Rotations and Reflections

So far these results simply show that two behavioral measures—one related directly to pattern goodness, and the other indirectly to pattern redundancy—are correlated. We do not know what specific properties of these particular stimuli lead to small or large inferred subsets, and thus presumably to differences in

FIG. 1.7. Two patterns forming unique R & R subsets. Each of these patterns simply reproduces itself if reflected about any axis or if rotated in 90° steps. The rated goodness of these patterns is excellent.

perceived pattern goodness. The next step is to search for some indication of the stimulus properties that produce this result. Or, put differently, what stimulus properties specify subsets of stimuli with different sizes, such that the different sizes are related to the rated goodness of the patterns? If we can find such properties, then we need not depend entirely on the behavioral measure of subset size to demonstrate the relation between pattern goodness and redundancy.

For these particular patterns, generated as they were in a square matrix, two obvious physical properties pertain to the number of reflections and 90° rotations of the patterns which lead to other patterns. We can form subsets of patterns in which all patterns in the given subset can generate each other by being reflected about any of the four axes—horizontal, vertical, right diagonal, and left diagonal—or by being rotated in 90° steps. In actual fact, as we shall see in a moment, these two stimulus properties are closely related, so we shall use them together as a single stimulus factor, and the subsets specified by the operations of rotation and reflection we shall call R & R subsets as a kind of shorthand. R & R subsets for these stimuli occur with sizes of 1, 4, or 8 patterns per subset. Thus we have a meaningful stimulus measure, one which generates subsets of different sizes, and the question is whether these subset sizes are related to the behavioral measure of pattern goodness.

Figure 1.7 shows two of these patterns, each of which forms a unique R & R subset, that is, a subset with just one member. Each of these patterns simply produces itself again if rotated in any number of 90° steps, or if reflected on itself about the vertical, the horizontal, or either diagonal axis, or if any combination of rotations and reflections is used. It is obvious that these are very good patterns, and in fact the rated goodness obtained in the actual experiment was 1.01. So these patterns with a subset size of 1 are very redundant and are rated as very good patterns.

Four more patterns are shown in Fig. 1.8, and these four patterns form a single R & R subset of four members. The pattern on the left is rotated in successive 90° steps to produce each of the other three patterns. As noted before, however, the rotation and reflection operations are intimately interrelated. The first pattern on the left is the reflection of the last pattern about a vertical axis. The first two patterns are reflections of each other about the horizontal axis. The first and third patterns are reflections of each other about the left diagonal axis, and the second and fourth patterns are reflections of each other about the right diagonal axis. But the essential point here is simply that these four patterns are in some sense the equivalent of each other: They form a subset of 4.

FIG. 1.8. An R & R subset of four patterns. Each of these patterns can form any of the others by the appropriate reflections and/or rotations. Thus they form a single R & R subset.

Altogether there are eight such R & R subsets of four patterns, for a total of 32 of the 90 patterns used in the experiment. A prototype of each of these patterns is shown in Fig. 1.9. The experimental result is that the 32 patterns represented by these eight prototypes were given an average goodness rating of 2.23. So with larger, thus less redundant, subsets, the pattern goodness is in fact poorer, although still fairly good.

Figure 1.10 shows still another R & R subset of patterns, this time with eight members in it. The pattern at the top left is rotated clockwise in 90° steps across the top. Each of the patterns on the top row is then reflected about its vertical axis to produce the pattern on the bottom row. Once again, however, the interrelations between the rotation and reflection criteria are intricate. For example, the top left pattern and the second pattern from the right on the bottom are reflections of each other about the horizontal axis. And the top left pattern is the reflection of the second pattern from the left on the bottom about its left diagonal axis. But the important point once again is that this is a larger, and thus even less redundant, subset. Altogether there are seven R & R subsets of eight patterns each, and a prototype of each of them is shown in Fig. 1.11. The mean goodness rating for these 56 patterns was 4.76, indicating quite poor patterns on the average.

Thus the point is made that redundancy, seen as related to the size of subsets of patterns, is indeed connected to the idea of pattern goodness. Good patterns exist in small subsets and are thus very redundant. Poor patterns exist in large subsets and are thus not very redundant. This result has been shown with a behavioral measure of subset size, and for these particular patterns it can be shown to hold

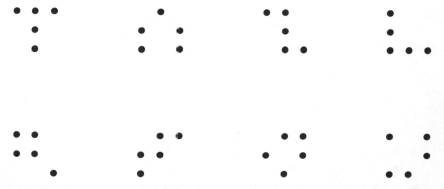

FIG. 1.9. Each of these patterns is one from R & R subsets of four patterns, since each can form three other patterns when rotated and/or reflected. Their rated goodness is intermediate.

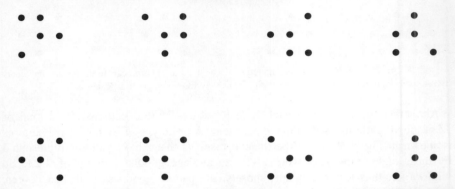

FIG. 1.10. An R & R subset of eight patterns. Each of these patterns can form any of the others by the appropriate reflections and/or rotations. Thus they form a single R & R subset.

with subset sizes determined by the stimulus properties of rotation and reflection of patterns. However, it must be remembered that subjects making the goodness ratings were never shown the patterns in either their behavioral or stimulus-specified subsets. Thus for each pattern seen alone, the subset of alternative patterns must be an inferred subset. Such inferred subsets are every bit as potent in determining perceived structure as are subsets physically arranged for the subject.

This relation between inferred subset size and pattern goodness makes excellent sense in terms of its connotations. Low redundancy is high uncertainty, so a poor pattern is one that is perceived as unstable, easily changed, as having, in fact, many alternatives. On the other hand, good patterns are those perceived as stable, not easily changed, and as having few alternatives. The best pattern of all is perceived as unique.

Symmetry

Redundancy is related to subset size in a fairly directly interpretable way with these dot patterns, in that the number of different patterns which can be formed

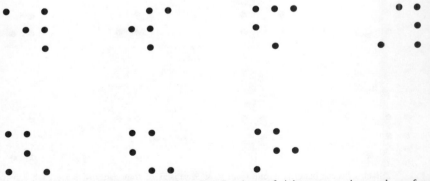

FIG. 1.11. Each of these patterns is one from R & R subsets of eight patterns, since each can form seven other patterns when rotated and/or reflected. Their rated goodness is poor.

by rotation and reflection is, in a sense, a measure of the amount of symmetry in the patterns. In fact, the reflection criterion is exactly what is meant by symmetry (on a plane surface), since if the pattern is reflected about an axis and reproduces itself, it is a symmetrical pattern. And amount of symmetry is interpretable in terms of the number of axes about which a given pattern is symmetric. To illustrate, the two unique patterns are symmetrical about four axes: the vertical, the horizontal, and the right and left diagonals. Thus these patterns are maximally symmetric.

Most of the patterns from R & R subsets of 4 are symmetric about one axis, although it may be any one of the four axes. Thus these patterns are less symmetric. Furthermore, all of the patterns from R & R subsets of 8 are symmetric about none of the axes, thus have zero amount of symmetry.

If symmetry is so directly related to pattern goodness, why don't we just say that symmetry is the pertinent factor, rather than subset size? The answer lies partly in the fact that symmetry is a sufficient but not necessary condition for producing small subset sizes, even with these simple stimuli. The pattern like a Z, for example, is not symmetric about any axis on the plane surface, yet has a subset size of four by the rotation-and-reflection criterion. Even further, as we shall see, the notion of inferred subset size has many more implications for other behavior related to pattern goodness than does the more restricted concept of symmetry. The size of real or inferred subsets is a critical factor in many phenomena pertaining to the perception of structure. Symmetry is simply one way in which the stimulus may be manipulated to produce variations in subset size, but its mode of action is via subset size rather than by symmetry *per se*.

Nested Subsets of Patterns

Our conception of the relation between the various subsets and the total set is essentially that illustrated in Fig 1.12: The total set of patterns is partitioned into mutually exclusive subsets, and these subsets differ in size. The subsets formed by rotations and reflections give such a partitioning, with any single stimulus

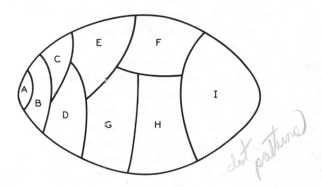

FIG. 1.12. A conception of subsets of unequal size produced by partitioning, with mutually exclusive subsets. (After Garner, 1966.)

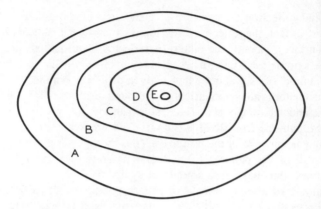

Fig. 1.13. A conception of subsets of unequal size produced by nesting, with each subset including all smaller subsets. (After Garner, 1966.)

existing in only a single subset. We could have subsets varying in size with another conception, however, as illustrated in Fig. 1.13: The total set contains successively smaller sets which are nested, so that all stimuli in the smallest subset (E, in the illustration) are contained in the next largest subset, and all of these are contained in still the next largest, and so on. Such a subset relation indicates an asymmetry between different patterns, since if a pattern is, for example, in subset C it is also in subset B; but if a pattern is in subset B, it is not necessarily in subset C.

In order to determine whether such asymmetric relations between patterns existed, we (Handel and Garner, 1966) carried out an experiment in pattern associations. This time we used all 120 of the patterns, and the patterns were drawn with the matrix lines visible, to facilitate the particular task we used. The subject was shown a card with one pattern on the left and an empty 3 × 3 matrix on the right. He was instructed to "draw a pattern of five dots, which is suggested by, but different from, the pattern in the left-hand matrix." Our idea in using this task was that if some degree of nesting of patterns exists, then the pattern associations should be asymmetric, with pattern A, for example, producing pattern B as an associate, but pattern B not producing pattern A as an associate. The conception of the association process that lies behind this idea is this: A pattern will be used as an associate to another pattern only if it lies in the smallest subset in which the stimulus pattern itself exists. Thus the associations can go from a larger subset to a smaller subset, but not conversely. The ultimate consequence of such an association process, of course, is that a sequence of associations, each given to the last pattern used as an associate, will lead ultimately to the patterns in the smallest subsets, which as we have seen are those that are the most redundant, thus are those with the greatest pattern goodness. Many experiments in the Gestalt tradition have shown exactly such an asymmetric association process, so the idea seemed to have some empirical basis.

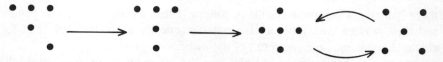

FIG. 1.14. An example of asymmetric associations of patterns. The patterns on the left progressively produce those to the right, but the reverse association process does not hold except for the two unique R & R patterns.

The results of the experiment led to the conclusion that both partitioning and nesting processes occur. The partitioning occurs with respect to the subsets formed by the criteria of rotation and reflection: Nearly 40 percent of all associations were to other patterns within the same subset, and these associations were clearly symmetric, with associations freely going back and forth between patterns within the given rotation and reflection subset.

Nesting, however, exists to a considerable extent when associations occur from stimulus patterns in one R & R subset to those in another R & R subset. The precise pattern of the nesting is a bit complex, since all the prototypical patterns did not form a perfect nesting relation. Nevertheless, the extent and nature of the asymmetry of association can be illustrated quite easily with specific patterns. Figure 1.14 shows one very common set of associations. The pattern on the left (from an R & R subset of eight members) frequently produces the "T" shown to its right (from an R & R subset of four members). That pattern in turn produces

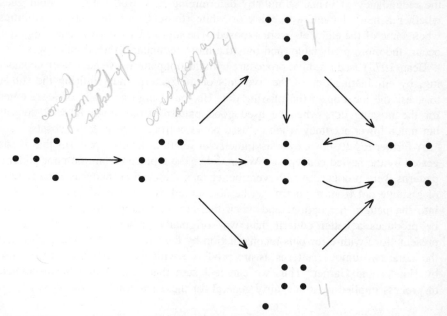

FIG. 1.15. A more complex example of asymmetric associations of patterns. Associations are produced unidirectionally for all patterns shown except for the two unique R & R patterns.

the + pattern, which produces the X pattern. These are the two unique patterns, and they produce each other as associates practically all of the time, and form the smallest subset—the end result of the association process.

Figure 1.15 shows a more complex but also common set of associations. The pattern on the left once again is from an R & R subset of eight members. It frequently produces the next pattern to the right as an associate, and it comes from an R & R subset of four patterns. This pattern, however, frequently produces two other patterns from R & R subsets of 4, as well as producing the + pattern as an associate. However, each of the two patterns from R & R subsets of 4 produce one or both of the + and X patterns as associates, and these two produce only each other as associates, as we have already seen. So once again, the end result of a sequential association process would be these very good patterns, although it might take a little longer getting there from this starting point.

Element Predictability and Nested Subsets

One of the earliest attempts to relate the information-theoretic concept of redundancy to the Gestalt concept of pattern goodness was made by Attneave (1954), using schematized pictures as stimuli. He emphasized primarily the fact that redundancy means that there is predictability, just as we saw earlier that redundancy means that there is correlation someplace in a subset of stimuli, even if the locus of the correlation may not be obvious. Attneave developed a procedure for estimating the redundancy of visual stimuli by determining how well subjects could guess whether a new element was black or white (those being the only possibilities) when some of the elements were exposed. The more easily correct guessing could occur, the more predictable, and thus the more redundant, the stimulus was.

Bear (1973) used a similar procedure with the dot patterns we have been considering, by eliminating one of the five dots of the pattern and requiring the subject to guess the location of the missing dot. He found high accuracy of replacement for the missing dots when he used good patterns from small R & R subsets, but much lower accuracy when he used patterns from large R & R subsets.

A further result showed the asymmetry of relation between patterns that is suggested by the nested conception. When dots were replaced from the poor patterns, patterns were produced which were better than the original patterns. The removal of a single dot from a pattern can be considered as a means of introducing error into the pattern perception, and when the subject attempts to correct the error, he produces a better pattern than was originally presented. A series of such presentations-with-error-plus-reconstruction by the subject will produce ultimately the same two unique patterns as are produced with the association process used by Handel and Garner. Thus we can feel sure that nesting and the asymmetry of process implied by it are fairly general for these patterns.

SUMMARY

The essential points discussed in this lecture, most of which will be pursued in later lectures, can be summarized as follows:

1. Total sets of stimuli can provide a dimensional structure for a set of stimuli, and conversely, the dimensional structure specifies the number and exact stimuli which exist in the total set. This total set is the ultimate reference group which determines the properties of the stimuli presumed to be relevant in any situation.

2. If a subset is selected from a total set, the subset is redundant. This redundancy constitutes correlational structure, although the nature of the correlational structure may be either simple or complex, the latter involving partial correlations.

3. The smaller the size of a subset for a total set of fixed size, the greater the amount of redundancy in the subset.

4. The properties (and meaning) of an individual stimulus derive from the properties of the total set and subset within which the stimulus exists, although these properties themselves derive from the totality of the individual stimuli forming the sets. Thus the properties of the total sets and subsets are at once the properties of each stimulus within the sets.

5. A single stimulus may lead to an inferred subset on the part of the perceiving organism, and while in one sense the properties of a single stimulus lead to the inferred subset, once again the perceived properties of the individual stimulus itself cannot be understood without knowing the nature of the inferred subset. To perceive is to perceive a stimulus and the nature and number of its alternatives.

6. Figural or pattern goodness, in the Gestalt sense, is high with redundant patterns and low with nonredundant patterns. This relation derives from the fact that redundant stimuli come from small subsets, while less redundant stimuli come from larger subsets. Thus patterns with low goodness have many alternative patterns, while the very best patterns are unique in the sense that they exist in subsets having only a single member.

7. The relations between perceived stimulus subsets within a total set involve both partitioning and nesting processes. Insofar as partitioning exists, relations between stimuli both within and between subsets are symmetrical. Insofar as nesting exists, relations between stimuli will be asymmetric. Such asymmetric relations lead to very good patterns or figures as the ultimate patterns in any process of sequential associations.

REFERENCES

Attneave, F. Some informational aspects of visual perception. *Psychological Review,* 1954, **61,** 183–193.

Bear, G. Figural goodness and the predictability of figural elements. *Perception & Psychophysics,* 1973, **13,** 32–40.

Garner, W. R. *Uncertainty and structure as psychological concepts.* New York: Wiley, 1962.

Garner, W. R. To perceive is to know. *American Psychologist,* 1966, **21,** 11–19.

Garner, W. R. Good patterns have few alternatives. *American Scientist,* 1970, **58,** 34–42.

Garner, W. R., & Clement, D. E. Goodness of pattern and pattern uncertainty. *Journal of Verbal Learning and Verbal Behavior,* 1963 **2,** 446–452.

Garner, W. R., Hake, H. W., & Eriksen, C. W. Operationism and the concept of perception. *Psychological Review,* 1956, **63,** 149–159.

Gibson, E. J. *Principles of perceptual learning and development*. New York: Appleton-Century-Crofts, 1969.

Gibson, J. J. *The senses considered as perceptual systems*. Boston: Houghton Mifflin, 1966.

Handel, S., & Garner, W. R. The structure of visual pattern associates and pattern goodness. *Perception & Psychophysics*, 1966, **1**, 33–38.

Mavrides, C. M. Selective attention and individual preferences in judgmental responses to multifeature patterns. *Psychonomic Science*, 1970, **21**, 67–68.

Neisser, U. *Cognitive psychology*. New York: Appleton-Century-Crofts, 1967.

LECTURE 2
PATTERN GOODNESS
IN INFORMATION PROCESSING

In the first lecture I showed that pattern goodness is related to the size of inferred subsets, good patterns being those with small inferred subsets. In this lecture I want to discuss some of the processing consequences of this idea, and to demonstrate that the inferred subset size—or actual subset size if deliberately manipulated experimentally—has clear consequences for such things as perceptual discrimination, recognition memory, paired-associates learning, and verbal encoding of stimulus patterns.

In a lighter vein I would have entitled this lecture: "What good is goodness?" It is a question I have often asked myself, since the Gestalt concept of pattern goodness is far less interesting if simply an epiphenomenon, than if it is a fundamental property of patterns that influences many different types of psychological process.

SIMPLE DISCRIMINATION

Probably the best way to start is to examine the effects of pattern goodness on simple discrimination between patterns. Clement and Varnadoe (1967) have provided data in which they measured speed of discrimination between various pairs of the dot patterns first used by Garner and Clement (1963). Some illustrative pairs of stimuli are shown in Fig. 2.1, ranked from easiest to most difficult. The experimental task was one of card sorting, with the subject sorting a deck of 50 stimulus cards into two piles. Each deck contained just two different patterns, in equal number. There were eight types of discrimination task, with the stimuli coming from different R & R subsets—those subsets in which all patterns are equivalent according to the operations of rotation and reflection.

In each code for the task types, the number refers to the size of the R & R subset and the letter to any particular R & R subset of that given size. Thus

23

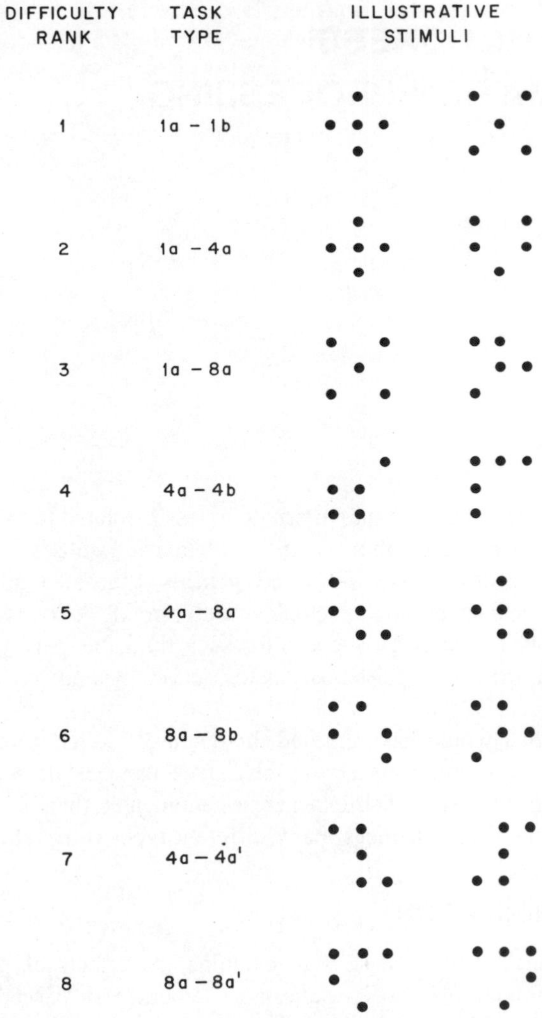

FIG. 2.1. Eight pattern discrimination tasks ranked from least to most difficult. Stimuli were dot patterns from R & R subsets of 1, 4, or 8 members; discrimination difficulty was determined from speed of sorting a deck of 50 stimulus cards. (Data from Clement and Varnadoe, 1967.)

the 1a–1b task required discrimination between the only two patterns that come from unique subsets. The 1a–4a condition required discrimination between one of the unique patterns and one member from an R & R subset of size 4. Many different comparisons of this type were used, and one pair of patterns is shown to illustrate each task type. When a letter is primed, it means that a different stimulus from the same R & R subset was used as the second stimulus for discrimination. Thus task 4a–4a' required discrimination between two patterns from the same R & R subset of size 4.

The easiest task involved discrimination between the two patterns which form unique R & R subsets, and this result seems intuitively reasonable. Then progressively more difficult were cases in which one pattern from a unique R & R subset was discriminated from a pattern coming from an R & R subset of size 4, and then of size 8.

The next most difficult task involved discrimination between two patterns from different R & R subsets of size 4, and then a 4a pattern compared to an 8a pattern. Next most difficult was discrimination between two patterns coming from different R & R subsets of size 8. Most difficult of all were the discriminations between patterns coming from the same R & R subset, with smaller subset sizes again being easier than larger subset sizes. A glance down the column of task types makes clear that there is a very regular ordering of task difficulty with respect to the sizes of the R & R subsets.

Discrimination as Stimulus Encoding and Comparison

Perhaps this ordering of difficulties seems self-evident to you, or even intuitively obvious. I (along with Clement and Varnadoe) would like to suggest that it is not, however, and that this ordering of difficulties implies that two different processes affect discrimination difficulty, one of them being stimulus encoding of the individual stimulus, and the other being a stimulus comparison of the two alternatives. Stimulus encoding implies (or at least allows) an asymmetric relation between the two stimuli being compared, and as we saw with the Handel and Garner (1966) data in the first lecture, the asymmetry involves relations between R & R subsets of different size. Stimulus comparison, on the other hand, implies a symmetric relation between the two stimuli.

Ordinarily we would expect speed of discrimination to be slowest when stimulus *similarity* is maximum, and fastest when stimulus *difference* is maximum. We already know from the association data that patterns within the same R & R subset are perceived as highly similar (and in fact in the Garner and Clement experiment, subjects nearly always kept patterns from the same R & R subset in the same group when doing free classification). Thus when discrimination involving patterns from the same R & R subset is the slowest, we are not surprised. Furthermore, it seems reasonable that when there are eight possible patterns in a single R & R subset, a pair of them should be more similar, and thus more difficult to discriminate, than when there are just four possible patterns in the R & R subset. This discrimination or comparison relation is symmetrical in the sense that the distance between one stimulus and the other is the same as the reverse distance. That is to say, stimuli are discriminated from each other, and it is not meaningful to say that stimulus A is more easily discriminated from stimulus B than stimulus B is from stimulus A.

The three tasks that involve discrimination between two patterns from different R & R subsets of the same size do not suggest an asymmetric relation. These three tasks have a difficulty ordering based solely on subset size. Thus task 1a–1b is easiest, 4a–4b next easiest, and 8a–8b most difficult.

The comparisons that do suggest an asymmetric relation are those involving stimuli from two different subset sizes. The first three tasks all involve one pattern from a unique R & R subset, and another pattern from either another unique R & R subset, or from R & R subsets of size 4 or 8. Now why would it be easier to discriminate between two unique patterns than to discriminate between one of the unique patterns and one from a larger R & R subset? Any kind of similarity measurement available now, such as frequency of association, or grouping in free classifications, indicates that the two unique patterns are more like each other than either of them is like a pattern from a larger R & R subset. But if so, then the ordering of these first three tasks should be reversed, as also should the ordering between the fourth and fifth most difficult tasks.

Consider, however, that each stimulus of a discrimination pair has its own component speed, and that the total or average discrimination time is a composite of these two speeds. Patterns from unique R & R subsets are processed most rapidly, and processing time increases as the size of the R & R subset from which the stimulus is taken becomes larger. Such a conception makes sense if we think of each stimulus as requiring formation of an internal representation, and that the processing factor really being affected by size of R & R subset is this stimulus encoding.

Total discrimination time, then, is a function of both the time required to encode each stimulus separately as well as the time required to compare the two stimuli (or each stimulus with the two internal representations). While time for stimulus encoding is, for these stimuli, primarily affected by size of R & R subset, comparison time would be most affected by stimulus similarity. This distinction between the formation of an internal representation and a comparison seems more natural and has been used more in recognition-type experiments, where the experimenter specifies which item is in memory and which is the "test" item. But it is just as appropriate in the context of a simple discrimination experiment.

We presently have some preliminary data in our laboratory which seem to validate an obvious implication of this idea, namely, that in a discrete reaction-time experiment reaction time to the better of two stimuli (better in the Gestalt sense) will be faster than reaction time to the poorer of the stimuli. Thus speed of discrimination is an asymmetric process, exactly the kind of thing implied by the nesting concept discussed before. In distance terms, such a relation suggests that the distance between the two points depends on where you start. But I don't really think this concept is as valid as the idea that the speed of reaction depends on speed of encoding the particular stimulus as well as on a stimulus comparison.

Our interest here is in pattern goodness. Which of these two processes in a discrimination task is affected by stimulus goodness, or the size of the R & R subset? The answer is very clear concerning the encoding stage: Good patterns are encoded more rapidly than poor ones. No other conclusion seems tenable from the orderings of difficulty of the several tasks used. The answer is less clear concerning the comparison stage. The speed of stimulus comparison should depend on stimulus similarity, but herein lies a difficulty. We really do not have a clear idea about similarity relations among different patterns, and thus we can only conjecture about them. So for the time being we can only conclude that pattern goodness affects stimulus encoding, and it may or may not affect stimulus comparison.

Discrimination of Configuration

All of the patterns used in this experiment by Clement and Varnadoe consisted of dots as the elements producing the configuration. Clearly the differences in speed of discrimination depend on these differences in configuration. Is it possible, however, that these results might be interpretable in more elementaristic terms, that such simple factors as correlations between elements in the dot patterns reduce the discrimination effectiveness of the patterns involved? The answer is no: The organism indeed processes patterns, not elements.

In brief support of this assertion, I will mention two experiments. Royer (1966) generated sets of eight different patterns and used speed of classification into the eight categories as his measure of performance. He started with a basic set of eight patterns and then rearranged rows and columns consistently to generate another set of eight patterns that had poorer overall pattern goodness. Nevertheless, by this method of creating the new patterns he ensured that all properties of the patterns involving relations between specific elements were held constant. The result he obtained is that the better patterns gave faster sorting speed, thus confirming the idea that it really is the configuration which is processed.

The second experiment was carried out by Clement and Weiman (1970). These authors wondered why pattern goodness, or the nature of the configuration, had so much to do with the efficiency with which two patterns were discriminated, since any two patterns can be perfectly discriminated on the basis of the difference in location of just one dot, or the presence or absence of a dot at a single location, if attention is paid to just the appropriate dot locations. If the discrimination task were carried out this way, discrimination should be quite easy, and there should be no differences in sorting speeds as a result of differences in pattern goodness. They tried to get their subjects to sort in this simpler way with a series of procedures, each procedure making it more difficult or less likely for discrimination to be on the basis of pattern. First they simply instructed their subjects on how much easier it would be to use locations of single dots. They then showed the subjects prototype cards that had just one corner of the patterns visible; thus, the entire pattern was not even shown for the prototype. Then the discrimination problem was made even more difficult by requiring true classification, with each response category being used for four different patterns from the same size of R & R subset. Finally, they rotated the patterns within one R & R subset, so that the classification could not depend solely on the overall configuration.

Only with these latter two conditions, each requiring classification of several different stimuli into a single category, did the advantage of small size of R & R subset disappear. Under these conditions the subjects indeed reverted to information processing of elements rather than configurations. But the extreme measures required to force processing of elements rather than pattern configuration make it ever so clear that configurational processing is the normal mode for human subjects, at least of the adult variety.

Additional Types of Stimuli

So much of the evidence concerning discrimination has involved the Garner-Clement dot patterns that we might feel some concern that the effects occur only with these particular stimuli. There is quite a bit of evidence, however, that the results are far more general and pertain to other types of stimuli as well. As one example, Royer (1971a) used stimuli formed from the four lines of a square plus the two lines of a plus sign inside the square. From these six elements stimuli can be formed which are unique by the R & R criterion, or are members of subsets of size 2, 4, or 8. Royer found that when subjects are required to substitute a designated digit for a figure, the speed of symbol-digit substitution was faster for the simpler, more redundant figures—those coming from small R & R subsets.

Snodgrass (1972) generated stimuli by filling in approximately equal numbers of black and white cells in a 9 × 9 matrix. She used a group of simple figures and another group of complex figures with a task in which the subject was required to decide whether two stimuli were the same or different. Reaction times were faster for the simpler figures, both when the figures were presented simultaneously and when they were presented successively.

As a last example, Pomerantz and Garner (1973) generated four stimuli by using two successive parentheses from an ordinary typewriter. This experiment will be treated in more detail in Lecture 7, but for now it is of interest that the fastest pair discrimination was between () and)(, and each of these stimuli comes from an R & R subset of two members; the slowest pair discrimination was between ((and)), and each of these comes from the same subset of four members. Thus in no sense are these discrimination results unique to the simple dot patterns.

RECOGNITION MEMORY

Recognition memory is, operationally speaking, only slightly different from simple discrimination. The experimental paradigm is that one or more items are held in memory, then one or more (usually one) items are displayed, and the subject is to state whether or not the displayed item is one of the memory set. In simplest form, if one item is held in memory and the second item (usually called the test item) is presented shortly thereafter, the task is simply one of successive discrimination, not so very different from a card-sorting discrimination experiment. Certainly the two tasks, discrimination and recognition memory, are so alike that similar principles should operate for both. We will examine in detail a recent experiment by Checkosky and Whitlock (1973) to see to what extent they do.

First, a general description of their experiment is in order. The stimuli were dot patterns of the Garner-Clement variety, just like those we have been discussing. A discrete reaction-time procedure was used. The subject held in memory either two or three of these patterns, and the items held in memory always were two or three patterns from different R & R subsets of the same size. Thus the memory items might have been three patterns from different R & R subsets of size 8 or of size 4, but the sizes were not mixed. The same memory set was used for

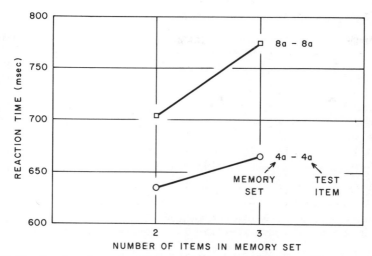

Fig. 2.2. Reaction times for correct YES responses in a recognition task with 2 or 3 items in the memory set. The stimulus items were dot patterns from R & R subsets of 4 or 8 members. (Data from Checkosky and Whitlock, 1973.)

54 consecutive stimulus presentations, and for each presentation the subject was required to push one key if YES the stimulus (the test item) was in the memory set, and another key if NO, it was not. Further aspects of the experiment will be mentioned along with a discussion of results.

Figure 2.2 summarizes the results for those test items that were in the memory set—the YES items. In this case the test item, of course, had the same properties as the two or three memory items, so there are really just two types of items, those coming from R & R subsets of size 4 and those coming from R & R subsets of size 8. The data show that items from the larger sized subsets are more difficult than those from the smaller sized subsets, in line with what we would now expect. Furthermore, an increase in number of memory items leads to an increased reaction time, interpreted as an increased processing time. The interaction between these two variables is of the greatest interest, because the shift from smaller to larger sizes of R & R subsets increases the slope of the function, although the intercepts of the two functions are practically identical. In line with Sternberg's (1967) argument, it seems reasonable to conclude that pattern goodness primarily affects the memorial comparison process rather than stimulus encoding as such, since the time cost per single comparison is greater with stimuli from the larger size of R & R subset. But let us examine this conclusion in more detail.

Discrimination and Recognition

Table 2.1 shows data from NO responses, when the test item was different from any of the memory items. There were only two ways in which items could lead to a YES response, but the experiment provided six different ways in which the test item could differ from the memory items and thus lead to a NO response. This table shows the results for these six ways for those cases in which the number

TABLE 2.1

Reaction Times (msec) for Correct NO Responses in a Recognition Task for Dot Patterns
with Two Items in the Memory Set (Data from Checkosky and Whitlock, 1973)

Pattern items		Reaction		Predicted[b]
Memory set	Test	time	Rank[a]	ranks
4B, 4C	4A	636	1	1, 1
4B, 4C	8A	647	2	2.5, 2.5
4A, 4B	4A′	686	4	5, 1
8B, 8C	4A	660	3	2.5, 2.5
8B, 8C	8A	701	5	4, 4
8A, 8B	8A′	741	6	6, 4

[a]Rank orders for the six different types of NO relation.
[b]Ranks predicted from Clement and Varnadoe (1967) discrimination data in Fig. 2.1.

of memory-set items was two. The coding used to describe these various kinds of difference is like that used in describing the discrimination data from Clement and Varnadoe. To be more specific, the first case involved two memory items from two different R & R subsets of size 4, and the test item was a pattern from still a third R & R subset of the same size. The last case involved two memory items from different R & R subsets of size 8, and the test item was another item from one of the same R & R subsets. The rest of the cases are interpreted in similar fashion. The obtained mean reaction times for each task type are given in the third column, but of more immediate interest for us are simply the rank orders shown in the fourth column.

Let us consider that there is a discrimination problem for the subject in this task, one in which the test item must be compared to each of the memory items. There are six different kinds of such discrimination possible in this situation, and for each of them we can determine the rank order which would obtain from the Clement and Varnadoe data shown in Fig. 2.1. These ranks (for each possible comparison between test and memory item) are shown in the last column, with new rank numbers for these six conditions. There are two cases which we cannot differentiate on the basis of the Clement and Varnadoe data, and these are cases in which patterns from R & R subsets of size 4 are compared with patterns from R & R subsets of size 8. What we do not know is whether there is an advantage to the better item being in the test or in the memory set. Only the second and fourth tasks involve this particular asymmetry, and for them we have simply used the average rank of 2.5.

To clarify these ranks further, consider the first task, in which the test item is from an R & R subset of size 4, and each of the memory items is from a different R & R subset of the same size. Both comparisons of test item to memory item are of the same difficulty and are the easiest possible in this experiment. The last task involves two different types of comparison: between a test item from an R & R subset of size 8 and a memory item from the same subset, or

TABLE 2.2

Reaction Times (msec) for Correct NO Responses in a Recognition Task
for Dot Patterns with Three Items in the Memory Set[a]

Pattern items		Reaction		Predicted
Memory set	Test	time	Rank	ranks
4B, 4C, 4D	4A	659	1	1, 1, 1
4B, 4C, 4D	8A	673	2	2.5, 2.5, 2.5
4A, 4B, 4C	4A'	710	3	5, 1, 1
8B, 8C, 8D	4A	713	4	2.5, 2.5, 2.5
8B, 8C, 8D	8A	769	5	4, 4, 4
8A, 8B, 8C	8A'	789	6	6, 4, 4

[a]Entries as in Table 2.1. (Data from Checkosky and Whitlock, 1973.)

another item from a different subset of the same size. The comparison involving
the same subset is the most difficult (ranked 6), while the other comparison is
ranked 4.

Comparison of the ranks for these experimental results and the ranks predicted
from the Clement and Varnadoe data certainly suggest that similar processes are
involved in simple discrimination and in recognition memory.

Table 2.2 shows the same sort of data when the memory set consisted of three
items. The generally good arrangement of predicted and obtained ranks continues
to hold. Only one task improved in obtained rank when three rather than two
items were in the memory set, and this is the task involving R & R subsets
of size 4 in the memory set with the test item coming from one of these subsets.
The addition of a third memory item has added an easy discrimination, and this
task improved rank position by one compared to its rank when there were just
two items in the memory set. So these data further confirm that recognition and
simple discrimination involve the same kinds of process.

Figure 2.3 shows the mean reaction times from these two tables in a manner
designed to elucidate the effects of changes in the test item and changes in the
memory items. In all cases an increase in the number of memory items leads
to an increase in processing time. However, the effects of size of R & R subsets
are quite different when we are considering the memory items and when we are
considering the test items. Consider first the three functions with dashed lines.
All these functions are for cases in which the memory set consists of two or
three patterns from different R & R subsets of size 4. If now the test item is
changed from an R & R subset of size 4 to one of size 8, the intercept of the
function is changed, but not the slope. Such a change suggests simply a greater
encoding time as a function of lower pattern goodness, just as we found for simple
discrimination data. However, if the test item is changed to one from an R & R
subset represented in the memory set (the 4a–4a' task), the intercept is increased
still further, but still with no change in the slope.

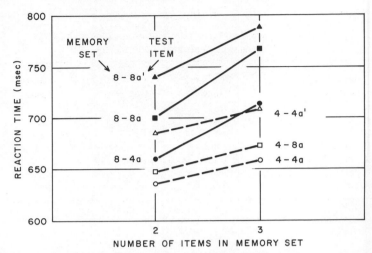

FIG. 2.3. Reaction times for correct NO responses in a recognition task with 2 or 3 items in the memory set. All memory items were dot patterns from R & R subsets of either 4 or 8 members (never mixed), and the test items were from either the same R & R subset, from a different subset of the same size, or from a subset of different size as the items in the memory set. (Data from Checkosky and Whitlock, 1973.)

Consider now the three functions with solid lines, all for memory sets from R & R subsets of size 8. This change in the nature of the memory set produces the change in slope we saw with YES responses, so clearly changes in the nature of the memory set to do something different than changes in the test items, presumably affecting the comparison process. However, the effects of changes in the nature of the test item parallel those obtained with the memory set of items from R & R subsets of size 4, namely, producing primarily a change in intercept, indicating an increased encoding time for poorer patterns.

It is very reasonable that a change in the goodness of the test item should simply change the intercept of these functions. A different encoding time for the one item is presumably required. It is less obvious that changing the test item so that it is one of the R & R subsets of the memory items should produce just a change in intercept, rather than a change of slope. Such a change in test item should produce an increase in similarity between test and memory item and thus ought to affect comparison time, and therefore the slope of the functions. It must be remembered, however, that in the present experiment, the primary change in discriminability (or similarity) is that the test item becomes a member of the same R & R subset as just one of the memory items. Thus conclusions concerning this effect with a larger number of memory items must be made very cautiously. It is unlikely that the effect is simply a change in the intercept constant.

Figure 2.4 will illustrate further that the effects of changes in the test item are separable from the effects of changes in the memory items. In this experiment, two different contrast levels were used for the presentation of the test stimulus, which we will call simply high or low, and which are labeled on this graph as

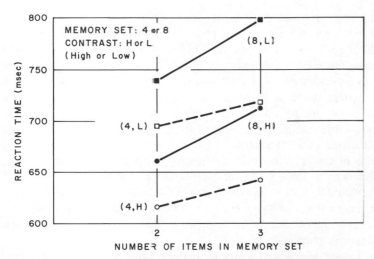

FIG. 2.4. Reaction times for correct NO responses in a recognition task with 2 or 3 items in the memory set. Memory items came from R & R subsets of 4 or 8 members, and reaction times are average for all types of NO relations of test and memory items. The test item was presented at either low or high visual contrast. (Data from Checkosky and Whitlock, 1973.)

H or L. If data are plotted separately for the two contrasts, averaged across all types of test item, we get exactly the same effect as with other changes in the test item shown in Fig. 2.3: The intercept of these functions is changed, but not the slopes. (This experimental manipulation corresponds most closely to the one Sternberg, 1967, had used, in which he degraded the test item and found it to affect primarily the intercepts of such functions rather than their slopes.)

Three Processes in Recognition

What can we conclude about pattern goodness and processes involved in recognition? Certainly it is clear that pattern goodness affects stimulus encoding, just as it does in simple discrimination. In this I am disagreeing with the conclusion drawn by Checkosky and Whitlock, yet it seems to me that the similar effects of goodness of test item and degradation of test item on the intercept of the functions argues strongly that pattern goodness affects stimulus encoding.

But what about the comparison process? As I argued in regard to discrimination processes, stimulus similarity should affect the comparison process and thus the slope of the function relating reaction time to number of memory items. But we know too little about similarity relations to draw clear conclusions, and what we can conjecture with some confidence does not lead to sensible conclusions. For example, if test items come from R & R subsets of size 4, then if we change the memory items from R & R subsets of size 4 to subsets of size 8, the slope of the recognition function is increased. But such a change should decrease similarity between test and memory items, thus producing a flatter rather than a steeper function.

Let us consider, however, that the effect of pattern goodness is on the memory process itself, not the comparison process. Checkosky and Whitlock argue this way and suggest that good patterns are more easily generated in memory. An alternative, but similar, argument is that it is easier to change from one good pattern to another than to change from one poor pattern to another in memory search. In fact, there well may be a factor of interitem similarity in memory which accounts for the change in slopes of the recognition functions. It seems more reasonable that different patterns from R & R subsets of size 8 are highly similar than that different patterns from R & R subsets of size 4 are. This conjectured difference in similarity between the items in memory would easily account for the differences in slope, with the steeper slope going with the poorer patterns. Thus we would have to accept the idea that there are at least three factors involved in such recognition tasks—encoding, memory generation, and comparison—and that pattern goodness affects the first two of these processes, but not necessarily the comparison process.

There is one last reservation I must draw now, and that is whether what I am calling memory generation is purely a memory factor. It is entirely possible that exactly the same effect might exist if we reversed the experimental paradigm, requiring the subject to hold one item in memory, then presenting him with a stimulus display of two or three items simultaneously, in what might be called a search task. It seems highly likely that the slopes of the functions relating reaction time to number of test items would be greater if the test items came from R & R subsets of size 8 rather than size 4. In such a case we could not conclude that there is something special about the memory process, but rather that in recognition or search there are two kinds of item similarity of concern: similarity between memory and test items, and similarity between items in the set providing choice of stimulus. A decrease of either type of similarity would lead to faster reaction.

REPRODUCTION MEMORY

One fact which is very clear from the Checkosky-Whitlock experiment is that pattern goodness directly affects the efficiency of the memory process. So it should be profitable to examine data on various types of learning and memory to determine whether the sizes of subsets and total sets affect these processes as well as those of discrimination and recognition memory. The evidence is clear that reproduction memory is so affected.

One of the very first experiments to use the concept of stimulus redundancy in memory was done by Attneave (1955), and his experiment is still worth describing in the present context of different set sizes. The experiment I shall describe involved stimuli like those shown in Fig. 2.5. First a pattern of dots was generated by random placement of dots (with probability of 0.5) in the cells of a 3 × 4 matrix, as illustrated in the upper left-hand corner. While this pattern is shown in the symmetric series, in effect it is the basic pattern for both the symmetric and random series. Then this pattern was duplicated around its right-hand column to produce

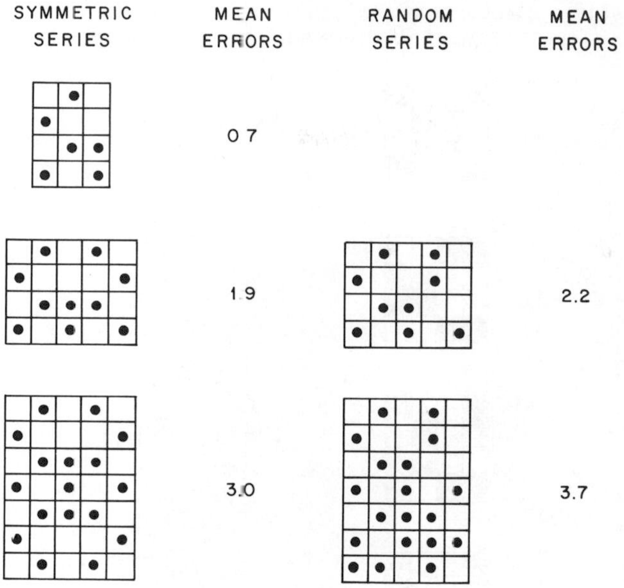

SYMMETRIC SERIES	MEAN ERRORS	RANDOM SERIES	MEAN ERRORS

FIG. 2.5. Mean errors in immediate reproduction of patterns. The symmetric series is generated by mirroring the top pattern first horizontally and then vertically. (After Attneave, 1955.)

the horizontally symmetric second pattern in the symmetric series, in a 5 × 4 matrix. Then this pattern was duplicated about its bottom row to produce still a third pattern, one which is now symmetric both vertically and horizontally. For each of these two larger patterns, control patterns were generated by placing dots randomly in cells of equal sized matrices. Each of five groups of subjects was required to reproduce 60 patterns of one of these five types, with the reproduction occurring immediately after each pattern was presented. Performance was measured by the mean number of errors per cell, and these are the numbers shown to the right of each pattern.

The results are quite straightforward: As the size of the matrix increases, so do the number of errors. However, for a given size of matrix, errors are fewer if the patterns are symmetric than if they are not. Yet symmetry alone is clearly inadequate to compensate for the increased size of matrix, since errors would have remained constant in the symmetric series if symmetry could compensate. In the language I have been using, the factor that makes the symmetric patterns easier than the random patterns of the same size is that the inferred subset size is smaller for the symmetric patterns. But the total set for patterns of the same matrix size is the same; thus, this comparison is a valid one to determine the effect of inferred subset size.

However, down the symmetric series itself, the increase in number of errors is due to the increased size of total set. I particularly wanted to bring in this classical paper at this time because in all the research I have discussed so far

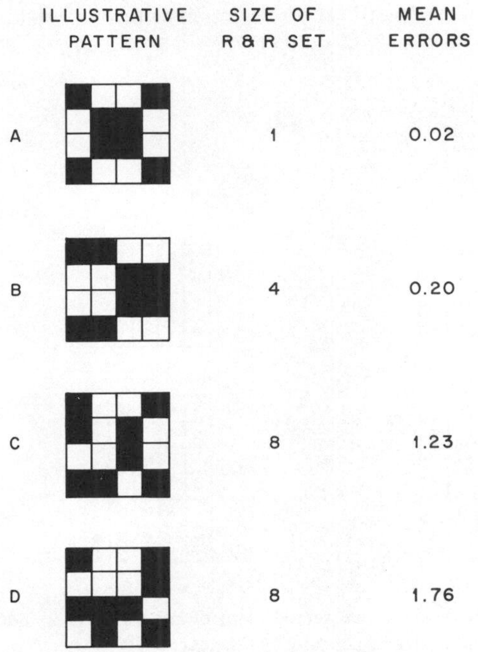

ILLUSTRATIVE PATTERN	SIZE OF R & R SET	MEAN ERRORS
A	1	0.02
B	4	0.20
C	8	1.23
D	8	1.76

FIG. 2.6. Mean errors in immediate reproduction of patterns. The size of the R & R subset for each type of pattern is as indicated. In addition, however, patterns of the C type have one half which is symmetric. (Data from Schnore and Partington, 1967.)

the total set has remained constant, with comparisons being between subsets of different sizes. But the individual stimulus is, as I remarked in the first lecture, a member of at least one subset and also a total set, and its properties are determined by the sizes and natures of both of these. In general, difficulty of processing becomes greater with an increase in either size of subset or size of total set.

One other experiment will illustrate the more common technique of using stimuli with a fixed size of total set, as shown in Fig. 2.6. These patterns were used in an experiment by Schnore and Partington (1967) and involved half of the cells being blackened in 4 × 4 matrix. With this square matrix, patterns can be generated by the rotation and reflection criteria with subset sizes of 1, 4, or 8 members. Just as in the Attneave experiment, immediate reproduction of these patterns after each single presentation was required, and scoring was in terms of the number of cells incorrectly reproduced. The data give an unequivocal result, namely, that as subset size increases, so do the number of reproduction errors.

There is one additional point of interest in Fig. 2.6, and that concerns pattern C. This pattern, strictly speaking, comes from an R & R subset of size 8, but its right half is symmetrical about the horizontal axis. This part-symmetry clearly provided some advantage in immediate reproduction of such patterns. The use of the single criterion of size of R & R subset has had such great experimental success that it becomes easy to forget that the human organism is not at all limited to that stimulus property in inferring subset sizes. We still have very little information on the number of ways in which size of inferred subset can be manipulated by various types of stimulus property.

There is one experiment where a free-recall technique showed similar results. Royer (1971b), using the same line figures mentioned earlier in connection with discrimination experiments, showed that free recall of sets of eight figures was better if the figures, on the average, came from smaller R & R subsets. Thus the particular learning and memory technique used does not seem to be crucial in determining the experimental results. And certainly all of these experiments do show that pattern goodness, and its corollary of subset size, influence memory processes as simple as those involved in immediate reproduction and free recall.

PAIRED-ASSOCIATES LEARNING

Probably the most commonly used learning paradigm in psychology is that of paired associates. I myself am not fond of that particular learning technique, because it contains more separate process factors than I care to put into a single experiment. Certainly at a minimum there is learning of the stimulus set, learning of the response set, discrimination between the stimulus items, discrimination between the response items, and associating the correct response with the correct stimulus. Nevertheless, if the technique can further clarify the role of pattern goodness in psychological processes, then it will have been valuable.

Attneave (1955), in the paper discussed previously, also used a paired-associates or identification task in which the subjects were required to learn a letter of the alphabet to identify each of 12 different patterns, some groups of subjects having the symmetrical patterns and others having random patterns. The results were, qualitatively, identical to those involving immediate reproduction, with symmetrical patterns being easier to learn than patterns of equal size, and with learning difficulty increasing as the size of the total set of patterns increased.

Clement (1967) carried out a paired-associates experiment using the 17 prototypical dot patterns he and I had used before, all within the same learning task. Patterns were used as stimuli, with two-digit numbers as responses; and in a separate experiment the numbers were used as stimuli with the patterns as responses. The good patterns were easier to learn either as responses or as stimuli. Thus the paired-associates task gives results similar to those found for discrimination, recognition, and immediate-memory tasks.

Dimensionally Defined Stimuli

I want to discuss in detail two experiments that used paired-associates learning, because they effectively clarify the role of subset size. The first of these is an experiment by Donderi (1967) using stimuli quite unlike these dot patterns, stimuli which incorporate a quite useful technique for generating subsets of different sizes. One set of his stimuli is shown in Fig. 2.7, along with some other appropriate data.

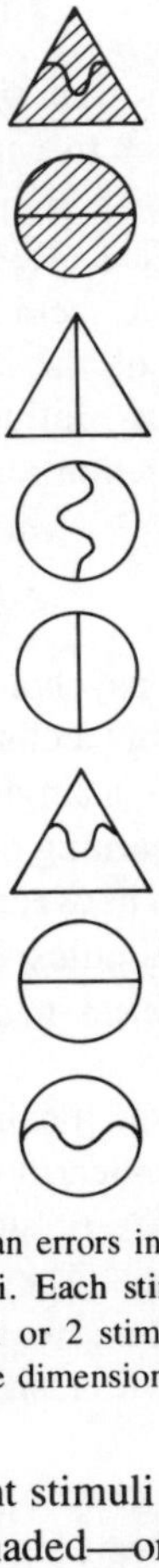

STIMULUS	MEAN ERRORS	SUBSET SIZE BY	
		1 DIMENSION	2 DIMENSIONS
A	1.11	2	1
B	2.00	2 (1.56)	1
C	2.00	3	1
D	2.55	3	1
E	1.66	3	2
F	2.33	3 (2.14)	2
G	2.66	4	2
H	3.22	4 (2.94)	2

FIG. 2.7. Mean errors in paired-associates learning of nonsense syllables as responses to geometric forms as stimuli. Each stimulus is a member of a subset of 2, 3, or 4 stimuli defined by a single dimension, or 1 or 2 stimuli defined by two dimensions. Mean errors for the three sizes of subset specified by one dimension are shown in parentheses. (Data from Donderi, 1967.)

These eight stimuli are generated from four dichotomous dimensions: color (red, shown as shaded—or green, shown as clear), shape (circle or triangle), wavy or straight center line, and vertical or horizontal center line. You will remember from the first lecture that if the total set of stimuli (in this case 16) is larger than the actual subset (in this case 8), then the subset is redundant. The cases I used as illustrations all were simpler than this one, however, because I used both levels on each dimension equally often, while in the present case the different levels are used in proportion of 6:2 for color, 5:3 for shape and direction of center line, and 4:4 only for the wavy-straight dimension. Thus all dimensions are not equally valuable in an information sense, and different stimuli in turn are more or less discriminable from all others. The numbers shown here indicate that analysis in terms of size of subset specified by one or possibly two dimensions is very effective.

The actual experimental technique was paired associates, with a nonsense syllable being learned as response to each of the eight stimuli. Errors to criterion were used as the dependent measure, and mean errors per trial per subject are shown in Fig. 2.7 for each stimulus. The middle column of numbers shows the number of stimuli existing in a single subset if that subset is defined by the total number of stimuli sharing the level of the particular stimulus on the single dimension that gives the smallest subset size. To illustrate, stimuli A and B are both red, and no other stimuli are red. Thus redness establishes these two stimuli as being in a subset of 2, and only enough further information to differentiate two stimuli is needed. These are easy stimuli to learn, mean errors being 1.56.

Stimulus C is a member of a subset of 3 by virtue of its being a triangle, since there are only two other triangles. It is also a member of a subset of 3 by having a vertical center line. Four patterns have first-order subset sizes of 3, and the mean number of errors for these four stimuli is 2.14. The only real anomaly occurs with pattern E, which was somewhat easier to learn than other stimuli of its general type, and I have no explanation for this. (The explanation is not that that particular pattern as shown is simpler, since different sets of logically equivalent patterns were used in the experiment to counterbalance for such things as salience of dimensions, levels, or combinations.)

Stimuli G and H are members of subsets of 4, because on each dimension their level was the one with more than four members except the dimension which was split 4:4. Thus having a straight or wavy line was the most differentiating property of these two stimuli. They were the most difficult to learn.

The last column shows the size of subset that is provided by the best two dimensions, and it clearly adds little to our understanding beyond the size of subset provided by the best single dimension. Thus of the four stimuli that are narrowed down to three possibilities with a single dimension, two of them are completely determined by two dimensions, while two of them still are in subsets of 2 with two dimensions. But there is no advantage to this status in terms of learning difficulty.

Total Sets and Subsets

The other experiment using paired-associates learning I want to discuss in detail is reported by Glanzer, Taub, and Murphy (1968), and once again it involves dot patterns, although of a slightly different type. The experiments reported are especially valuable because they provide comparisons of different subset sizes within a set to be learned, as well as differences in total set size for given subset sizes. Still further, the subsets of stimuli actually used did not correspond in some cases to the number of subset items which could be used.

The experimental paradigm used by these authors was paired associates, with eight patterns as stimuli and eight consonant letters as responses. Four different sets of dot patterns were used, each learned by a different group of subjects, and the patterns are illustrated in Fig. 2.8. Each pattern consisted of two rows,

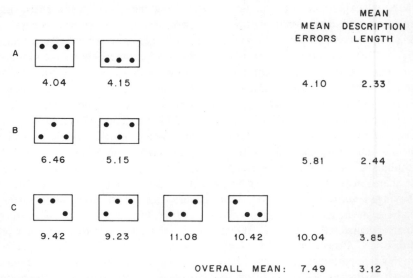

		MEAN ERRORS	MEAN DESCRIPTION LENGTH
A 4.04 4.15		4.10	2.33
B 6.46 5.15		5.81	2.44
C 9.42 9.23 11.08 10.42		10.04	3.85
OVERALL MEAN:		7.49	3.12

FIG. 2.8. Paired-associates learning of letters as responses to 3-dot patterns as stimuli. Mean errors to learn each of the eight patterns are shown under the pattern, and mean errors for each of the three R & R subsets are to the right. At the far right are shown mean lengths of verbal descriptions, obtained in a separate experiment. (Data from Glanzer et al., 1968.)

and each column had one dot in either the upper or lower row. (These dot patterns had earlier been used in a learning experiment by Bricker, 1955.)

In Fig. 2.8, there were three columns, so that there were eight possible stimuli all together; that is to say, the total set of stimuli was eight. All eight stimuli were used, so that overall no redundancy was involved. However, as can be seen, the eight stimuli group themselves into three R & R subsets, two of size 2 and one of size 4. The mean errors for each single stimulus are shown under the pattern, and averages for the R & R subsets to the right. It is quite apparent that the size of the R & R subset is the dominant factor in determining individual item difficulty and that the overall difficulty of learning these eight patterns is some function of the sizes of the subsets of stimuli forming the total set. Patterns within a subset are learned with essentially equal difficulty. (For the moment, please ignore the last column of data, the mean description length. We will return to it later.)

Figure 2.9 shows two new groups of eight patterns. For these patterns a fourth dot position has been added, so that each actual set of eight patterns is a redundant subset of the total set, which now has 16 members. These 16 patterns have six R & R subsets. Four of them are of size 2, and these were used to form one set of patterns to be learned, as shown at the top of this figure, labeled Set 4-2. Since there are only trivial differences in difficulty between patterns in the same R & R subset, only a prototype is shown for each R & R subset, along with mean errors for both patterns in each subset. There is some variation in difficulty

	PATTERN PROTOTYPE	NO. IN R & R SET	MEAN ERRORS	MEAN DESCRIPTION LENGTH
A	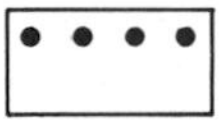	2	4.12	1.90
B	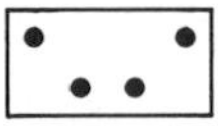	2	7.91	2.40
C	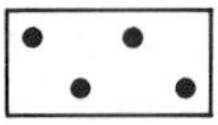	2	10.81	2.65
D	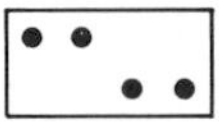	2	11.11	2.57
	OVERALL MEAN:		8.49	2.38
A	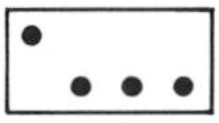	4	14.59	3.16
B	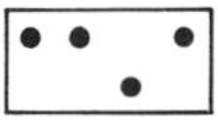	4	16.03	3.98
	OVERALL MEAN:		15.31	3.57

SET 4-2 (rows A–D); SET 4-4 (rows A–B).

FIG. 2.9. Paired-associates learning of letters as responses to 4-dot patterns as stimuli. Two sets of eight stimuli were learned, one set containing stimuli from R & R subsets of 2 members and the other containing stimuli from R & R subsets of 4 members. Mean errors and mean description length are indicated, as in Fig. 2.8. (Data from Glanzer et al., 1968.)

among the four R & R subsets, with those having vertical symmetry (patterns A and B) being easier than those requiring 180° rotation to reproduce themselves. Nevertheless, overall, these are fairly easy patterns to learn.

At the bottom are shown the two R & R subsets of size 4, and these were used to form another set of eight patterns to be learned, labeled Set 4-4. Once again, only mean errors for all patterns in each R & R subset are shown. What is very obvious is that this is a much more difficult set of patterns to learn than Set 4-2. Not one pattern from Set 4-2 was as difficult to learn as any pattern from Set 4-4. Technically, of course, each of these two sets of patterns has the same amount of redundancy, since each is itself a subset of 8 patterns from a total set of 16. But the really controlling factor in learning difficulty is the size of the R & R subset within the actual set to be learned.

Bricker (1955) has used Set 4-4 in his experiment, but not Set 4-2. He found his set with four elements more difficult than one with five (which we shall discuss in a moment). This result seemed anomalous, since a set of eight patterns constructed with five dots is more redundant than a set of eight patterns constructed with four dots, and usually increased redundancy leads to greater difficulty of learning if the actual set size is constant. However, what is now apparent is that the size of the R & R subsets constituting the actual set is even more important than the amount of redundancy overall in the actual set to be learned.

Nevertheless, difficulty of learning with an actual set of fixed size is a function of total set size. The overall mean errors for Set 4-2, involving only R & R subsets of size 2, is greater than the overall mean for 3-dot patterns, which was 7.49 as shown in Fig. 2.8, even though in that condition half of the patterns came from an R & R subset of size 4. Thus both the size of the subsets within the actual set to be learned and the size of the total set influence learning difficulty.

Figure 2.10 shows the stimulus patterns used in a last condition. These eight stimuli contained five dots, so the total set has now become 32, and the possible choices of R & R subset size have become much greater. The 32 patterns are composed of four R & R subsets of size 2, and six R & R subsets of size 4. The prototypical patterns and R & R subset sizes actually used are shown in this figure. Notice particularly, however, that even though three of the R & R subsets have 4 members, only two of them were used in the actual experiment. So actual subset size and R & R subset size were not the same. Which is the more important?

PATTERN PROTOTYPE	NO. IN R & R SET	NO. USED	MEAN ERRORS	MEAN DESCRIPTION LENGTH
A	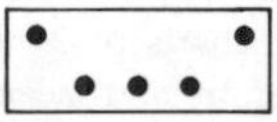 2	2	9.74	2.29
B	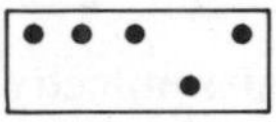 4	2	13.58	2.48
C	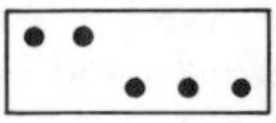 4	2	14.39	2.89
D	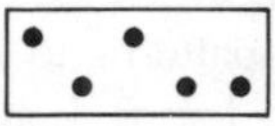 4	2	15.64	3.03

OVERALL MEAN: 13.23

FIG. 2.10. Paired-associates learning of letters as responses to 5-dot patterns as stimuli. The size of the R & R subset was 2 or 4, but when 4, only two members were used. Mean errors and description length are indicated as in Fig. 2.8. (Data from Glanzer et al., 1968.)

TABLE 2.3

Summary Measures for Paired-Associates Learning
of 3-, 4-, and 5-Dot Patterns, and for Description Lengths[a]

Set of patterns	Mean R & R size	Mean no. used	Mean errors	Mean length description
3	3.0	3.0	7.49	3.12
4-2	2.0	2.0	8.49	2.38
4-4	4.0	4.0	15.31	3.57
5	3.5	2.0	15.64	3.03

[a]See Figs. 2.8, 2.9, and 2.10 for details. (Data from Glanzer et al., 1968.)

The first-order answer certainly has to be that R & R subset size is the more important in this task. All patterns from R & R subsets of 4 were more difficult than the two patterns from an R & R subset of 2, even though only two patterns were used from each subset. Furthermore, in Fig. 2.9 the mean errors for the eight patterns involving two R & R subsets of size 4 was 15.31, a figure not too different from those shown here for equivalent sized R & R subsets. Since, however, total set was increased in this instance, there should have been an increase in number of errors. But there was actually a slight decrease in these cases, so we may conclude that although R & R subset size is the more important factor, there is some advantage if not all patterns from a given R & R subset are actually used. And, more generally speaking, inferred subset size is at least as important as actual subset size in such experiments.

As a summary, and to provide a better comparison between the different conditions in these experiments, consider Table 2.3. The mean number of errors for all eight stimulus patterns of each of the four sets of patterns is shown. Certainly the easiest patterns to learn are the nonredundant ones, Set 3, where the actual set is the same size as the total set. When the total set is increased, as for Set 4-2, learning difficulty increases, even though all R & R subsets were of size 2 in that condition. But learning difficulty is drastically greater if size of both total set and subset are increased, as in Set 4-4. Set 5 is quite confounded, but since it is slightly more difficult to learn than Set 4-4, certainly size of total set is important. And the size of subsets actually used is a relatively weak factor, a fact most clearly seen by comparing mean errors for Set 5 and Set 4-2. Mean number of patterns used in a given R & R subset is the same for these two conditions, but errors are almost twice as great for Condition 5. Again, the confounding doesn't allow us to say whether the increase in size of total set or size of R & R subset is the critical factor here. Both clearly operate, however.

One can almost summarize these results by stating that good paired-associates learning occurs when the set of stimuli used is perceived as a total set, and when each stimulus within the set is perceived as unique. Thus increased size, whether of the subset or the total set, whether actual or inferred, deters learning.

VERBAL ENCODING

Patterns are discriminated, recognized, and learned. They can also be described verbally, either for purposes of internal encoding, or for purposes of long-term memory and reproduction. Certainly if size of subset and total set are such important factors in so many psychological processes, it seems only inevitable that they should be important in verbal encoding processes also.

Length of Encoding

Glanzer and Clark (1963), using linear arrays of black and white elements, showed that accuracy of reproduction of patterns was correlated with the length of description of the patterns. They further showed (1964), using various outline figures, that the length of the description was correlated with judged complexity of the figures. These experiments led to their verbal-loop hypothesis, in which they assumed that pattern goodness is a function of the length of the description; thus, the idea of a loop. It is not necessary to subscribe to this causal assumption to be convinced that length of a description is related to pattern goodness, for the critical factor in much of the processing of pattern is the size of the subsets and total sets of stimuli, and these must necessarily affect length of description. But lengths of description are not quite synonymous with learning difficulty, as we shall see by considering the several sets of patterns used by Glanzer et al. again, since these authors obtained description lengths for patterns in each of the sets. The descriptions were obtained from different subjects than those used in the learning experiments, and the subjects had full knowledge of all patterns in the actual set in each case by being given preliminary trials before the actual descriptions. The data for description lengths are given in the last column in Figs. 2.8, 2.9, and 2.10, and in Table 2.3. Data on lengths of description can thus be directly compared with data on learning difficulty.

Figure 2.8 shows data for Set 3, with two R & R subsets of two patterns and one R & R subset of four patterns. Mean description length (in number of words) clearly parallels the learning results: Longer descriptions were required for the larger R & R subset. So longer descriptions go with greater difficulty of learning, both of them being natural consequences of subset size.

Figure 2.9 shows data for the two different sets of patterns with four dots in them. In this case intra-set comparisons are less important, since R & R subset size is the same for all items in each set of patterns to be learned. Inter-set comparison, however, shows that Set 4-4, with R & R subsets of size 4, required considerably greater description length than Set 4-2, with R & R subsets of size 2. Although definitive conclusions cannot be drawn, it appears that description length is unaffected by the increase in total set size. That is to say, these description lengths are about the same as those obtained with Set 3.

Figure 2.10 shows the results for the patterns with five dots. Once again the size of the R & R subset affects length of description, but much less so than in the previous sets, and much less than the learning data show. Remember that in this set the number of patterns actually used from any one R & R subset was always two, regardless of the size of the subset. It would appear, then, that verbal descriptions are more sensitive to the actualities of the set than to inferred subsets that do not exist in the actual set of stimuli.

Further evidence for this point is shown in the comparisons between sets of patterns in Table 2.3. Here the mean length of descriptions for Set 5 is actually shorter than that for Set 3, although the shortest of all is for Set 4-2, which has the lowest mean size of R & R subset. These verbal descriptions, then, are clearly related to subset and total set size, and thus to learning difficulty, but there is a difference between the effect of set size on learning and its effect on length of verbal descriptions.

This difference is that the verbal descriptions depend much more on the actual set size, and the actual subsets used, than on total set and inferred subset, both of which are not measures of the stimuli actually presented. Why should this be so? Possibly verbal descriptions are much more reality-prone, being concerned more with actualities and less with possibilities. I suspect another reason, however, and it is that the task used in this experiment to check the subjects in their verbal descriptions was one in which they were presented the eight appropriate patterns and were required to match their descriptions to them. Such a task puts little burden on memory for the set of patterns and emphasizes discrimination between items. Such a task makes more efficient use of actual information and structure, rather than potential information and structure.

Verbal Association

Length of a description is only one way in which pattern goodness can affect verbal factors associated with it. Naturally, the longer a description is, the more possible descriptions there are of a given class. But Clement (1964) has shown that this greater variability of verbal response to a pattern can exist simply by use of a greater vocabulary of free associations to the patterns. In addition, he has shown that another aspect of this greater variability, longer latency of response, also occurs. We have known for some time that reaction time increases with the number of response alternatives that a subject must choose between, so this relation between latency and free verbal associations is a quite natural, almost-to-be-expected consequence.

Clement used two kinds of stimulus patterns in his experiments, and the first, the familiar five-dot patterns, is shown in Fig. 2.11. Altogether Clement used 50 different patterns, but results are presented here for just nine representative patterns. His experimental procedure was to present a single pattern and to require the subject to make a one-word verbal response to the pattern. The response was supposed to be appropriate to the pattern. Each subject made one response to each of the 50 patterns. Two measures were obtained for each pattern: One was the mean latency of response, shown in the second row of data, and the other was the inter-subject variability of responses, measured in bits of uncertainty and shown in the bottom line. Since Clement used 60 subjects, the maximum response

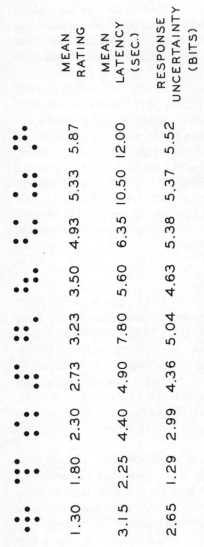

FIG. 2.11. Some illustrative dot patterns (from 50 actually used), with mean goodness rating, mean latency to produce a verbal associate, and variability of verbal responses (in bits of uncertainty) to the patterns. (After Clement, 1964.)

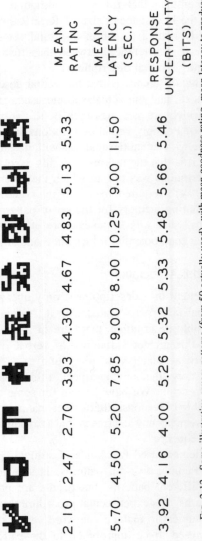

FIG. 2.12. Some illustrative square patterns (from 50 actually used), with mean goodness rating, mean latency to produce a verbal associate, and variability of verbal responses (in bits of uncertainty) to the patterns. (After Clement, 1964.)

uncertainty was just under 6 bits. Another group of subjects made goodness ratings of the patterns, which we already know to be highly correlated with the size of the R & R subset, or with direct behavioral measures of goodness. There is little need to go further with these data. The results are clear: High pattern goodness (low rating) is associated with low variability of verbal response and with short latency of response.

Clement duplicated this experiment with a different class of patterns, shown in Fig. 2.12. The cells of a 9 × 9 matrix were filled in with a probability of 0.5, and a set of 50 such patterns was selected to give a good range of pattern goodness. Again, nine sample patterns are shown in this figure, with the measures of rated pattern goodness, mean latency of verbal response, and response uncertainty in bits. The result is equally clear with these patterns that all three measures are highly correlated, with good patterns producing relatively few alternative responses, and these are produced with short latencies.

SUMMARY

The lecture has demonstrated that there are many processing consequences of pattern goodness, most of them being direct effects of the fact that good patterns come from small subsets, whether actual or inferred. In addition, however, the effect of the size of the total set is also evident in these various types of information processing.

1. Simple discrimination of patterns is better when the patterns come from small subsets defined by rotation and reflection. The data suggest that two processing factors can be delimited: One is a comparison between the two stimulus patterns, and this factor is symmetric in that a comparison of A with B is as fast as a comparison of B with A. The other factor is an encoding one and is potentially different for each pattern in the comparison, being faster for patterns from small R & R subsets. Thus an asymmetric process exists in which speed of responding to A is not necessarily the same as speed of responding to B.

2. Recognition memory involves three processing factors: encoding of the test item, generation of the memory items, and comparison of the test item with the memory items. Each of the first two processes is faster with items from small R & R subsets, but the role of pattern goodness is less clear with respect to the comparison process.

3. Reproduction memory is better for patterns from small R & R subsets but is poorer if the total set from which the patterns are drawn is larger.

4. Paired-associates learning is better for those items in a set that come from small R & R subsets. The effect of the inferred subset is greater than the effect of the actual subset within the set to be learned. However, learning is poorer if the total set is large compared to the actual set of stimuli used, that is, if there is redundancy in the set of stimuli to be learned.

5. Verbal descriptions are shorter for patterns from small R & R subsets and are relatively unaffected by the size of the total set. Also, descriptions are more influenced by the size of the actual subset than by the size of the inferred subset.

6. Single-word associates to patterns are less variable to good than to poor patterns, and latencies of the verbal response are shorter.

REFERENCES

Attneave, F. Symmetry, information, and memory for patterns. *American Journal of Psychology*, 1955, **68**, 209–222.

Bricker, P. D. The identification of redundant stimulus patterns. *Journal of Experimental Psychology*, 1955, **49**, 73–81.

Checkosky, S. F., & Whitlock, D. The effects of pattern goodness on recognition time in a memory search task. *Journal of Experimental Psychology*, 1973, **100**, 341–348.

Clement, D. E. Uncertainty and latency of verbal naming responses as correlates of pattern goodness. *Journal of Verbal Learning and Verbal Behavior*, 1964, **3**, 150–157.

Clement, D. E. Paired-associate learning as a correlate of pattern goodness. *Journal of Verbal Learning and Verbal Behavior*, 1967, **6**, 112–116.

Clement, D. E., & Varnadoe, K. W. Pattern uncertainty and the discrimination of visual patterns. *Perception & Psychophysics*, 1967, **2**, 427–431.

Clement, D. E., & Weiman, C. F. R. Instructions, strategies, and pattern uncertainty in a visual discrimination task. *Perception & Psychophysics*, 1970, **7**, 333–336.

Donderi, D. C. Information measurement of single multidimensional stimuli. *Canadian Journal of Psychology*, 1967, **21**, 93–110.

Garner, W. R., & Clement, D. E. Goodness of pattern and pattern uncertainty. *Journal of Verbal Learning and Verbal Behavior*, 1963, **2**, 446–452.

Glanzer, M., & Clark, W. H. Accuracy of perceptual recall: An analysis of organization. *Journal of Verbal Learning and Verbal Behavior*, 1963, **1**, 289–299.

Glanzer, M., & Clark, W. H. The verbal-loop hypothesis: Conventional figures. *American Journal of Psychology*, 1964, **77**, 621–626.

Glanzer, M., Taub, T., & Murphy, R. An evaluation of three theories of figural organization. *American Journal of Psychology*, 1968, **81**, 53–66.

Handel, S., & Garner, W. R. The structure of visual pattern associates and pattern goodness. *Perception & Psychophysics*, 1966, **1**, 33–38.

Pomerantz, J. R., & Garner, W. R. Stimulus configuration in selective attention tasks. *Perception & Psychophysics*, 1973, in press.

Royer, F. L. Figural goodness and internal structure in perceptual discrimination. *Perception & Psychophysics*, 1966, **1**, 311–314.

Royer, F. L. Information processing of visual figures in the digit-symbol substitution task. *Journal of Experimental Psychology*, 1971, **87**, 335–342. (a)

Royer, F. L. Spatial orientational and figural information in free recall of visual figures. *Journal of Experimental Psychology*, 1971, **91**, 326–332. (b)

Schnore, M. M., & Partington, J. T. Immediate memory for visual patterns: Symmetry and amount of information. *Psychonomic Science*, 1967, **8**, 421–422.

Snodgrass, J. G. Matching patterns *vs* matching digits: The effect of memory dependence and complexity on "same"–"different" reaction times. *Perception & Psychophysics*, 1972, **11**, 341–349.

Sternberg, S. Two operations in character recognition: Some evidence from reaction-time measurements. *Perception & Psychophysics*, 1967, **2**, 45–53.

LECTURE 3
THE PERCEPTION AND LEARNING
OF TEMPORAL PATTERNS

We now know that there is a direct relation between pattern goodness and the number of alternative patterns, even though the alternative patterns are inferred rather than being part of the stimulus presentation. Still further, the discriminability, recognition, immediate reproduction, identification learning, and verbal encoding of visual patterns are all affected by pattern goodness in ways quite sensibly explainable on the assumption that each pattern is perceived both as itself and as a member of a subset of alternative patterns. The greater the number of such alternatives, the more difficult are all of the various information-processing tasks.

PERCEIVED PATTERN ALTERNATIVES

In this lecture I shall describe research on temporal patterns and will introduce a variation on this idea of number of alternative patterns. Rather than inferred alternatives, we will use the concept of perceived alternatives, and we shall see that the idea of number of perceived alternatives makes very good sense of some phenomena associated with the learning and perception of relatively simple temporal patterns.

All of our experiments involve the use of repeating temporal patterns. The patterns consist of either visual or auditory stimulus elements presented at different rates, but with the time between successive stimuli being uniform so that the pattern is formed by arrangement of the elements and not by temporal variations. Table 3.1 will help me explain the problem we have been investigating and the approach we have taken. On the top line is a particular succession of eight events, an event being the occurrence of one of two possible elements, shown here as either X's or O's. We start such a pattern and then continue it indefinitely without pause between successive whole patterns. The dots before and after the patterns are

TABLE 3.1

Eight Alternative Organizations for One Temporal Pattern

```
. . . X X X O X O X O . . .
  . . . X X O X O X O X . . .
    . . . X O X O X O X X . . .
      . . . O X O X O X X X . . .
        . . . X O X O X X X O . . .
          . . . O X O X X X O X . . .
            . . . X O X X X O X O . . .
              . . . O X X X O X O X . . .
```

Note.—All of these patterns are identical when repeated indefinitely and without pause; they form one basic pattern. Each specific pattern differs from the others only in its starting point, thus being one alternative organization of the same basic pattern. (After Garner, 1970.)

simply reminders that the single pattern of eight events shown is pulled out of an ongoing sequence of events.

On the next line is another pattern of eight events, also pulled out of an ongoing sequence. By our realignment of it to the right we have shown that this pattern cannot be distinguished from the one above, once it is an ongoing sequence. In the language we use, each of these two patterns is the same *basic pattern* but with a different *starting point*. Even though this second pattern is as available in the ongoing sequence as the first pattern, it is rarely perceived in the ongoing sequence. On the third line is still another pattern, and again it is one that is rarely perceived even though it is as available in the ongoing sequence as the first pattern. It is the same basic pattern as the first two, being distinguishable from them only in terms of its starting point.

I think by now you have got the idea that in an ongoing sequence of events of this sort there isn't a single pattern at all, but eight different patterns; or, more generally, one pattern for each possible starting point of the same basic pattern. However, because there are eight different patterns in objective fact does not mean that all of these patterns will be perceived by human observers.

Our interest in these patterns is, first, whether basic patterns of the same number of alternatives as determined by pattern length differ in the number of perceived alternatives, and second, whether this difference in number of perceived alternatives is related to the difficulty of pattern perception. If this relation is found, we would have an excellent parallel to the finding that the difficulty of processing visual patterns is related to the number of alternative patterns.

The first experiment we (Royer and Garner, 1966) carried out on this question involved auditory stimuli. We used two doorbell buzzers bought at the local dime store as our two alternative stimulus elements. We generated all possible patterns of eight events. There are 256 such patterns, but as you have seen, these reduce to many fewer basic patterns. After excluding patterns that reduce to shorter effective lengths, and pooling patterns in which the elements simply are reversed (complemen-

TABLE 3.2

Temporal Patterns
Having Two Perceived
Organizations, Whose
Starting Points Are Indicated
by the Underlined Events[a]

X̲	X	X	X	X	X	X	O̲
X̲	X	X	X	X	X	O̲	O
X̲	X	X	X	X	O̲	O	O
X̲	X	X	X	O̲	O	O	O
X̲	X	X	X	X	O̲	X	O
X̲	X	X	X	O̲	X	O	O
X̲	X	X	O̲	X	O	X	O

[a]The mean number of
events required for correct
description of these patterns
was 22. (Data from Royer and
Garner, 1966.)

tary patterns), we ended up with 16 basic patterns. These patterns were played at the rate of two events per second.

The procedure was relatively simple: The pattern was started, and then played continuously. The subject listened, and when he had perceived the pattern, he then tracked it by tapping the pattern out on two telegraph keys, in synchrony to the continuing stimulus. We used three measures:

1. *Which* patterns were perceived, determined by how the subject began to tap the pattern out. We assumed that he started tapping at what was for him the beginning of the pattern as he perceived its organization.

2. The *number* of different patterns or organizations that were used for each basic pattern by different subjects. This measure, of course, is derived from the first and is the one of most immediate interest. This was our measure of number of alternative perceived patterns.

3. The delay from the beginning of the stimulus sequence until the subject began to tap the pattern out, measured in number of stimulus events. This was our measure of difficulty of pattern perception.

Our results can be summarized by placing the 16 basic patterns into three groups according to the number of pattern organizations used by the subjects.

Table 3.2 shows the seven basic patterns for which only two of the eight different pattern organizations were used. The perceived organizations are indicated by the underlining of the event that starts the pattern as perceived. The mean number of events heard before these patterns were tracked was 22. This is a quite low value, less than three complete cycles, indicating that these are quite easy patterns to perceive.

TABLE 3.3

Temporal Patterns
Having Three Perceived
Organizations, as Indicated
by the Underlined Events[a]

X	X	X	X	O	O	X	O	
X	X	X	X	O	X	X	O	
X	X	X	O	X	O	O	O	
X	X	X	O	X	X	O	O	
X	X	X	O	O	X	X	O	
X	X	X	O	O	X	O	O	
X	X	O	X	O	X	O	O	

[a] The mean number of events required for correct description of these patterns was 34. (Data from Royer and Garner, 1966.)

Note that when the pattern has only two runs, the beginnings of these two runs are the two alternative starting points. Thus the number of runs provides a limiting factor in the number of perceived patterns. However, number of runs is at best a weak determiner of the number of perceived alternatives, since these patterns include cases with two, four, and six runs of identical elements. With a greater number of runs, the patterns are perceived as either starting or ending with the longest run in the pattern.

In Table 3.3 are the seven basic patterns for which three different perceived organizations were used. The mean delay before tracking of these patterns began was 34 events; thus these patterns are substantially more difficult than those which have just two alternative organizations.

The principles which determine the particular organizations used are less clear here: Patterns beginning or ending with the longest run are always preferred. What is not clear is what determines the choice of the third organization. Length of run has something to do with it, but it is not a pre-emptive factor, since the second pattern from the bottom, for example, has the third starting point as a single event between two runs of two identical events. Also notice again that number of runs is not a strong determiner of number of organizations and difficulty, since a six-run pattern at the bottom is included with four-run patterns.

Table 3.4 shows the two basic patterns for which six perceived organizations were used, although with patterns this difficult and complex, it is equally difficult to determine from the diluted data exactly how many organizations are perceived, and I will later show that four is probably a better estimate than the six apparently shown in this first experiment. Yet it is clear that many organizations were used, and that these patterns were very difficult, with the top one requiring 49 events before correct perception and the bottom one requiring 104 events.

TABLE 3.4

Temporal Patterns
Having Six Perceived
Organizations, as Indicated
by the Underlined Events[a]

X X O X X O X O
(49 events)
X X O X O O X O
(104 events)

---

[a]The mean number of
events required for correct
description of these patterns
is indicated for each of the two
patterns. (Data from Royer
and Garner, 1966.)

This first experiment clearly established what we were seeking: Each basic pattern had eight different possible pattern organizations to be perceived, but not all of them were perceived. Furthermore, different basic patterns had different numbers of perceived alternatives. Lastly, the greater the number of perceived alternatives, the more difficult perception of them was. This result is, in one sense, counter-intuitive, since it would seem reasonable that tracking of the patterns could begin sooner the more acceptable patterns there are. The result does correspond to intuition, or common sense, however, if we realize that the subject must select from a greater number of perceivable alternatives.

HOLISTIC ORGANIZING PRINCIPLES

The next step in such research is to find out what properties of the stimulus patterns determine when a basic pattern has a small or a large number of perceived alternatives. The first experiment gave us only some limited clues, namely, that runs of identical elements are never broken and that when there are more than two runs, the patterns perceived tend to begin or end with the longest run.

In order to provide more clarification about these organizing principles, Royer and I (1970) did a further experiment. This time we used all basic patterns of two elements (tones, this time) nine events long. The use of nine events, rather than eight, doubles the total number of patterns and makes possible many additional and more complex types of organization.

We also changed our technique. A pattern was started at a fairly high rate—too fast for pattern to be perceived—and then the rate was reduced gradually until the pattern could be heard, and then reduced still further so that the subject could write a description of the pattern, actually in terms of X's and O's. While I don't want to dwell on technique, this particular technique has some advantages worth noting: The pattern can be perceived at higher rates than the subject can respond to it, yet the subject continues hearing the same pattern as the rate is decreased, so he can describe it. But by starting at a high rate, there is no effect of the particular point at which the pattern itself is started. Thus each basic pattern can be presented just once. Lastly, the technique is amenable to group testing, which is exactly what we did, using college students in classes.

I will do scant justice to this experiment, since I only want to use it as a transition to the next experiment. It provided some clarification of the organizing principles, however, and I will illustrate these with a few specific examples.

Temporal Balance

Table 3.5 describes some nine-event patterns, but I have changed the coding of them to take into account the fact that perceived organizations never break a run of identical elements. Therefore we can describe a pattern in terms of its successive run lengths, and that is what has been done here. So the pattern 2115 is actually X X O X O O O O O, or its complement O O X O X X X X X.

These are some patterns which are written in their most preferred organizational form, that is, the form most frequently used, and they illustrate that the preferred organizations are those that provide the best possible balance, with long runs at both ends of the pattern. For each basic pattern, of course, there is no guarantee

TABLE 3.5

Preferred Pattern Organizations
Illustrating Temporal Balance,
with the Longest Runs at the Ends
of the Perceived Pattern

	2	1	1	5	
	5	1	1	2	
	3	1	1	4	
	4	1	1	3	
	3	2	1	3	
	3	1	2	3	
2	1	1	1	1	3
3	1	1	1	1	2

Note.—Each pattern is described in terms of its successive run lengths, and each pattern shown is usually the most preferred from its basic pattern. The pairs of patterns are temporal reversals of each other, each from a different basic pattern. (Data from Royer and Garner, 1970.)

that perfect balance can be found, since the alternatives are limited by the structure of the basic pattern itself.

A secondary point to be noted here is that each of these patterns in a pair is a temporal reversal of the other, and they are not alternative organizations of the same basic pattern. Thus if a given organization is preferred in one basic pattern, so is its temporal reversal in some other basic pattern.

Temporal Progression

Next, in Table 3.6, are some pattern preferences illustrating another principle, that of temporal progression of length of run. All of these patterns show either an increasing or decreasing run length, again insofar as the basic pattern allows. These patterns are usually second in preference to patterns that have temporal balance. Notice once again that pairs of these patterns are reversals of each other, each pattern coming from a different basic pattern. (Most of these patterns are the same basic patterns as shown in Table 3.5, and the property of temporal reversal is true for the basic patterns and therefore for any specific patterns or organizations from the basic patterns.)

These two principles, of temporal balance with long runs at the ends, and of temporal progression, really clarify what had been found in the first experiment. There we noted that preferred patterns usually began or ended with the longest run. We now know that a still better pattern is one that both begins *and* ends

TABLE 3.6

Preferred Pattern Organizations
Illustrating Progression, with Run
Lengths Increasing or Decreasing

	5	2	1	1	
	1	1	2	5	
	4	3	1	1	
	1	1	3	4	
	4	2	2	1	
	1	2	2	4	
3	2	1	1	1	1
	1	1	1	2	3

Note.—Each pattern is described in terms of its successive run lengths, and each pattern shown is usually the second most preferred from its basic pattern. The pairs of patterns are temporal reversals of each other, each from a different basic pattern. (Data from Royer and Garner, 1970.)

with a long run, or that begins *or* ends with a long run either preceded or followed by a run of next shorter length, with regular progression in length beyond that.

The more general point of these principles is that they are somewhat holistic in nature. It's not just a matter of beginning a pattern with a long run that's important—it's the relation of that run length to other run lengths in the pattern that matters.

Temporal Reversals

Further evidence that we should be looking for more holistic principles of perceptual organization comes from the fact already noted—that when a pattern is preferred, so is its temporal reversal—the point being that what's in common between two patterns that are reversals of each other is a total configuration that is the same only in the sense that a mirror reflection of either pattern produces the other. Further evidence on this matter of pattern reversals is provided in Table 3.7.

What we have seen so far is the preference for patterns that are temporal reversals of each other, but with each of the patterns coming from a different basic pattern. Here in Table 3.7 are some patterns in which each of the pairs is a reversal of the other, but now both patterns come from the same basic pattern. For example, the pattern 1215 is the pattern 5121 started after the run of five identical elements. Each of these pairs of patterns contains the two most preferred patterns in the particular basic pattern.

To illustrate still further that this equal preference for reversal patterns suggests that holistic, configurational principles are operative, consider in Table 3.8 a more detailed illustration of pattern reversals that are not in the same basic pattern. The top pattern ends with the run of four identical elements. When we look at

TABLE 3.7

Preferred Pattern Organizations
Within the Same Basic Pattern

5	1	2	1
1	2	1	5
1	3	1	4
4	1	3	1
2	1	2	4
4	2	1	2
3	1	3	2
2	3	1	3

Note.—Each pair of patterns, indicated in terms of successive run lengths, are the two most preferred within the same basic pattern and are temporal reversals of each other. (Data from Royer and Garner, 1970.)

TABLE 3.8

A Detailed Illustration of the Preference
for Patterns That Are Temporal
Reversals of Each Other

If this:	O O X X O X X X
Then this:	X X X X O X X O O
Not this:	O X X O O X X X

Note.—The top pattern is the most preferred from its basic pattern, and the second
pattern, a temporal reversal of the first, is the
most preferred from its basic pattern. However, the third pattern could have been
chosen from the second basic pattern, and it is
more like the top pattern in terms of matching
elements. (Data from Royer and Garner,
1970.)

what happens in the basic pattern that contains the reversal of the top pattern,
we find that the reversal pattern is also the most preferred organization, as shown
on the second line. But an alternative organization to this second pattern is shown
on the bottom, and it ends with the run of four identical elements just as the
top pattern did. And the structure of the first five elements is really not changed
very much from the first to the third pattern.

As a last illustration, consider the patterns in Table 3.9. The top one is preferred.
So also is its reversal, which comes from a different basic pattern and is shown
on the second line. The bottom line shows an alternative organization to this
second pattern, and a close look will show that the movement of the single X
in that bottom pattern one event forward produces the top pattern. Surely the
top and bottom patterns are more alike than the top two—unless alike means
total configuration.

All right. This experiment primarily convinced us that the principles we were
trying to understand were holistic in nature, involving things like temporal configura-

TABLE 3.9

Another Illustration of the Preference
for Patterns That Are Temporal Reversals
of Each Other

If this:	X X O X X O X O O
Then this:	O O X O X X O X X
Not this:	X X O X X O O X O

Note.—Meanings are as in Table 3.8.
(Data from Royer and Garner, 1970.)

tion. However, the idea that the phenomenal perception is holistic has never to me precluded the idea that we as scientists can be analytic about it and can try to understand the configurational whole as an interaction—even a complex interaction—between parts with identifiable properties.

One-Element Patterns as Components

In order to understand these holistic principles as a complex interaction of identifiable components, Preusser, Garner, and Gottwald (1970) carried out further experiments. An obvious component of two-element patterns is the individual element itself. A two-element pattern may be considered as a series of events in which one of two alternative elements occurs in a given unit of time. A one-element pattern may be considered as a series of events in which a single element does or does not occur. Any two-element pattern may then further be considered as the interlocking of two appropriate one-element patterns, as shown in Table 3.10.

The top pattern in Table 3.10 is one in which a run of three positive events (the X's) is followed by two empty events (the apostrophes), then by one X and three empty events. The complement of this one-element pattern is another one-element pattern, shown on the next line, where the positive events of the first pattern are now the empty events of the second pattern—and vice versa. (Zeros are the positive events in this second pattern.) If these two one-element patterns are interposed, the two-element pattern shown on the bottom line is obtained.

We carried out an experiment to determine what organizing principles were appropriate for these one-element patterns, and then we applied these principles to an understanding of the organizing principles that operate with two-element patterns. We used patterns with 7, 8, 9, or 10 events, in each case using all basic patterns that contained temporal reversals of each other. Then we had our subjects listen to these patterns, played at a rate of three events per second. When

TABLE 3.10

A Two-Element Pattern
as the Composite of Two
One-Element Patterns

X X X ' ' X ' ' '

\+

' ' ' O O ' O O O

\=

X X X O O X O O O

Note.—The two top patterns have an element that occurs or does not (indicated as '). When these are interlocked, they form the two-element pattern at the bottom.

the pattern was turned off by the experimenter the subject tapped the pattern he had perceived on one or two telegraph keys, depending on whether a one- or two-element pattern had been presented. The stimulus elements in this case were the old doorbell buzzers placed to the right and left of the subject, and also two lights placed side-by-side. Both lights and buzzers were played together, so the two elements were either right-light-and-buzzer, or left-light-and-buzzer. With either one- or two-element patterns, the pattern was played for a fixed period of time. Thus only pattern descriptions or organizations were obtained, but not measures of pattern difficulty.

One-Element Pattern Principles

First, let us consider the organizing principles that evolved from descriptions of one-element patterns. There are two major factors that can operate with these patterns—the relative lengths of the runs and the relative lengths of the gaps. Over-all analyses made it clear that there were just two principles operating: Start the pattern with the longest run; end the pattern with the longest gap.

The combination of these two principles complicates the picture, since these two principles may be compatible, in that they lead to the same organization; or they may be incompatible, in that they lead to conflicting organizations. These two principles are compatible for the top pattern in Table 3.10, both leading to the organization as shown, and they are incompatible for the second one-element pattern, the run principle calling for the pattern to start with the run of three elements and the gap principle calling for it to start with the run of two elements, thus ending with the gap of three elements.

TABLE 3.11

Some One-Element Patterns
with Compatible Gap and Run
Principles: Both Principles
Predict the Same Preferred
Organization

X X X ' X ' '
X X X X ' X ' ' '
X X X X X ' X X ' '
X X X ' X X ' ' ' '

X X X ' X ' X ' '
X X X X ' X ' X ' '

Note.—The organizations are used as shown 90 percent of the time for the patterns with two runs of positive events, and 81 percent of the time for the patterns with three runs of positive events. (Data from Preusser et al., 1970.)

TABLE 3.12

Some One-Element Patterns
with Incompatible Gap and Run Principles:
Each Principle Predicts
a Different Preferred Organization[a]

X X ' X X X ' ' ' '	Gap > Run
X ' ' X X ' ' ' ' '	(86)
X X X ' X X X X ' '	Gap = Run
X ' ' X X X ' ' ' '	(71)
X ' X X X ' '	Gap < Run
X ' X X X X ' ' '	(49)

[a]The relations between the two principles are shown at the right, with the percent use of the gap principle indicated in parentheses. (Data from Preusser et al., 1970.)

Table 3.11 shows some more patterns all of which have run and gap principles compatible. In each of the top four patterns—those with two runs of positive events—the pattern is shown both starting with the longest run and ending with the longest gap. For such patterns, the subjects' use of the organization called for by the compatible run and gap principles was 90 percent. In other words, all but the usual small number of perverse subjects used the organization as shown.

The situation is a bit more complicated with patterns of three runs of positive events in that sometimes the run or gap principle is nondifferentiating, but in Table 3.11 are a couple of patterns in which both the principles of starting with the longest run and ending with the longest gap predict a single organization—and that organization was used 81 percent of the time for such patterns. Thus when these two principles predict the same organization, we have little question about what organization is perceived.

When the gap and run principles are incompatible, we have to make differentiations having to do with the relative strengths of the two organizing principles, as shown in Table 3.12. We used the absolute difference in the lengths of the runs or the gaps to establish relative strength of the two principles on a stimulus basis. The two top patterns are cases in which the differences in the lengths of the gaps are greater than the differences in the lengths of the runs. In these cases the gap principle determined the organization used 86 percent of the time, almost as frequently as when the gap and run principles were compatible. Thus these patterns were perceived as shown.

When the gap differences were equal to the run differences, the gap principle determined perceived organization 71 percent of the time—so again the patterns were perceived mostly as shown in Table 3.12, but with considerably less frequency. When the gap principle was less strong than the run principle, as illustrated in the two bottom patterns, then each of the two organizations shown was used about equally often. Thus the gap principle is more potent than the run principle.

Two-Element Patterns as Composites

How do these relatively simple organizing principles for one-element patterns relate to the perceived organizations of two-element patterns? The first-order answer is that the perceived organizations of the two-element patterns are simply composites of the perceived organizations of the two one-element patterns that produce the two-element patterns. Table 3.13 illustrates one such composition: The two-element pattern to be understood is 4112 in run-length notation. It is a pattern that had two perceived organizations in the first Royer and Garner (1966) study, and they start at the underlined events. The numbers under them show the frequency of use of these two organizations obtained in the earlier study, and the important point is that these two organizations were used about equally often.

Now let us examine each component one-element pattern. The first pattern as shown starts with the longer run and ends with the longer gap. Thus the two organizing principles are compatible and predict a single organization, starting with the run of four elements. In the second one-element pattern these two principles are incompatible in that each calls for a different organization. However, since the gap principle is much stronger than the run principle, it will dominate, and only one organization will be used—that ending with the longest gap. To summarize, each one-element pattern has just a single perceived organization, and the composite pattern has just two. This pattern is an easy one, as we learned before.

Note also, however, that one of these organizations leads to the best balance with long runs at the ends, and the other leads to a relatively simple upward progression. Thus the holistic principles come from rather simple component principles.

Now let us consider another pattern, as shown in Table 3.14. You may by now recognize this pattern as a reversal of the last one. It, however, had three perceived organizations in the original study, although not all were used with equal frequency, as indicated by the numbers in parentheses. Let us once again examine the component one-element patterns. The one-element pattern containing

TABLE 3.13

The Perceived Organizations of a Two-Element Pattern
Analyzed in Terms of the Organizing Principles for the Component One-Element Patterns
(Data from Royer and Garner, 1966)

X X X X O X O O	Two perceived organizations
(54)[a] (45)[a]	
X X X X ' X ' '	Gap and Run compatible: One organization
' ' ' ' O ' O O	Gap > Run: One organization

[a]Numbers in parentheses are frequencies of use of organization starting at that event.

TABLE 3.14

The Perceived Organizations of a Two-Element Pattern
Analyzed in Terms of the Organizing Principles
for the Component One-Element Patterns, as in Table 3.13
(Data from Royer and Garner, 1966)

X X X X O O X O	Three perceived organizations
(36) (61) (16)	
X X X X ' ' X '	Gap < Run: Two organizations
' ' ' ' O O ' O	Gap and Run compatible: One organization

the run of four elements has gap and run principles incompatible. It will have two organizations used, with at least equal frequency and possibly with the run principle being the stronger, because the difference in run length is much greater than the difference in gap length. Both of these organizations were used in the original two-element pattern, but with the longer run being used more frequently. The other one-element pattern has only a single perceived organization because the run and gap principles are compatible in it. So here we have a two-element pattern with three perceived organizations, but both the particular patterns and the number of them can be understood from principles operating in one-element patterns.

It is worth pausing just a moment here to refute slightly what we had seen earlier. The fact that reversal patterns were always preferred is itself a simple conclusion. But here we see that simple principles pertinent to one-element patterns explain the effect quite nicely. At the same time, they show a more complex interaction in that these simple component principles when applied to reversal patterns lead to unequal variability of perceived organization and to a consequent unequal difficulty. The reversal of the pattern 4112 to 2114 does lead to the prediction that the two organizations with temporal balance will be the most preferred. However, the reversal also leads to a predicted increase in number of perceived alternative organizations from two to three, and the data from the earlier experiment confirm this prediction as well as the resultant increase in delay before tracking started. Thus the use of analytic explanation is in one sense simpler, but in another, more complex, in that the interactions between simple component factors may be very complex. I will return to this point in a moment.

Figure-Ground Effects

If the perceived organizations for two-element patterns are simply the composites of the perceived organizations for the two one-element patterns that form the two-element patterns, we can still ask which of the appropriate one-element patterns will determine the organization in any particular case. Preusser, Gottwald, and I had originally undertaken this experiment with the idea that the simplicity or "goodness" of the structure or organization within each component one-element pattern would determine which would dominate, the simpler organization being the one we expected to dominate, to become the figure against the ground provided by the other element. The data utterly refute this idea, even though I am still rather fond of it.

On the contrary, the very fact that the two-element organizations are composites of one-element organizations indicates that no preferential treatment is being given to the better component organization. In the original Royer and Garner experiment we had no evidence that anything other than transitory effects determined which of the two elements would have the controlling influence. Possibly chance fluctuations, or possibly what the subject had done on the last pattern were influencing it. Since we always counterbalanced the use of actual stimulus elements in these experiments, we ran no risk that one element could always dominate and determine the perceived organization of the patterns.

In this last experiment, however, where we used both lights and tones clearly differentiated on a laterality basis, individual subjects showed distinct preferences for starting their pattern descriptions with either the right or the left elements—and of course we do not know whether this effect was due to a stimulus bias or to a response bias. What we do know is that each subject had a strong preference to use one element as "figure" and the other element as "ground." Our analysis of this factor was made easier by the fact that an equal number of subjects used each element as "figure." By knowing, for each subject, which element was predisposed to be figure, we could tell with great certainty exactly which perceptual organizations he would use. In fact, by segregating data according to element preference (or salience, if you like), we were nearly able to duplicate the data from one-element patterns in our analyses of two-element patterns.

The point of this figure-ground business is simply this: Structure, goodness, or simplicity of organization do not determine which is figure and which is ground. Rather, other factors determine which element is figure and which is ground, and that determination then affects perceived goodness and difficulty of pattern. We actually have no direct measures of either goodness or perceptual difficulty for the one-element components of these patterns, but we do know that variability of pattern organization is affected by which element is figure, and by now we feel quite certain that goodness and perceptual difficulty are functions of number of perceived alternatives.

Interaction of Principles

Now let me return to the point I mentioned a moment ago, that because we have shown that the perceived organizations can be understood from analysis into relatively simple, one-component factors does not mean that the perceptual principles are any less holistic, configurational, or even much simpler. The interaction of these simple principles in realizable patterns can be very complex indeed. I will give some illustrations that will also show that neither length of pattern nor number of runs are *per se* terribly valuable explanations of pattern complexity or difficulty. Rather, the interaction of the simple principles of run and gap is.

TABLE 3.15

A Pattern of Seven Events Analyzed into Its One-Element Components
to Predict That Two Organizations Will Be Perceived

X̲ X O̲ X O X O	Two organizations
X̲ X ′ X ′ X ′	Gap non-differentiating, Run predicts:
	One organization
′ ′ O̲ ′ O ′ O	Run non-differentiating, Gap predicts:
	One organization

As shown in Table 3.15, we will start with a simple pattern of seven events and six runs. We have never used this pattern in an actual experiment, but we can see that it would be a very easy pattern to perceive, because each one-element pattern gives a clear prediction for a single organization—either the gap or run principle predicts in each pattern, but not both.

Now I will add one event to the pattern, giving us an eight-event pattern. There are only four ways in which this can be done to lead to a different basic pattern, and we shall examine each. In the pattern shown in Table 3.16 we have simply increased the length of the longest run, and this pattern still has two one-element patterns each of which leads to a single organization. So it will be an easy pattern. In the original data from Royer and Garner (1966), this pattern required 21 events for it to be perceived.

In the pattern shown in Table 3.17 we have added the extra event to the last single run, giving us two runs of two events. Analysis of this pattern shows that one of the one-element patterns has run and gap principles compatible, so a single organization is perceived. The second one-element pattern has the run and gap principles incompatible and equally strong. This result produces two alternative organizations. The original data showed a total of three organizations used, with 31 events required before perception of the pattern.

In Table 3.18 is still a third way of adding the extra event. If we look at the component one-element patterns, we see that neither the gap nor the run principle

TABLE 3.16

A Pattern of Eight Events Analyzed into Its One-Element Components
to Predict That Two Organizations Will Be Perceived

X̲ X X O̲ X O X O	Two organizations
X̲ X X ′ X ′ X ′	Gap non-differentiating, Run predicts strongly:
	One organization
′ ′ ′ O̲ ′ O ′ O	Run non-differentiating, Gap predicts strongly:
	One organization

TABLE 3.17

A Pattern of Eight Events Analyzed into Its One-Element Components
to Predict that Three Organizations Will Be Perceived

X X <u>O</u> X O X <u>O</u> O	Three organizations
<u>X</u> X ' X ' X ' '	Gap and Run compatible:
	One organization
' ' <u>O</u> ' O ' <u>O</u> O	Gap and Run incompatible, equal strength:
	Two organizations

TABLE 3.18

A Pattern of Eight Events Analyzed into Its One-Element Components
to Predict That Four Organizations Will Be Perceived

X X <u>O</u> <u>X</u> X <u>O</u> X O	Four organizations
<u>X</u> X ' <u>X</u> X ' X '	Gap non-differentiating, two longest runs:
	Two organizations
' ' <u>O</u> ' ' <u>O</u> ' O	Run non-differentiating, two longest gaps:
	Two organizations

TABLE 3.19

A Pattern of Eight Events Analyzed into Its One-Element Components
to Predict That Four Organizations Will Be Perceived

X X <u>O</u> X <u>O</u> O X O	Four organizations
<u>X</u> X ' X ' ' <u>X</u> '	Gap and Run incompatible, equal strength:
	Two organizations
' ' <u>O</u> ' <u>O</u> O ' O	Gap and Run incompatible, equal strength:
	Two organizations

predicts a single organization for either of the component patterns. Each pattern has two organizations; thus we should have four organizations, causing increased difficulty for the two-element pattern. The original data had shown six perceived organizations, and 49 events were required for perception.

Table 3.19 shows the last way of adding that extra event. Now we have the worst possible case from the point of view of difficulty, since both gap and run principles predict an organization for each of the component one-element patterns, but in each pattern the principles are incompatible. Thus we have four organizations again, but with active competition between them. The original data had shown six organizations, and 104 events were required before perception of the pattern.

So the number of perceived two-element patterns for a given basic pattern, and the difficulty of these patterns, can be understood in terms of two rather simple principles pertinent to the perception of the component one-element patterns: The one-element pattern is perceived as beginning with the longest run and/or ending with the longest gap. These principles may be compatible or incompatible for a given one-element pattern, and when the principles are incompatible, there is greater variability in perceived organization. (Of course, in some patterns one principle will be nondifferentiating and thus will be inoperative in determining perceived organization.) For the two-element pattern, some factor other than structure or pattern variability determines which element will be used as figure, or as starting the perceived organization. Thus pattern difficulty and goodness should be to some extent a consequence of figure-ground relations rather than a cause.

Simple or Complex Principles?

The picture I have presented here suggests that the basic processes that determine perceived organization of these patterns are really rather simple: The two elements are segregated into figure and ground, then the perceived organization of the figure is determined by the relative lengths of the runs and the gaps. Certainly as a perceptual process from the viewpoint of the subject in an experiment, this process of perceiving organization is quite straightforward and does not involve any very high level of cognitive processing at all.

There have been alternative approaches to the processing of temporal patterns, however, and these usually assume a far more complex process involving rule learning of complex strings of elements, or grammatical analyses of the two-element patterns. Such approaches are exemplified in recent papers by Restle and Brown (1970), Vitz and Todd (1969), and Kotovsky and Simon (1973). Since these various rule-learning approaches are quite successful in predicting performance, it is clear that some rapprochement is possible between the approach I have favored and these other approaches. We are, after all, trying to understand the same phenomena, and if the data are valid (which I certainly believe to be so), then alternative successful explanations must be capable of rationalization. However, I would argue that the picture I have presented of a fairly simple perceptual process is far more parsimonious, assuming lower-level cognitive functioning, and must be considered as the alternative of choice until it is clearly shown to be inadequate.

There is a real possibility that the two approaches will interrelate, but not perfectly. If so, then I would expect the approach I and my coworkers use to be more successful in situations that are clearly perceptual, and at rates of presentation not allowing much high-level cognizing on the part of the subject. Alternatively, the rule-learning approaches should be more successful in situations where more complex behavior can be engaged in.

PERCEPTION OR LEARNING

Stimuli quite comparable to these two-element temporal patterns have, of course, been used in many studies of learning, studies with stimuli presented at rates

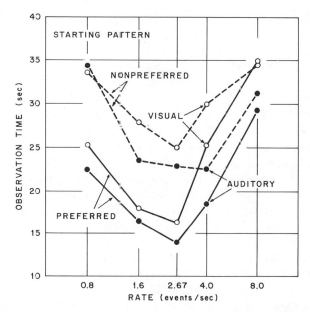

FIG. 3... Observation time required to describe two-element temporal patterns as a function of rate of presentation. The patterns were presented either visually or auditorily and were started at the beginning of the preferred description or of a nonpreferred description. (After Garner and Gottwald, 1968.)

of about one every four seconds, where each event is indeed perceived as a distinct entity. It certainly seems natural to speak of learning rather than perception at such rates. At the same time, it seems natural to speak of perception of patterns when the rate of presentation is 2 or 3 events per second, as in the experiments I have described. Certainly the subjective experience with these faster rates is one of perceptual organization, an experience so strong that the pattern has a distinct beginning and end, and if the pattern is terminated at some point other than its natural ending, a sense of incompletion occurs. Are there two separate classes of phenomena, and do they obey entirely different rules, or are there at least some principles of organization in common between them?

In one attempt to clarify this issue, Garner and Gottwald (1968) varied the rate of presentation of the pattern events from less than one event per second to eight events per second. A subject observed a pattern until he could describe it, at which time he stopped the pattern and then described it verbally. Thus both descriptions of patterns and measures of delay were obtained.

Several different patterns of eight events were used, and two further experimental variables were introduced, as indicated in Fig. 3.1. One variable was modality, with the pattern elements being either the two doorbell buzzers or two lights close together on a board. The other variable was the point at which the pattern was started, either at the point corresponding to the preferred organization or at a point corresponding to a nonpreferred organization. The results shown in this figure indicate a very interesting relation between these two variables and rate of presentation.

First, notice that the overall time required for correct perception (or learning) of these patterns is at a minimum in the region of 2 to 3 events per second. Thus our consistent use of these rates in our perceptual experiments was an efficient choice. Evidence that these tasks are processed quite differently at slow and fast speeds is given by the effects of the other two experimental variables. At slow speeds, how the pattern is started has a very great effect on performance, with patterns starting at nonpreferred organizations being much more difficult. At a rate of about four events per second, however, this variable ceases to be very important. On the other hand, notice that at slow speeds the modality used is unimportant, but it becomes important at about four events per second.

The differential effects of these two variables with rate of event presentation certainly suggests that processing at the slow speeds and at the high speeds is not identical. At high speeds, modality has some effect and indicates that temporal patterns are processed more easily with the auditory mode. That seems reasonable enough, since audition is much better adapted to cope with temporal properties of stimuli. But at slow speeds modality has no effect, a result which also seems reasonable and suggests that probably each event is encoded into a different form, and learning then occurs with respect to the encoded form, probably verbal. The fact that such encoding occurs early, on essentially the first trial, is suggested by the strong interfering effect of starting the pattern in a way that will not be used as the final preferred organization.

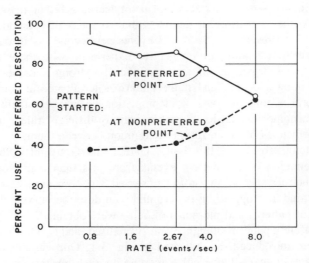

FIG. 3.2. Use of the preferred description of two-element temporal patterns as a function of rate of presentation. The patterns were started at the beginning of the preferred description or of a nonpreferred description. (After Garner and Gottwald, 1968.)

Figure 3.2 further clarifies the effect of starting the pattern at a nonpreferred organization. It shows, as a function of rate, what percent of descriptions correspond to the preferred description used as one of the starting organizations. As would be expected, at slow speeds the pattern is described as presented practically all of the time if it is presented in a preferred form, but this extreme preference drops off, again at a rate of about four events per second. When the pattern is presented in a nonpreferred form, the preferred description is used less than half the time, largely because the pattern is described as actually presented a much greater proportion of the time. Once again this effect begins to disappear at a rate of about four events per second. And we suspect that these effects are due to the ability of the subject to use verbal encoding of discrete events at the slower rates of presentation.

VERBAL ENCODING

Further evidence that the role of form of encoding is important in differentiating learning from perception comes from an experiment by Preusser (1972). He used a variety of two-element patterns ranging in length from 5 to 12 events, at three different rates of presentation. He introduced a variation in technique which avoided the effects of how the stimulus pattern was started by starting all patterns as a series of random events which then shifted to the repeating pattern at some later time. The subject stopped the pattern as soon as he could describe it. Preusser

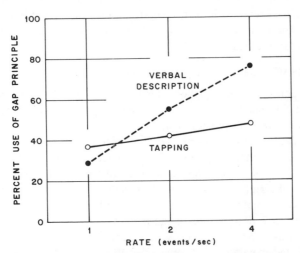

FIG. 3.3. Descriptions of two-element temporal patterns as a function of rate of presentation. The ordinate shows the percent use of descriptions in which the one-element pattern ended with the longest gap, and data are shown only when there was an alternative in which the description could have started with the longest run. The descriptions were either verbal or tapped out on two telegraph keys. (Data from Preusser, 1972.)

measured the delay before the subject stopped the pattern and the actual description given by the subject after he had stopped the pattern.

The variable of most interest to us here is the mode of description used by the subject, as indicated in Fig. 3.3. Some of his subjects were required to give a verbal description of the pattern, and these were usually given by describing successive run lengths; other subjects were required to tap the pattern out on two telegraph keys. The results shown in Fig. 3.3 are for those patterns in which one of the one-element component patterns had incompatible run and gap principles operating, and these data are only for descriptions starting with that element having these incompatible principles. (The other one-element pattern had compatible run and gap principles and thus provides no differentiation on this matter.) The results are clear enough: For both modes of responding there is an increase in the use of the gap principle with increased rate of presentation. But of even more interest is that this increase is much greater for verbal descriptions than for tapped descriptions. The complement of this graph, of course, would show the percent use of the run principle.

An additional result obtained by Preusser was that at a rate of two events per second, this same difference was obtained for both tapping and verbal descriptions when patterns were separated into long and short ones. Specifically, pattern descriptions (either verbal or tapped) of short patterns used the gap principle 61 percent of the time, while descriptions of the longer patterns began with the longest run 64 percent of the time. In summary, then, at slower rates and with longer patterns, descriptions tend more to begin with the longest run rather than end with the longest run. To us it seems most reasonable that this result would hold if the patterns are indeed recoded into run lengths, such as is probably done with verbal descriptions. The particular role of verbal encoding is less clear when the subject is required to tap the pattern out.

Expectancies with Simple Pattern Learning

Further evidence concerning the different way in which the subjects cope with the learning of slow patterns comes from another experiment by Garner and Gottwald (1967). Briefly, we had subjects learn two different sequential patterns of five events, presented at the rate of one event every four seconds, and with the subject required to respond in anticipation of (i.e., guess) each single event. We were thus able to obtain error data for each event in the pattern. The actual stimulus elements were the right or left position of a light. The patterns were started at each of the five possible starting points for each basic pattern.

The subjects gave descriptions of the patterns after they had learned them, and these descriptions showed that the same organizing principles that I have been describing for faster patterns still operate at these lower rates. For example, one basic pattern was nearly always described as either R R R L L or L L R R R (L and R for left and right position of the light), and these are the same descriptions which would occur at a faster rate. The other pattern was described most frequently as L L R L R or R L R L L, and once again these descriptions are those expected at faster rates.

Analysis of errors and trials to criterion, however, show that the subjects are engaging in more cognitive activity at these slower rates, albeit activity involving fairly simple expectancies about the whole pattern they are learning. To illustrate with the simple pattern of two runs, the most errors were made at the third R position in the pattern, and this result suggests that the subjects were trying to learn a simple double alternation. That this expectancy was operating is further established by noting the difficulty of learning the pattern when it was started at different points. The easiest starting point was R R R L L, and this is the starting point that disconfirms the double alternation earliest, on the third trial. On the other hand, the most difficult starting point was R R L L R, which does not disconfirm the double-alternation hypothesis until the seventh trial. Thus the way to make learning of such a pattern easy is to disconfirm as quickly as possible the most likely erroneous expectancy about what the pattern is.

Similar results were obtained with the more complex pattern. Many errors were made at the second L in the run of two L's, and this fact suggests that an expectancy of a single alternation was operating. The starting pattern that most quickly disconfirms the single alternation hypothesis is L L R L R, and it was very easy. The most difficult starting pattern was R L R L L, and the single alternation is not disconfirmed until the fifth trial. Another easy starting pattern, however, was L R L R L, and this does not disconfirm the single alternation hypothesis until the sixth trial. However, this sequence can be learned as a repeating single alternation of L R L R L—L R L R L, etc.

The total picture here is that even though similar organizational principles operate with slow and more rapid pattern presentation, a distinction needs to be made between the learning of patterns at slow speeds and the perception of patterns at higher rates of presentation. Pattern perception is phenomenally integrated, immediate, compelling, and relatively passive, while pattern learning is unintegrated, derived or recoded, intellectualized, and very active on the part of the learner. However, this active cognition on the part of the learner may involve relatively simple expectancies, and we do not necessarily have to invoke unduly complex processes requiring probabilistic rule learning.

SUMMARY

In summary, then:

1. If a temporal pattern of two alternative elements is generated and repeated continuously without pause, there exists the basic pattern and as many specific patterns with different starting points as there are events in the pattern.

2. The number of specific patterns which are perceived differs from one basic pattern to another.

3. The difficulty of pattern perception increases with the number of perceived alternatives.

4. The nature and number of perceived organizations can be understood by considering the two-element patterns to be composites of two one-element patterns.

5. The organizing principles appropriate to these one-element patterns are to start the pattern with the longest run, or to terminate the pattern with the longest gap, or do both.

6. These two principles may be compatible or incompatible for a given one-element pattern, and more alternative patterns are perceived when they are incompatible.

7. Similar organizational principles operate for learning of patterns presented at slow rates and perception of patterns presented at faster rates. Nevertheless, the learning process is much more active and intellectualized than the perceiving process.

REFERENCES

Garner, W. R. Good patterns have few alternatives. *American Scientist*, 1970, **58**, 34–42.

Garner, W. R., & Gottwald, R. L. Some perceptual factors in the learning of sequential patterns of binary events. *Journal of Verbal Learning and Verbal Behavior*, 1967, **6**, 582–589.

Garner, W. W., & Gottwald, R. L. The perception and learning of temporal patterns. *Quarterly Journal of Experimental Psychology*, 1968, **20**, 97–109.

Kotovsky, K., & Simon, H. A. Empirical tests of a theory of human acquisition of concepts for sequential patterns. *Cognitive Psychology*, 1973, **4**, 399–424.

Preusser, D. The effect of structure and rate on the recognition and description of auditory temporal patterns. *Perception & Psychophysics*, 1972, **11**, 233–240.

Preusser, D., Garner, W. R., & Gottwald, R. L. Perceptual organization of two-element temporal patterns as a function of their component one-element patterns. *American Journal of Psychology*, 1970, **83**, 151–170.

Restle, F., & Brown, E. R. Serial pattern learning. *Journal of Experimental Psychology*, 1970, **83**, 120–125.

Royer, F. L., & Garner, W. R. Response uncertainty and perceptual difficulty of auditory temporal patterns. *Perception & Psychophysics*, 1966, **1**, 41–47.

Royer, F. L., & Garner, W. R. Perceptual organization of nine-element auditory temporal patterns. *Perception & Psychophysics*, 1970, **7**, 115–120.

Vitz, P. C., & Todd, T. C. A coded element model of the perceptual processing of sequential stimuli. *Psychological Review*, 1969, **76**, 433–449.

LECTURE 4
LEARNING OF DIMENSIONAL AND CORRELATIONAL STRUCTURE OF STIMULI

Now I want to return to a discussion of psychological tasks requiring that the subject learn properties of sets of stimuli. Specifically, I shall deal with learning of the dimensional structure of stimulus sets, and with learning the correlational structure which exists if the set of stimuli to be learned is a subset of a total set. The stimulus materials used include visual figures, nonsense words, and real words. The psychological tasks include free-recall learning, concept or classification learning, and discrimination learning.

Any stimulus set, whether a total set or a subset, has two different aspects that must be learned, aspects that are almost antitheses of each other. One of these aspects is that the stimuli in a set are somehow the same or similar in that they share occupancy in the same set or subset. The other aspect of the stimuli in a set is that they are all somehow different from each other. So there must be two different psychological processes involved in learning the properties of a stimulus set, one being learning what stimuli go together by being in the set, and the other being learning to discriminate one stimulus from another. In normal, everyday circumstances, probably both aspects are learned more or less concurrently. In research on the problem, however, it is better if we can find ways of disentangling the two aspects.

FREE-RECALL LEARNING

Free-recall learning has always had a special appeal to me, since I think it comes closest, of the many learning procedures used by psychologists, to measuring reasonably directly the first aspect of the problem, namely, learning what stimuli exist in the set to be learned and thus go together. It is not, of course, a perfect technique in that it deals only with this aspect of the problem, since any free-recall

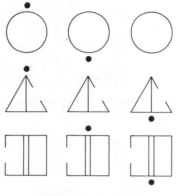

MEDIAN TRIALS: 2
(RANGE: 1-7)

FIG. 4.1. Free-recall learning of a subset of visual figures with three simple contingencies. (After Whitman and Garner, 1962.)

procedure does require that the subject at least know that he is not repeating an item in his recall; but this technique emphasizes discrimination less than do techniques such as paired-associates learning.

Geometric Figures

One of the first experiments we undertook to determine the effect of stimulus structure on free-recall learning was carried out by Whitman and Garner (1962). In this experiment we were concerned with learning of different kinds of correlational structure. We used geometric figures generated by four trichotomous dimensions, so we had a total set of 81 figures. The dimensions and their levels can be seen in Fig. 4.1.

The four dimensions were: form—circle, triangle or square; gap—on the left, on the right, or none at all; vertical line—none, one, or two; and dot—above, below, or none at all. (We have since ceased using dimensions on which one of the levels is a null, but the use of such dimensions actually seems to create little difficulty for the subject.)

A subset of nine of the possible 81 figures is shown in Fig. 4.1. Selection of a subset creates redundancy, or correlational structure, and the amount of redundancy is a function of the size of the subset in relation to the size of the total set. However, if we know the amount of redundancy, we still need to specify its form. In this set of figures it consists of three simple contingencies between pairs of dimensions: The gap is always on the left of the squares, on the right of the triangles, and missing in the circles. Furthermore, the circles have no lines, the triangles have one line, and the squares have two vertical lines. So form and gap position are correlated, form and number of lines are correlated, and therefore gap position and number of lines are also correlated. Thus this subset of stimuli has three simple contingencies or nonmetric correlations.

The task consisted of presentation, one at a time, of all nine figures, after

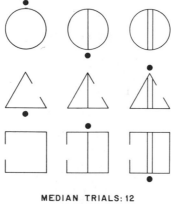

MEDIAN TRIALS: 12
(RANGE: 7-19)

FIG. 4.2. Free-recall learning of a subset of visual figures with one simple contingency. (After Whitman and Garner, 1962.)

which the subject was required to reproduce them by drawing all nine figures, and this procedure constituted one trial. Presentation was in random order, different for each trial, and recall was in any order. The results indicate that this subset is extremely easy to learn, with a median of two trials, and with no subject requiring more than seven trials to learn all nine figures.

Before turning to the next subset of figures, please note the three figures on the secondary diagonal—the circle with the dot on top; the triangle in the middle; and the square with the gap on the left, two lines, and a dot below. The results for these three particular figures were the same as for all figures together. That is, they were neither easier nor more difficult to learn than the other six figures.

Figure 4.2 shows another subset of nine figures, for which there is just one simple contingency, or correlation between variables, and that is between form and position of the gap: The gap is missing in the circles, on the right of the triangles, and on the left of the squares. This one correlation is not enough to account for the total amount of redundancy, since even if this correlation is allowed, 27 different figures could be generated. The rest of the redundancy is in the more complex form of interaction uncertainty and is expected to be less easily perceived and learned. That it is so can be seen from the results shown at the bottom. Instead of a median two trials to learn, the median is now 12, and there was barely an overlap between the results for this subset and those shown in Fig. 4.1.

Now notice the three figures on the secondary diagonal. They are the same as the equivalent figures in the first subset. Yet in this second subset, learning of these figures was identical to learning of the whole set. So they are no more or less difficult than the other six figures. However, since when these three figures occurred in the first subset learning difficulty was appropriate to that subset, it is clear that subjects in no sense learn individual items, but rather they learn sets of items. So our concern with the properties of sets of items is very valid, since that is what subjects seem to learn. And my earlier comment that the properties

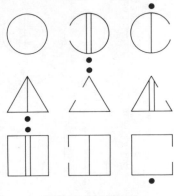

MEDIAN TRIALS: 19
(RANGE: 9–20+)

FIG. 4.3. Free-recall learning of a subset of visual figures with no simple contingency (complex structure). (After Whitman and Garner, 1962.)

of the total set and subset are at once the properties of each item in the set to be learned has clear experimental validity.

Figure 4.3 shows the last subset of nine figures we required subjects to learn, and in this case no pair of dimensions is correlated with a simple contingency. This is the sort of correlational structure that I will refer to as complex from now on, and the results we obtained with this subset certainly show that such subsets are very difficult for subjects to learn. Median trials to learn were 19, and since we terminated learning at 20 trials, we just barely obtained a median. I might remark that the subjects in this particular experiment were, for the most part, professional personnel in a veteran's hospital, and they were not happy about being unable to learn just nine stimuli within 20 trials. But as we have since learned, subsets with only a complex correlational structure are always very difficult to learn, and one almost wants to say that complete free-recall learning will not occur without some structure more perceptible than these interactions provide. That statement is, of course, too strong, but not by much.

Before leaving this experiment, I want once again to remind you that our evidence is very good that properties of the individual figure—as isolated from the properties of the set in which it exists—were not important in learning of subsets. Further evidence of this fact comes from an experiment by Garner and Degerman (1967), using nonsense syllables of a type I will describe in a moment. We used free-recall learning with a transfer paradigm in which half of subsets of eight words were retained in learning another subset of eight words. There was very little advantage to those words that were carried over, a result again supporting the idea that subjects really do learn sets and not items.

Nonsense Words

This first experiment established that correlational structure makes free-recall learning easy or difficult depending on whether the structure is simple or complex.

TABLE 4.1

The Sets of Nonsense Words Used
by Garner and Whitman (1965)

4A		4C		
BROZ		BLAZ		
BRAJ	+	BLOJ	=	8C
PLOZ		PRAZ		
PLAJ		PROJ		
+		+		+
4B		4D		
BRAZ		BLAJ		
BROJ	+	BLOZ	=	8C'
PLAZ		PRAJ		
PLOJ		PROZ		
‖		‖		‖
8S	+	8S'	=	16T

Note.—Each subset of four has two simple contingencies. When combined vertically into subsets of eight, a
simple structure is produced; when combined horizontally, a complex structure is produced.

It further established that with such material learning is of the actual set presented
for learning, and not of individual items. We needed to know some further things,
such as whether the same effects would be obtained with nonsense syllables, and
what the relations were between learning of subsets and of total sets.

The stimulus sets and subsets used in a further experiment by Garner and Whitman
(1965) are shown in Table 4.1. Nonsense words were generated by using two
alternative letters in each of four letter positions, as shown in the table. Thus
the total set, labeled 16T in the lower right hand corner, has 16 members in
it. We formed various subsets of size four or eight, and the relations between
them are shown here. We started with four subsets of four members each, and
these are labeled 4A, 4B, 4C, and 4D. In each of these subsets there are two
simple contingencies: The first two letters are correlated, and the last two letters
are correlated. So each of these subsets of four has the same correlational structure,
and it is a simple structure.

These subsets were then combined into subsets of eight so as to give a simple
or complex form of structure. If we combine subsets downward, to get subsets
8S and 8S' (S is for simple), then the subset has one simple contingency, with
the first two letters being correlated. However, if the subsets are combined horizontally, then subsets 8C and 8C' (C is for complex) are formed. In these subsets
there is no pair contingency at all, so the correlational structure is in the form
of interactions. Several learning experiments were carried out with these nonsense
words.

TABLE 4.2

Median Trials to Criterion for Initial Learning
of Different Sets of Nonsense Words Shown in Table 4.1
(Data from Garner and Whitman, 1965)

Set	4A	8S	8C	16T
Trials	2.3	4.8	>10	4.3

The experimental procedure was always to present words in a list in random order, with a different random order on each trial, and after a complete presentation the subject wrote down all the words he could in any order. Table 4.2 shows results in median trials to a criterion of two perfect recalls. First note the two middle conditions in which subjects learned subsets of eight words with simple or complex correlational structure. This result confirms what we had found out with figures, namely, that simple structure is much easier to learn than complex structure. In the present experiment, trials were discontinued after 10, and hardly any subject ever learned the subset with complex structure within the allotted 10 trials. Now if we shift to the 4A condition, we see that learning of four nonsense words, with quite simple structure, was easier than learning eight nonsense words even with simple structure. This result seems reasonable enough, since we have long known that it takes more trials to learn more items.

The results with the total set, 16T, however, complicate this picture a great deal, since slightly fewer trials were required to learn all 16 words than to learn the subset of 8 words with simple structure. For subsets of eight, the simplest structure that can be obtained is to have one simple contingency, as was done in the present experiment. Thus no simpler, and thus easier, subset of eight words can be formed. Any random sample of eight words would have a structure somewhere between the limits of our simple structure and our complex structure, so learning difficulty would be somewhere between the performance we obtained for simple and complex structure, which is to say that learning would be more difficult for randomly selected subsets of eight than for the total set of 16 words.

In learning a total set, dimensional structure must be learned. In learning a subset, not only must the dimensional structure of the total set be learned, but also the correlational structure of the subset itself. Thus it is eminently reasonable, as in fact I had argued in 1962, that it should be more difficult to learn a redundant subset than to learn a nonredundant total set. This line of reasoning argues also that it should be easier to learn a total set of eight items than a subset of eight items. In this experiment we did not use a total set of eight nonsense words, but Nelson, Garland, and Crank (1970) did, and they found that indeed total sets of eight items were much easier to learn than subsets of eight items.

The point of this discussion is that redundancy is not necessarily a good thing. We have already seen in the second lecture, from the results of Glanzer, Taub, and Murphy (1968), that overall paired-associates learning was more difficult if the eight stimulus items were redundant, even though individual items within the subset were easier to learn if they came from smaller, thus more redundant, subsets. It is difficult to untangle exactly when redundancy is good and when it is not, because few psychological tasks used in actual experiments represent reasonably pure psychological skills. However, we shall see that results for discrimination tasks are different from results for free-recall learning.

To return to the present experiment, let us consider that when a subset is learned, the dimensional structure of the total set must be learned as well as the correlational structure of the subset. Is the learning of the dimensional structure of the total set done as easily with complex structure of the subset as with simple structure? Table 4.3 shows some results pertinent to this question.

Five different ways in which subjects learned the total set are shown in this table. These ways involve either learning of the total set immediately, as with Group I; or learning two halves first and then learning the total set, as with Groups II and III; or learning two subsets of four, followed by the appropriate subset of eight, and then the total set, as with Groups IV and V.

Two measures of performance are shown: the total number of individual word exposures before learning of the total set of 16 was accomplished, and the median number of trials required when just the total set of 16 was presented for recall. This latter measure ignores all previous learning of parts of the total set of 16.

The first group is the control group, and total word exposures were 69, with median trials of 4.3. Group II first learned a subset of eight with simple structure, then the complementary subset (which necessarily also had simple structure). Then the subjects were required to learn the total set, but only 0.2 median trials were required. In other words, once the subjects had learned each half, they knew the total set and required no more trials. Furthermore, it is not at all clear that they needed exposure to both halves in order to know what the total set was, since Group IV learned one-half of the stimuli, with simple structure again, after learning each half of the half, and then required a median of just 1.1 exposures of the total set to have complete learning of it. In other words, it strongly appears that when a subset with simple structure is learned, the total set is learned at

TABLE 4.3

Total Word Exposures and Median Trials Required
to Learn Total Set of 16 Nonsense Words
(Data from Garner and Whitman, 1965)

Group		Total word exposures	Median trials of 16
I	16T	69	4.3
II	8S—8S'—16T	53	0.2
III	8C—8C'—16T	240	5.0
IV	4A—4B—8S—16T	44	1.1
V	4A—4C—8C—16T	135	2.0

the same time. Actual data for total number of word exposures show a decrease from Groups I to II to IV, and while these differences did not reach statistical significance, it is quite possible that the most efficient way to learn a total set is not to bother with all of it; just half, with simple structure, is quite enough to accomplish learning of the total set while at the same time learning the subset. It appears that two birds can be killed with one stone after all.

Note how different are the results, however, when the learning is of two halves, each subset having complex structure, as with Group III. In this case 240 total word exposures were required, and even after 10 trials with each half had been provided, there was absolutely no saving on learning the total set of 16 words. Group V learned only one subset of eight with complex structure and did not fare quite so poorly. This group had considerable savings in learning the total set of 16, requiring only 2.0 median trials. So it would appear that the less subsets with complex structure are learned, the easier it is to learn the total set. And the evidence is that little learning of the total set goes on at the same time that learning of the subset is occurring.

Thus, to summarize briefly, the properties of the single stimulus are at once those of the subset and the total set within which it is contained, and learning of the subset is simultaneously learning of the total set. However, if the subset has a complex structure, one which is not easily perceived, neither that structure nor the dimensional structure of the total set is learned very effectively.

Stimulus Similarity and Correlational Structure

The topic of this particular lecture is the learning of dimensional and correlational structure, and such structure requires the use, experimentally, of stimulus sets with dimensions and their levels well-defined. Even with such stimuli, however, it is possible for other forms of structure to exist, and with nonsense syllables the interstimulus similarity constitutes one form of structure which has been of interest to people working in the area of verbal learning. We will, in the next lecture, be concerned quite specifically with contrasting structure based on the dimensions of stimuli and structure based upon the similarities of stimuli. Now, however, let us at least consider briefly the relative roles of similarity and dimensional structure in free-recall learning of nonsense words.

Horowitz (1961) investigated the role of stimulus similarity in free-recall learning of trigrams composed of three consonants. He used two lists of 12 trigrams each. His high-similarity trigrams were constructed from just four different letters, F, S, V, and X, and these letters were used equally often in each letter position. His low-similarity trigrams were constructed from 12 different letters, and these were assigned to the different letter positions so that no letter appeared twice in the same trigram. Thus the high-similarity items had many letters in common, and the low-similarity items had few letters in common. His experimental result with the free-recall technique is quite straightforward: In early stages of learning, free recall was better for high-similarity items, although in later stages, free recall was better with low-similarity items. In a similar experiment, again using the free-

TABLE 4.4

Percent Subjects Learning Three Lists of Nonsense Words
(Data from Koeppel, 1968)

High similarity		Low similarity
Simple structure	Complex structure	
BFG	GXM	FLD
BFL	GJS	WPF
BFD	GDB	MGJ
KHD	QDM	VHB
KHL	QJB	BQC
KHG	QXS	CTM
ZJG	PXB	SKW
ZJD	PDS	RJT
ZJL	PJM	NXP
92	17	53

recall technique, Underwood, Ekstrand, and Keppel (1964) found a consistent superiority for items of low similarity, and again similarity was manipulated by varying the number of letters in common between different items on the list. So the effect of similarity on free-recall learning is not a simple one.

Let us consider this problem within the context of amount and form of redundancy or correlational structure. The necessary argument is best made by direct reference to an experiment by Koeppel (1968) in which he manipulated both similarity and form of correlational structure in the same experiment. His word lists are shown in Table 4.4. The summary measure of performance shown in this table is the percentage of subjects, out of 36, who learned a list perfectly within 10 trials of a complete presentation of the lists.

The list shown on the right is a low-similarity list, with practically no duplication of letters either in the same word or across words. Such a list has high redundancy, since the total set of items that can be generated with all the English consonants used randomly is quite high. We would expect, therefore, that free-recall learning would be reasonably difficult, since high redundancy makes for difficult learning. In actual fact, about half the subjects learned to criterion within the allotted 10 trials. Notice that when items are generated with minimum overlap of letters there can be no correlational structure. So it is meaningless to ask whether this list has a simple or complex structure.

Now consider the two lists with high similarity. Only three letters are used at each letter position, so that there is a fair amount of interitem similarity, if similarity is defined in terms of the number of letters in common among different words on the list. In this case, however, correlations can exist between different letter positions, and this correlational structure can be simple or complex, depending on whether it exists as simple contingencies between letter positions or as the complex interactions. In the left-hand list, the first two letter positions are perfectly correlated, so this list has simple structure, and nearly all of the subjects learned the list. In fact, 20 of the 36 subjects actually learned this list within five trials. The middle list contains items with no simple contingency, and only 17 percent of the subjects learned this list within the 10-trial limit.

This result with high-similarity lists confirms what Whitman and I had found with geometric figures and with nonsense words: Simple structure leads to easy free-recall learning, while complex structure leads to very little learning.

With regard to the problem of similarity, however, it is now clear that the question concerning the effect of interitem similarity has no meaningful answer until the correlational structure of the high-similarity lists is known. Low-similarity sets are much easier to learn than high-similarity sets if the high-similarity sets of words have complex structure, but low-similarity sets are much more difficult to learn if the high-similarity sets have simple structure. One is tempted to ask whether correlational structure is more or less important than similarity structure, but the temptation should be avoided. The question cannot be answered except within such a specific context of total set sizes, nature of material, etc., that the general question itself becomes meaningless. What can be said, however, is that both similarity structure and correlational structure are very important stimulus factors in controlling the rate of free-recall learning.

CLASSIFICATION AND CONCEPT LEARNING

I have used the free-recall technique in studies of learning primarily because I think it comes close to tapping in a reasonably pure way one aspect of the learning problem—learning what exists in a given set or subset. The other aspect of the learning problem—learning to discriminate the items from each other—has been emphasized more in American psychology, and the frequently used paired-associates technique is certainly much the better technique when discrimination between items is the most important consideration. However, I feel that the stimulus-response paradigm, which is so suitable for discrimination learning, has often been used in circumstances where it might really be inappropriate and thus might obscure some very important psychological functions.

Consider the classification or concept-learning task with stimuli defined multidimensionally. A good operational definition of the learning problem is that the experimenter defines a many-to-one mapping of stimuli to responses such that several stimuli lead to the same response. The subjects' task, then, is to learn the appropriate pairings of stimuli to responses. Clearly such an operational definition makes the concept-learning task differ only trivially from a paired-associates task, and it seems most natural that a paired-associates technique be used experimentally to investigate the difficulty of learning different types of stimulus-response mappings, that is to say different logical types of concept. The emphasis clearly is on having the subject learn to differentiate the circumstances under which he says

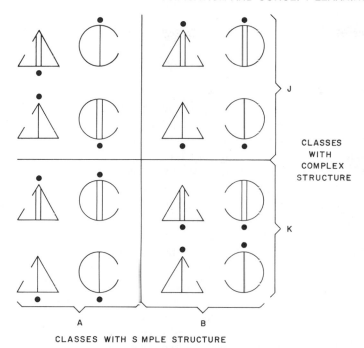

CLASSES
WITH
COMPLEX
STRUCTURE

J

K

A   B

CLASSES WITH S MPLE STRUCTURE

FIG. 4.4. Stimuli used in classification or concept learning by Whitman and Garner (1963). Subsets of eight stimuli formed vertically have simple structure; those formed horizontally have complex structure.

A, for example, from those under which he says B. Stimuli are intermixed, one trial is given at a time, and sooner or later the subject learns when to say A and when to say B. Alternatively he may be learning to push the left-hand button or the right-hand button, or to say "yes" or "no." But whatever the nature of the response, the emphasis is on the discriminative aspect of learning. Specifically, the subject is required to discriminate instances of one subset from those of another.

Suppose, however, that the important part of a concept problem is not to tell the positive instances from the negative ones, or the A's from the B's, but rather to learn what goes together to form the single class—in other words, to learn what the subset is that is called A, or "yes," or is the right-hand button. If the concept problem is really more a matter of learning subsets within defined total sets rather than one of discriminating subset from subset, then learning techniques more like free recall are the appropriate ones, and just possibly the use of the paired-associates paradigm inappropriately changes the nature of the problem for the subject.

Whitman and I (1963) undertook an investigation concerning this problem, with the help of the stimuli shown in Fig. 4.4. Here is a total set of 16 stimuli formed from four dichotomous dimensions, similar to those we had used in our first free-recall learning experiment, except that we eliminated the square and the levels of the other three dimensions that were null levels—i.e., those in which the dimension effectively did not exist. So there are triangles or circles, gap on the left or on the right, one or two vertical lines, and a dot either above or below. We divided these stimuli into the two subsets (or classes or concepts) in two different ways. As the stimuli are actually arranged, when divided in half vertically each subset has simple structure with position of the gap correlated with form, always being on the left of the triangles and on the right of the circles for the "A" subset, and with these relations reversed for the "B" subset. When the stimuli are divided in half horizontally, then each subset has correlational structure only in interaction form, which we have been calling complex.

In the literature on concept learning, many investigators have found that of the different logical types of concept, such as simple affirmation, conjunction, and disjunction, the biconditional concept is the most difficult to learn. A biconditional concept is one in which, to illustrate, the positive instances of the concept might be red squares and blue triangles, while negative instances of the concept would be blue squares and red triangles. In a concept experiment form and color would constitute the relevant dimensions (those that define the biconditional concept), and there would be additional irrelevant dimensions which are correlated with neither of the relevant dimensions nor with the set of response alternatives.

What is interesting about this problem is that a subset containing simple structure with a single pair of dimensions correlated is actually completely identical to this very difficult biconditional concept, as those of you familiar with the concept literature may have been aware. For example, in Fig. 4.4 the class labeled "A" can be described as all those stimuli containing a triangle with a gap on the left or a circle with a gap on the right. Likewise, the class labeled "B" contains all the triangles with a gap on the right or the circles with a gap on the left. Location of the dot and number of vertical lines are irrelevant variables, being correlated with neither of the relevant variables within either subset. But if such a subset is so very difficult to learn when it is called a concept or class, why is it almost absurdly easy to learn when all the subject has to do is learn, for free recall, what the members of a subset are? We decided to find out.

First we carried out the concept-learning experiment as closely as possible to the usual method, varying it to make the comparisons we were interested in possible. One stimulus was presented at a time, and stimuli from the two classes were intermixed. On each stimulus card was the appropriate label, "A" or "B" when classes with simple structure were used, and "J" or "K" when classes with complex structure were used. After each stimulus in the total set had been presented once, thus constituting one trial, the subject was given a deck of cards containing the total set (but without labels), and he was required to sort the stimuli into two classes appropriately. Errors per trial were recorded, and results are shown in Fig. 4.5. Learning was very slow, and there was no difference in the rate of learning with simple structure and complex structure. Certainly given this result alone we would be justified in arguing that biconditional concepts are very difficult to learn; in fact, as difficult as a classification for which there is no statable rule to use at all, where an apparently completely arbitrary classification scheme is used.

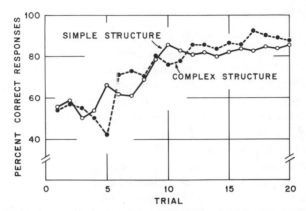

Fɪɢ. 4.5. Learning of classes with simple and complex structure (see Fig. 4.4) when the two classes are intermixed in learning trials. (After Whitman and Garner, 1963.)

Then we changed our learning procedure to make it more like that used in free-recall learning. Just one class was presented to the subject, again one stimulus at a time. After all eight stimuli in a single class were presented, the subject was given the deck with all 16 stimuli and required to sort into two classes, as before. The results with this method are shown in Fig. 4.6.

Here, the classification with simple structure is much easier to learn than that with complex structure, a result in accord with what we know about free-recall learning. The results with the complex structure were essentially the same as with the previous method, however. Thus, there was no facilitation in learning the classification with complex structure by presenting just one class. (Incidentally, the same result obtained when we presented both classes during learning, but first one and then the other. In other words, the important thing is to keep the classes well-separated in the learning stage.)

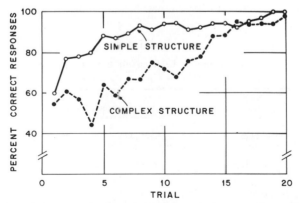

Fɪɢ. 4.6. Learning of classes with simple and complex structure (see Fig. 4.4) when only one class is presented for learning. (After Whitman and Garner, 1963.)

Response Methods in Concept Learning

A similar effect on concept learning can be obtained by the use of labeling systems which induce the subject to focus on the properties of the positive set of stimuli. Two different experiments, by Peters and Denny (1971) and by Gottwald (1971), have shown that learning of a biconditional concept can be facilitated by the use of positive-negative labeling, as shown in Table 4.5. Peters and Denny used stimuli with four trichotomous levels: shape, color, number of items, and number of borders. Because of their use of three levels, their biconditional concept was somewhat more complicated than that Whitman and Garner used. The easiest way to describe the positive instances of such a biconditional concept is, for example, to state that the concept includes all stimuli that are red and square or that are neither red nor square. Gottwald used some bug-like stimuli, varying in body shape, spot color, leg number, and antenna type, dichotomously in all cases. As the results indicate, these dimensions provide a difficult learning task. In both experiments stimuli were presented one at a time, classes intermixed, and the subject learned the appropriate response in the usual paired-associates fashion.

The variable of importance is the mode of responding. With neutral response labels, all stimuli were responded to as "A" or "B" in the Peters and Denny experiment, and as "alpha" or "beta" in the Gottwald experiment. With positive-negative responding, Peters and Denny required the subjects to say "yes" or "no," depending on whether the stimulus was a positive instance of the concept, while Gottwald required his subjects to say "alpha" or "not-alpha." The differences in detail are of little importance since both experiments showed that learning of the biconditional concept was facilitated with the use of positive-negative labels. Apparently such labeling does make the subject attend more to the properties of the positive set, thus facilitating learning in exactly the same way as Whitman and Garner did by only presenting the positive set.

These results certainly indicate that concept and classification learning should be considered in terms of the learning of subsets of stimuli with specifiable structure. While the ability of a subject to discriminate between positive and negative instances,

TABLE 4.5

Trials to Criterion for Learning of a Biconditional Concept
with Two Kinds of Response

Experiment	Response labels	
	Neutral	Positive-negative
Peters & Denny (1971)	19	14
Gottwald (1971)	256	54

or just between different classes of stimuli, is an ultimate consequence of a subject's learning what stimuli go into each class, it is a secondary consequence that does not define or establish the essence of concept learning. Concept learning is the learning of properties of subsets of stimuli, of the structure of subsets and total sets, and as such is closely related to free-recall learning. Techniques that may indeed be appropriate to the study of stimulus-response associative learning are not appropriate to the learning of concepts, because such techniques focus on the secondary consequence of the learning of concepts rather than on the primary process of learning what the properties of sets and subsets are.

DISCRIMINATION LEARNING

In free-recall learning, simple correlational structure in the set of stimuli to be learned is highly advantageous compared to the complex structure in which the correlations consist of interactions between the stimulus dimensions. Does this fact mean that simple structure is advantageous for all kinds of learning of the properties of sets of stimuli? In particular, is simple structure advantageous when the learning procedure places much greater emphasis on the problem of discrimination between the items within a subset of stimuli? As noted before, free recall requires learning what exists, and it is thus facilitated by simple structure within the subset. But if the subject in an experiment is required to learn to discriminate the stimulus items within the subset, the advantage of simple structure may be lost.

I had argued in 1962 that form of structure of subsets should affect discrimination learning in exactly the opposite way it affects free-recall learning. Where discrimination between stimuli is important, simple structure is disadvantageous, because the simple correlation produces literal duplication of differentiating information, and this is inefficient. Conversely, however, the very lack of simple contingencies or correlations which make learning what exists so very difficult will make discrimination between stimulus items relatively easy, because independent differentiating information is provided by the dimensions. Thus any type of learning in which discrimination between stimulus items is an important, or the most important, aspect of the learning should show that complex structure is better than simple structure.

In the second lecture I discussed some experiments which emphasized discrimination learning, as indeed many types of paired-associates task do, especially those in which the response terms are already well-known by the subject and are highly differentiated. The experiment by Donderi (1967) was certainly of this type, since he required subjects to learn a nonsense syllable as a response term to each of the geometric figures, but the nonsense syllables were highly dissimilar and were furthermore always available to the subject. Thus he never actually had to learn the response terms, and this aspect of the paired-associates task was therefore minimized. In that experiment, the concern was, if I may remind you, with showing how the learning of individual items within a single list of stimuli was influenced by the equivalent number of items defined by the sharing of levels of any single dimension defining the stimuli. In other words, the concern at that time was with intralist comparisons of learning difficulty. In the present case we are concerned with interlist comparisons, comparisons based on differences in the structure of the subsets of items to be learned.

There is good reason to believe that free-recall and discrimination learning are not identical or even parallel processes. Earlier I briefly discussed an experiment by Horowitz (1961) in which free-recall learning was found to be easier early in learning with similar items, as contrasted to learning with dissimilar items. Horowitz also used a serial-learning procedure in which the stimulus items were given to the subject on cards, and he was required to arrange the stimuli in the same order as they had been presented to him. Thus the subject did not have to learn what the set of stimuli was at all, but only to arrange them in a proper order. Certainly this procedure is one which emphasizes discrimination. Horowitz found, with the serial task, that learning was consistently easier with dissimilar items.

Another experiment showing a difference between the two types of learning was reported by Waugh (1961). She presented words on a screen and required the subjects either to recall them in any order or to recall them in the order presented. She found that the serial-recall procedure led to a linear curve in early trials, while the free-recall procedure led to a negatively accelerated function. So the two processes are certainly not identical.

TABLE 4.6

Percent Correct Responses for Free and Ordered Recall
of Lists of Nonsense Words with Simple and Complex Structure
(Data from Whitman, 1966)

Recall	Structure	
	Simple	Complex
	TAJ	TAS
	TEJ	TEF
	TOJ	TOJ
	YAF	YAF
	YEF	YEJ
	YOF	YOS
	XAS	XAJ
	XES	XES
	XOS	XOF
Free recall	85	54
Ordered recall	66	88

Whitman (1966) carried out an experiment directly testing the effect of type of subset structure on the two kinds of learning. He used the stimuli shown in Table 4.6. As you can see, the stimuli were consonant-vowel-consonant trigrams. Those with simple structure had the first and last letters correlated, while those with the complex structure had no pair of dimensions correlated. Summary results are shown at the bottom of the table. When the free-recall procedure was used, simple structure led to considerably better learning than did complex structure—a familiar result by now.

A few words need to be said about the procedure for discrimination learning. After the subjects had learned the lists of words, they were then required to carry out a second learning task with the words they had just finished learning. In this second task the same words were presented in a fixed serial order, and the subject was required to write the words down in the order in which they had been presented. Correct responses for this task are shown at the bottom of Table 4.6 and give a very clear result, but quite the reverse of that obtained with free recall. With ordered recall, the stimulus subset with complex structure was definitely the easier list.

This experiment emphasizes part of what I have been trying to say here: Learning is not a single process, and different aspects of the learning process will be differentially affected by changes in the structure of the subsets to be learned. At the barest minimum, even when the learning task is constructed so as to be primarily concerned with stimulus learning rather than response learning or stimulus-response association, learning *what* exists is a quite different psychological process from learning to differentiate or discriminate the items *that* exist. Since our function as scientists is to analyze these separate processes, we must be willing to use deliberate variation in the procedures, trying, even though seldom succeeding, to find tasks that tap a single psychological process.

SEMANTIC CONSIDERATIONS

In all the experiments described in this lecture so far, the stimuli—whether geometric figures or nonsense words—have dimensions that are unambiguous, both to the experimenter and to the subject in the experiment. Thus it seems perfectly reasonable to talk about the correlational structure of these nonsense words, because they are almost certainly perceived by the subject as having dimensions and levels. But suppose the same kind of structure is used where the letters combine to form words, and the subject is apt to think of the stimuli as unitary words rather than as multidimensional stimuli. Does the structure of the dimensions defining the subset still have an effect? In other words, are the subsets and total sets defined by these dimensions perceived by the subject in any meaningful way, or are the subsets and total sets perceived entirely in terms of the words as the units?

Words and Form of Structure

Whitman (1966), in the same experiment just reported, provides a partial answer to this question. The stimuli he used for the second part of the experiment are shown in Table 4.7. Notice that the same letters, both consonants and vowels, were used that had been used in generating the nonsense syllables, but Whitman was able to produce highly meaningful units—actual words in almost every case—simply by reversing the beginning and ending consonants. Once again, there is simple and complex structure, and the free-recall procedure was used, followed by ordered recall as before. The results are shown at the bottom. Overall performance was improved by the use of words, and most importantly, the effects of form of structure were nearly eliminated. Thus when the subject can encode the stimuli as words, the dimensional structure provided by the letters, even though it exists in the stimuli, becomes relatively unimportant.

However, it is interesting to note that what effects exist are in the same direction as before: Simple structure provides better free recall, while complex structure provides better ordered recall. The difference for ordered recall is the only significant one, but as we shall see in a moment, another experiment also shows that the differences due to dimensional factors are attenuated rather than eliminated when the letters form words.

TABLE 4.7

Percent Correct Responses for Free and Ordered Recall
of Lists of Meaningful Words with Simple and Complex Structure
(Data from Whitman, 1966)

Recall	Structure	
	Simple	Complex
	JAT	JAX
	JET	JET
	JOT	JOY
	FAY	FAT
	FEY	FEY
	FOY	FOX
	SAX	SAY
	SEX	SEX
	SOX	SOT
Free recall	93	90
Ordered recall	80	93

Words, Similarity, and Form of Structure

Earlier I described an experiment by Koeppel (1968) showing that difficulty of free-recall learning is affected both by the similarity between nonsense words and by form of structure with nonsense words of high similarity. A more recent experiment expands on this point and adds some rather relevant information. Table 4.8 shows the stimuli and results obtained by Nelson et al. (1970). The stimuli are consonant-vowel-consonant in form, and the letters used do not form words. Twelve learning trials were used for each subset. The two subsets of stimuli on the left show the usual result that free-recall learning is easier with simple structure than with complex structure. The right-hand subset shows also that nonsense syllables of low similarity, as defined by the items having few letters in common, provide learning of intermediate difficulty. So far, this result completely duplicates that of Koeppel. The fourth subset of stimuli adds a new condition to which I alluded earlier, namely, a total set of nine nonsense syllables made by using a single vowel. And as I had mentioned, learning of this total set is easier than learning even the easiest of the subsets of the same size. Thus in free-recall learning, it is indeed more difficult to learn a redundant subset than to learn a total set of the same size. Redundancy does not make the task easier, but rather it gives the subject something additional to learn.

But let us return to our concern with words. Table 4.9 shows this experiment duplicated but with letters that form words in each of the four conditions. The major overall result, as before, is that the availability of higher-order encoding thoroughly diminishes the effect of structural factors in the subsets of stimuli.

TABLE 4.8

Percent Correct Responses for Free Recall of Four Lists of Nonsense Words
(Data from Nelson et al., 1970)

High similarity			Low similarity
Simple structure	Complex structure	Total set	
XAF	XAJ	XOJ	QAZ
XEF	XEQ	XOQ	XAL
XUF	XUF	XOF	DEJ
ZAQ	ZAQ	ZOJ	BIW
ZEQ	ZEF	ZOQ	ZOF
ZUQ	ZUJ	ZOF	VUB
VAJ	VAF	VOJ	XYV
VEJ	VEJ	VOQ	YEC
VUJ	VUQ	VOF	JIH
55	30	71	45

TABLE 4.9

Percent Correct Responses for Free Recall of Four Lists of Meaningful Words
(Data from Nelson et al., 1970)

	High similarity		Low similarity
Simple structure	Complex structure	Total set	
BAG	MAN	BAN	FAN
BEG	MET	BAT	REX
BUG	MUG	BAR	WIG
PAN	PAT	PAN	BOW
PEN	PEG	PAT	DUZ
PUN	PUN	PAR	GYM
MAT	BAG	MAN	SHY
MET	BEN	MAT	END
MUT	BUT	MAR	ALP
72	69	77	80

Furthermore, the general level of performance is considerably higher with meaning-ful words than with nonsense syllables.

However, once again, the actual ordering of results for the three conditions involving differences in structure with high-similarity words is exactly the same with meaningful words as it was with nonsense words: Learning of the total set is easiest, followed by learning of the redundant subset with simple structure, followed by the redundant subset with complex structure. However, the items with low similarity were learned easiest of all, and this result does not correspond to that obtained with nonsense words. Nevertheless, the general conclusion can be drawn that the effects of dimensional structure are reduced when the letters form real words, but they are not eliminated. It would be interesting to have a comparable result for geometric figures, with one set of figures in which the dimensions used provide easy Gestalt integration, and another set in which they do not.

Words as Dimensional Levels

In the preceding two experiments, a higher-order encoding unit was available with meaningful words, and the dominant factor in learning was these words as contrasted with the letters as dimensional elements. Perhaps, however, the use of words in any way eliminates or attenuates the tendency for multidimensional structural factors to operate. An experiment by Musgrave and Gerritz (1968) gives some evidence on this point. In their experiment, words rather than letters were the multidimensional units.

Their stimulus material was formed from descriptions of—to use one exam-

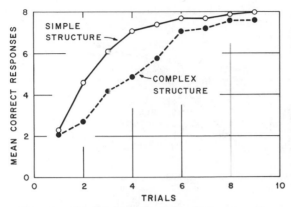

FiG. 4.7. Free-recall learning of verbal descriptions with simple and complex structure. (Data from Musgrave and Gerritz, 1968.)

ple—eight hypothetical Chinese fish, each with a label. The descriptions were based on four dichotomous attributes: color, availability, edibility, and markings. An illustrative passage presented to the subject is:

A green, abundant species of Chinese freshwater fish, Yungtai, are edible. They are spotted. Huso are green and abundant. These fish are inedible and spotted. Brown and scarce, Kimure are edible. They are a striped variety. Green fish which are abundant and inedible, Anhei, are striped.

Tschang are brown, scarce fish. They are edible and spotted. Green fish, Oshima, are abundant and edible. They are striped. Brown, scarce and inedible, Mori are a spotted species. A brown fish, Chungan, are scarce. They are inedible and striped [p. 1089]

I think you can see how simple and complex structure can be formed with these descriptions which are completely analogous to the nonsense words used in the Garner and Whitman experiment described earlier. The experiment was completely replicated with descriptions of boys and of musical compositions, and I shall describe average results for all three topics.

After the passage was presented, the subjects were required either to write down the descriptions for the free-recall task, or to match the descriptions to the labels in a paired-associates task which would hopefully provide a learning task emphasizing discrimination. Results for the free-recall task are shown in Fig. 4.7. As is clear, free recall of the descriptions is considerably easier when the subset of descriptions forms a simple structure than when the subset forms a complex structure. In this respect the result is the same as that obtained with the structurally equivalent nonsense words. However, notice that learning is really quite good by the end of nine trials, even with the complex structure, and this result is not what we obtained with nonsense words, since very little learning occurred within 10 trials. So the use of words as units, in meaningful paragraphs, does seem to reduce the extent to which structural properties are important.

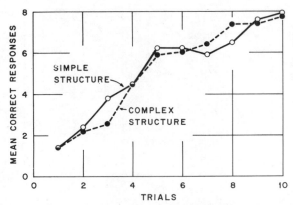

FIG. 4.8. Recall for matching of labels to verbal descriptions with simple and complex structure. (Data from Musgrave and Gerritz, 1968.)

Figure 4.8 shows results for the matching task, and in this case there simply was no consistent difference in learning difficulty between the two forms of structure. Insofar as the task used by these authors provides the ability to test discrimination in learning, this result is contrary to what was obtained for both nonsense words and meaningful words. While I cannot be sure why no difference was obtained, my own guess is simply that this matching task emphasizes the stimulus-response association aspect of the learning process too much, and there is no reason for the form of structure of subsets to affect this aspect of learning.

SUMMARY

In summary:

1. Free-recall learning taps one of two important processes involved in stimulus learning, namely, learning what exists in a subset and the total set from which the subset comes. When stimuli are dimensionally defined, such learning involves learning of the dimensional structure of the total set as well as the correlational structure of the subset.

2. Learning what exists in a subset is more difficult than learning what exists in a total set of the same size. The redundancy or correlational structure that is in the subset provides an additional load in learning. In many cases, learning of a subset is actually more difficult than learning the total set from which the subset comes, unless the subset is much smaller than the total set.

3. The correlational structure or redundancy in a subset may be simple, having simple contingencies between dimensions; or complex, having interactions. Free-recall learning of subsets is much easier with simple structure. Furthermore, with simple structure, the total set is learned along with the subset much more easily than is so with complex structure.

4. Concept classification or learning is very similar to free-recall learning in that the task is to learn what exists in a specified subset. However, techniques such as paired-associates learning make the learning of concepts more difficult than techniques more analogous to free-recall procedures and may make relatively easy concepts, such as the biconditional, appear to be very difficult to learn.

5. The second important process in stimulus learning involves discrimination between the items in the total set or subset. Discrimination-learning techniques show quite different effects than free-recall techniques. In particular, complex structure of subsets is much better for discrimination learning than simple structure. Thus the best form of correlational structure depends on whether free-recall or discrimination processes are involved in a learning task.

6. If letters are used as the levels and dimensions of multidimensional stimuli, and these letters form real words rather than nonsense words, the effects of form of dimensional structure on either free-recall or discrimination learning are considerably attenuated. This fact indicates that the stimuli are encoded as words, and that these are the meaningful units in learning.

REFERENCES

Donderi, D. C. Information measurement of single multidimensional stimuli. *Canadian Journal of Psychology,* 1967, **21**, 93–110.

Garner, W. R., & Degerman, R. L. Transfer in free-recall learning of overlapping lists of nonsense words. *Journal of Verbal Learning and Verbal Behavior,* 1967, **6**, 922–927.

Garner, W. R., & Whitman, J. R. Form and amount of internal structure as factors in free-recall learning of nonsense words. *Journal of Verbal Learning and Verbal Behavior,* 1965, **4**, 257–266.

Glanzer, M., Taub, T., & Murphy, R. An evaluation of three theories of figural organization. *American Journal of Psychology,* 1968, **81**, 53–66.

Gottwald, R. L. Effects of response labels in concept attainment. *Journal of Experimental Psychology,* 1971, **91**, 30–33.

Horowitz, L. M. Free recall and ordering of trigrams. *Journal of Experimental Psychology,* 1961, **62**, 51–57.

Koeppel, J. C. Intralist similarity, internal structure, and free recall. *Journal of Verbal Learning and Verbal Behavior,* 1968, **7**, 882–886.

Musgrave, B. S., & Gerritz, K. Effects of form of internal structure on recall and matching with prose passages. *Journal of Verbal Learning and Verbal Behavior,* 1968, **7**, 1088–1094.

Nelson, D. L., Garland, R. M., & Crank, D. Free recall as a function of meaningfulness, formal similarity, form and amount of internal structure, and locus of contingency. *Journal of Verbal Learning and Verbal Behavior,* 1970, **9**, 417–424.

Peters, K. G., & Denny, J. P. Labeling and memory effects on categorizing and hypothesizing behavior for biconditional and conditional conceptual rules. *Journal of Experimental Psychology,* 1971, **87**, 229–233.

Underwood, B. J., Ekstrand, B. R., & Keppel, G. Studies of distributed practice: XXIII. Variations in response-term interference. *Journal of Experimental Psychology,* 1964, **68**, 201–212.

Waugh, N. C. Free versus serial recall. *Journal of Experimental Psychology,* 1961, **62**, 496–502.

Whitman, J. R. Form of internal and external structure as factors in free recall and ordered recall of nonsense and meaningful words. *Journal of Verbal Learning and Verbal Behavior,* 1966, **5**, 68–74.

Whitman, J. R., & Garner, W. R. Free-recall learning of visual figures as a function of form of internal structure. *Journal of Experimental Psychology,* 1962, **64**, 558–564.

Whitman, J. R., & Garner, W. R. Concept learning as a function of form of internal structure. *Journal of Verbal Learning and Verbal Behavior,* 1963, **2**, 195–202.

LECTURE 5
DIMENSIONAL AND SIMILARITY
STRUCTURE IN CLASSIFICATION

When a total set of stimuli is partitioned into subsets or classes, all of the stimuli within a class are alike in some way, and at the same time they are all different from the stimuli in other classes. As I mentioned in the last lecture, both aspects must be learned in classification or concept learning. Now I want to discuss two major ways in which sets of stimuli can be structured, or perceived as structured, since these are the ways in which stimuli can be like other stimuli in the same class while being different from those in other classes.

Figure 5.1 will help to outline the nature of the problem for this discussion. We, the experimenters, that is, generate a set of stimuli by defining two dimensions on which the stimuli can vary. These dimensions are here called "X" and "Y." In order for a dimension to exist, it must have at least two levels. These two dichotomous dimensions provide a minimum orthogonal set of four stimuli, each stimulus being specifiable by its level on each of the two dimensions, and these are labeled in Fig. 5.1 as A, B, C, and D.

We ask a subject to divide these four stimuli into two classes. Typically the result of such a simple classification procedure is that the subject divides the stimuli into two classes of two stimuli each, the two classes being differentiated by one or the other of the two dimensions. If the subject groups stimuli A and C into one class and stimuli B and D into another class, we infer that he has classified the stimuli by dimension "X." If he groups stimuli A with B, and C with D, we infer that he has classified by dimension "Y." Fortunately for the simplicity of this discussion, subjects hardly ever use the biconditional classification of A with D and C with B.

Given either of these two "natural" modes of classification, what do we know about the perceptual basis of the classification? We could argue that the subject classifies by dimensions, using the two levels of one dimension to differentiate

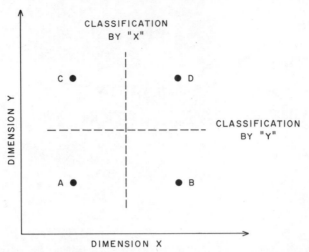

FIG. 5.1. The basic classification paradigm. Four stimuli are formed from two dichotomous dimensions, and the subject is required to divide them into two classes.

the classes, and using each level on that dimension as the means of establishing that all stimuli sharing that level are alike. Thus one dimension becomes the relevant one, serving both to differentiate and to establish alikeness, while the other dimension is irrelevant. This is certainly the explanation that comes quickly to mind if we think that the dimensions used by the experimenter are those perceived and used by the subject.

There is, however, at least one important alternative explanation of the natural classifications that must be considered. It is that the subject classifies the stimuli so that he maximizes the perceived differences between classes while at the same time maximizing the perceived similarities within classes. From this point of view the only function of the dimensions is that they serve as the means of generating stimuli that have a set of perceived similarities.

Thus these four stimuli may be considered to have a structure based upon the stimulus similarities. Furthermore, the relation between similarity structure and dimensional structure may not be a simple one and may itself depend on the particular dimensions used to generate a set of stimuli.

SIMILARITY SCALING

To begin to provide an understanding of the role of dimensional and similarity structure in perceptual classification, let us first consider the considerable body of research concerned directly with the measurement of stimulus similarities with multidimensional stimuli. Figure 5.2 diagrammatically illustrates a basic issue involved in all of this research, namely, how the perceived similarity of stimuli that differ on two dimensions relates to the perceived similarity of stimuli that differ on each of the two dimensions separately. In our diagram, there are three stimuli, A, B, and C. Stimulus A differs from B only on dimension "X," and

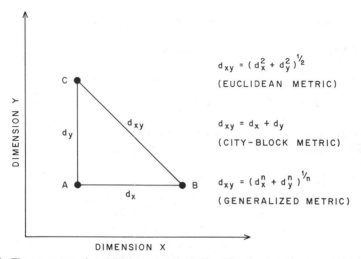

$$d_{xy} = (d_x^2 + d_y^2)^{1/2}$$

(EUCLIDEAN METRIC)

$$d_{xy} = d_x + d_y$$

(CITY-BLOCK METRIC)

$$d_{xy} = (d_x^n + d_y^n)^{1/n}$$

(GENERALIZED METRIC)

FIG. 5.2. The geometry of multidimensional similarity. The distance between stimuli B and C, differing on dimensions X and Y, can bear several relations to the distances between each of these stimuli and stimulus A, each pair differing on a single dimension.

the perceived similarity is indicated as d_x. (Actually, while most commonly the experiments are done in terms of similarity, the converse concept is more appropriate for measurement, and fortunately the symbol d can stand for distance, difference, discriminability, or even just dissimilarity.) Also, stimulus A differs from C only on dimension ''Y,'' and the perceived similarity is indicated as d_y. The experimental question is: If we know the values of d_x and d_y, what is the value of d_{xy}, the distance between stimuli C and B, which differ on both dimensions?

If similarity is thought of as distance, then it is appropriate to use the ordinary geometry which defines distances for us on plane surfaces. In this case the distance between B and C is defined by the Pythagorean relation of the Euclidean metric indicated at the top right. It is the familiar relation in which the hypotenuse of a right triangle is the square root of the sum of the squares of the two sides.

If you hadn't learned about the Pythagorean relation, you might have assumed an even simpler relation between these three distances, namely, that stimuli that differ on two dimensions have a perceived dissimilarity which is the sum of the two perceived dissimilarities for stimulus pairs differing on just one dimension at a time. This is the relation shown in the middle on the right, and it is commonly referred to as the city-block metric. The reason is that if the city streets are at right angles to each other, then to get from any point to another, you must traverse a set of sides of right angles and can never walk on the hypotenuse because they have buildings on them, not streets. Thus the distance between two points is the sum of the distances along each dimension separately.

These two relations can be considered as special cases of a more generalized metric, as pointed out by Torgerson in 1958. That generalized metric is indicated at the bottom on the right, and it has the unknown exponent, *n*, which is both the power to which each distance is raised, and also the extracted root of the sum. If this exponent is 2, then we have the Euclidean metric. If the exponent is 1, then we have the city-block metric. It does not seem very reasonable that any experimental result should have an exponent less than 1 or greater than 2, and fortunately various experimental results have always comfortably fitted between these two exponents, so that our rationality limits are not strained. Furthermore, it is usually fairly clear whether a given experimental result corresponds more to one metric than the other. So ordinarily we do not have to be concerned about intermediate solutions of the generalized metric but can act as though there are just two possible outcomes without doing great disservice to data.

There is actually a third value of the exponent that defines a logically important condition, as pointed out by Coombs, Dawes, and Tversky (1970). That value is infinity, and it establishes the dominance model, in which the perceived distances are a function of a single dimension only, that dimension being the one with the greatest distance. There are, to my knowledge, no data showing such an extreme relation, but some data which I discussed in the first lecture certainly tend toward the dominance model. These were the data obtained by Mavrides (1970), in which she found that the single dimension most differentiating a particular pair of stimuli had a far greater influence on the judgments of perceived difference than appropriate in terms of its overall effectiveness in influencing the judgments. Perhaps the dominance model should be investigated more than it has been so far.

City-Block or Euclidean Metric

Research on the perceived similarities of multidimensional stimuli has gone on for some time, and it has become clear that the question concerning whether the city-block or the Euclidean metric better describes the psychological process is too limited. There is no single answer. Rather, the question has become one of finding which pairs of dimensions give one metric rather than the other, and then of trying to determine the basic properties of the dimensions that lead to each of the metrics.

Many different experimental techniques have been used in studying this problem, ranging from direct numeric estimations of similarities, to forced choice with the method of triads, to the use of error distributions to establish similarity. I shall not discuss specific methodology because (*a*) it is not terribly pertinent, and (*b*) there is a consistency to the results obtained by various researchers with different methods that makes it clear that the results are general beyond the artifactual constraints of any particular method.

Attneave (1950) used visual stimuli varying in size and form, and in a second experiment, in size and brightness. In both cases he found that the city-block metric described his experimental results better than the Euclidean metric. Torgerson (1958), in describing his 1951 doctoral dissertation, showed that the Munsell dimensions of value and chroma (or brightness and saturation) gave results consistent with the Euclidean metric. In contrasting his results and those of Attneave, Torgerson suggested that the city-block metric might be appropriate where the dimensions are "obvious and compelling" but that the Euclidean metric might be appropriate otherwise.

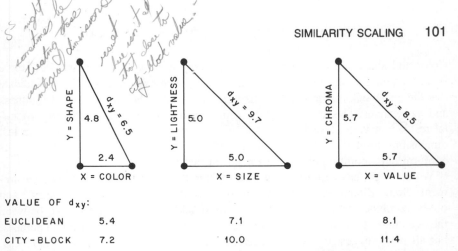

VALUE OF d_{xy}:

EUCLIDEAN	5.4	7.1	8.1
CITY-BLOCK	7.2	10.0	11.4

FIG. 5.3. Similarity judgments for stimuli generated from three pairs of dimensions. The numbers on each diagram are experimental data. The numbers given below are computed from the one-dimensional distances for the two metrics. (Data from Handel and Imai, 1972.)

Further data came from Shepard (1964), who used as stimuli circles in which a radius lay. The circles varied in size, and the radii varied in angle. Shepard found, with a variety of experiments, that the Euclidean metric did not provide an adequate representation of the data, and that some metric closer to the city-block was more satisfactory. He used the terms "unitary" and "analyzable" to describe multidimensional stimuli that would produce the Euclidean and city-block metrics, respectively.

Hyman and Well (1967, 1968) confirmed previous results that the Euclidean metric was appropriate for dimensions of value and chroma, but that the city-block metric was appropriate for size and form, as Attneave had shown, and for circles with radii, as Shepard had shown. These authors, however, further clarified the issue by presenting value and chroma as separate dimensions in two different color chips on the same card and found that when the dimensions were thus separated, they also gave results in line with the city-block metric. These results, comparing different stimulus dimensions within the same experimental paradigm, clarify that there really is something different about dimensions themselves and that previously found differences were not an accident of variations in experimental procedure. Furthermore, the differences are clearly related to the general ideas of unitariness, analyzability, separability, etc.

Data from one further experiment are shown in Fig. 5.3. These data come from Handel and Imai (1972) and involve comparisons between three pairs of stimulus dimensions as indicated. For each pair of dimensions, the values of dissimilarity (on a 10-point scale) are shown as values on the sides of triangles. The values when stimuli differed on just one dimension are indicated within each triangle, and the obtained value for dissimilarity when stimuli differed on both dimensions is shown on the hypotenuse. The tabled values underneath show the value that would have been obtained for the hypotenuse if either the Euclidean or city-block metric held exactly.

These three pairs of dimensions were used because of their different properties.

Color and shape are dimensions on which only nominal levels exist (i.e., there is no meaningful way to order sizes or colors). The experimental results indicate that the city-block metric is better than the Euclidean. The dimensions of lightness and size were used because both of these are scalable, and in this case the experimental result is a very close fit to that expected with the city-block metric. The last dimensions used were Munsell value and chroma, and in this case the results conform quite comfortably to the Euclidean metric.

We do, then, have a fairly clear picture from the research on similarity measurement. Some dimensions combine so as to conform to a Euclidean metric, and others combine so as to conform to a city-block metric. The difference between the two kinds of dimensions has been described in various ways by different authors, but all have suggested that the difference has to do with unitariness, singleness, or compactness, as contrasted with distinctiveness, analyzability, or separability. I shall refer to this property of dimensions to produce the Euclidean metric as integrality, a term first used by Lockhead (1966) in a context different from the present one, but related to it. The complementary concept, applicable with dimensions producing the city-block metric, is separability.

Two Kinds of Structure

What do we conclude about the differences in perceptual process between integral and separable dimensions? There are two approaches we can take. One of them is to accept as face valid that we are in fact dealing with similarity, since the data were obtained from experiments, in most cases, in which the subjects were judging similarity. That is the operationally respectable thing to do. But then we must, as Torgerson (1965) argues, conclude that similarity is not a unitary concept, that its essential meaning for stimuli defined by integral dimensions is different from those defined by separable dimensions.

The second approach, which I shall try to show is preferable, is that two quite different properties of sets of stimuli are involved when they are generated with the two kinds of dimensions. Each of these properties can serve as the basis of the perceived structure of a set of stimuli. One of these is truly a similarity structure, and it is the one in which the Euclidean metric holds, in which ordinary distance relations are meaningful. The other structure is based upon dimensions, and in this case similarity in the ordinary sense of the word, and certainly in the sense of distance, is quite unimportant.

If the task given the subject is to judge similarity, he will do it whether that is his normal mode of perception or not. If we change our task to one of perceptual classsification, however, we can get more directly at the structure of sets of stimuli as perceived by subjects. With this technique it is possible to show that factors that should affect similarity and distance relationships have relatively little effect on classifications with separable stimuli, while factors pertinent to the defining dimensions themselves have relatively little effect on classifications with integral stimuli.

PERCEPTUAL CLASSIFICATION

Before reporting some actual data on our classification studies, a few general words need to be said about procedures. Essentially, in these classification studies, a subject is presented with a set of stimuli and his task is to form classes. The subject may be asked to form one, two, or more classes. He may be required to form any number of classes he chooses from a fixed set of stimuli. Or he may be required to form a specified number of classes with a fixed number of stimuli. We have tried to develop a nomenclature for these tasks, with only limited success. We do use the term *free classification* when the subject is simply given a set of stimuli and told to divide them into as many classes as he likes, and of whatever sizes. We also use the term *restricted classification* when the experimenter limits what the subject may do in some manner, such as requiring that the subject form a specified number of classes, or use particular stimuli in his classes. When we revert to more traditional methodology and tell the subject what classes he is to create or learn, and then measure some performance consequence, such as learning trials, errors, or speed, we use the term *constrained classification*.

In this lecture I will describe experiments using free and restricted classification. The important point to remember about these methods is that the experimental outcome is an actual classification not an indirect measure of performance. Thus we want to know how the subject classifies, not how well he can perform with the classifications we insist he use or learn. With many such classifications, we attempt to determine or at least conjecture what the nature of the perceived structure must have been to lead to these classifications.

Nominal Dimensions

First let us consider some data on classifications of nominal dimensions. As an introduction, let us examine the data in Table 5.1. Imai (1966) asked subjects to classify 12 stimuli with no restrictions on numbers or sizes of classes. In one case the stimuli were in fact all identical. As you can see in the second column, well over half of the subjects formed two classes (nearly always of 6 members

TABLE 5.1

Percent Use of Two and Four Classes in Free Classification of Sets of 12 Stimuli of Three Different Types (Data from Imai, 1966)

No. of classes formed	Stimulus set		
	Identical	4 Colors	2 Colors × 2 sizes
2	62	7	56
4	24	77	33

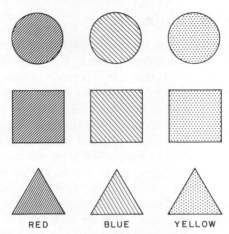

FIG. 5.4. Stimuli used by Imai and Garner (1968) in classification experiments. Three levels on nominal dimensions of form and color generated a total set of nine stimuli.

each), and the only other number of classes used with any consistency was four. Thus there is a basic tendency for subjects to use a small number of classes, preferably two. Furthermore, although not shown in Table 5.1, they use these with balanced numbers of instances per class.

The data in the next column show, however, that if the stimuli differed categorically by being of four different colors, and in many cases with an uneven distribution of colors, then the number of classifications using four classes increased dramatically. So we know that a stimulus property can dominate a simple preference for a smaller number of classes. The data in the last column show what happened when the four categories were formed from the two dimensions of color and size (with only color, of course, being a nominal dimension): Once again there was a majority use of just two categories. Thus classification by categories is not the major mode when the categories themselves are formed from two dimensions rather than being nominal levels on a single dimension. Certainly this result suggests that stimulus dimensions are important in the classification process, and that the function of stimulus dimensions is not simply to produce categories but is to provide a perceived property of the set of stimuli themselves.

Several further experiments by Imai and Garner (1968) confirm the importance of the dimensional structure in classification of stimuli formed from two nominal dimensions. Figure 5.4 shows the total set of stimuli we used in these experiments. We used two dimensions with three levels on each: color, with red, blue, and yellow as levels; and form, with circles, squares, and triangles as levels. A preliminary experiment with a similarity-judgment procedure established that these two dimensions provided equally dissimilar levels and that within each level the three possible differences were equal. Thus we were assured that the stimuli were not perceived as ordered. This fact means that many different actual classes of stimuli are logically equivalent and could thus be pooled in our analysis of the classifications.

Single subset selections. The first classification experiment, with some results

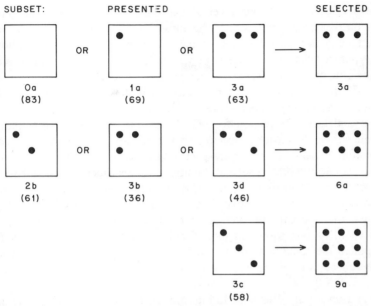

FIG. 5.5. Single subset selections for different presented subsets of stimuli from total set in Fig. 5.4. Each presented subset led to the selected subset more often than to any other selected subset, with the percent used indicated in parentheses. (Data from Imai and Garner, 1968).

indicated in Fig. 5.5, involved the selection or production of single subsets by the subject. The procedure was simple: The subject was given a total of nine stimuli (actually plastic chips which were easily handled). The experimenter on a single trial presented the subject with a subset of none, one, two, or three stimuli. The subject then selected the identical stimuli from his set and added any stimuli he wanted to the original ones.

Both the subset presented and the subsets selected can be diagrammed as cells in the 3 × 3 matrix of stimuli representing the total set. What are shown in Fig. 5.5 are logical types of subsets, for each of which there are many representations involving variations in the dimensions and their levels. To illustrate, subset 3a might be a red triangle plus a blue triangle plus a yellow triangle. Or it might be all three of the blue stimuli. Or, to take a more complex one, subset 3d might be a blue square plus a yellow square plus a red circle. All possible representations of the logical types of subset actually were used in the experiment, but fortunately the specific representations had little effect on the results, so that summary data in terms of the logical forms of subset are quite sufficient.

For all subsets presented, the vast majority of selected subsets were the three shown in the column on the right. The percentages of times that different presented subsets produced the particular selected subset are shown in parentheses under the presented subset. In each case, the selected subset shown was the most frequently selected one. You can look at these various subsets in detail if you like, but the total result can be stated fairly simply: For a single selected subset, subjects prefer subset 3a, in which one level of one dimension is represented, but with all levels on the other dimension. If the subset presented makes such a selection possible, then it is used. However, if the subset presented does not allow that possibility, then subset 6a is used, in which two levels of one dimension are represented, but once again for each of these levels, all levels on the other dimension are used. If that possibility does not exist, then the total set, 9a, is selected.

To summarize, orthogonal subsets are selected, but orthogonal subsets in which there is complete representation for one dimension. Thus there is a preference to maintain simple dimensional structure, but at the same time to maintain accurate representation of the total set with respect to at least one dimension.

Two subset selections. A second classification experiment required that subjects select two subsets from the total set, as diagrammatically illustrated in Fig. 5.6. The procedure was similar to that used for single subset selections, except that on a single trial the experimenter presented two subsets: of no stimuli, of one stimulus each, or one subset of one stimulus and another of two stimuli. The subject pulled the same stimuli out from his total set and then added any other stimuli he chose to each subset. Filled circles represent the stimuli in one subset and open circles the stimuli in the other.

The major results are illustrated in Fig. 5.6. Just two selected subsets dominated the classifications and were used whenever possible. The percentage of use for each logical type of presented subset is shown as the number in parentheses under

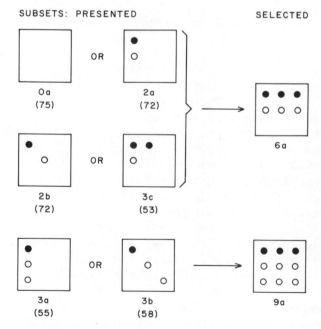

FIG. 5.6. Two subset selections for different presented subsets of stimuli from total set in Fig. 5.4. Each pair of presented subsets led to the pair of selected subsets with the percent used indicated in parentheses. Open and closed circles differentiate the subsets. (Data from Imai and Garner, 1968.)

the type of presented subsets. As you can see, if the presented subsets together involved only two levels on a single dimension, then the selected subsets were two subsets, each representing a single level on one dimension but containing all possible stimuli on the other level. These are the subsets labeled 6a. If the presented subsets made such a selection impossible, then the total set was used, divided into one subset representing all levels on one dimension for a single level on the other, the other subset being the complementary orthogonal subset. These are the subsets labeled 9a. By comparison with the data for single subset selections, you can see that the preferred single subsets were simply combined when the subjects were required to select two subsets. Thus here, too, the dimensional structure of the total set is maintained insofar as possible in the subset selections.

Free classification. We carried out further experiments in which the experimenter presented a subset of 4, 5, or 6 stimuli to the subject, who was then required to make a free classification, that is, to sort the stimuli into as many classes and of whatever type he wanted. The data from these experiments are too numerous to attempt presentation in any detail, but I can show selected data.

Figure 5.7 shows two presented subsets of four stimuli each and the most frequently used free classifications of them. The same logical classes are represented as before. On the right, the classifications are indicated by the lines separating the stimuli. The results with these particular presented subsets are of interest primarily because they show the extent to which the dimensional structure of the stimuli will cause the subject to violate the strong preference for forming two classes of two members each. For presented subset 4a, most of the classifications were three and one, dividing the stimuli so that the classes are differentiated by the two levels on one of the dimensions. Alternatively, the subjects divided the stimuli into three classes according to the three levels on the other dimensions. What they did not

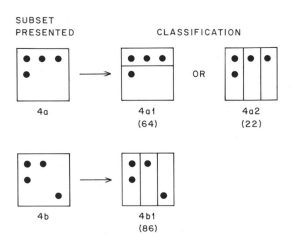

SUBSET
PRESENTED

CLASSIFICATION

4a

4a1
(64)

OR

4a2
(22)

4b

4b1
(86)

FIG. 5.7. Free classification of subsets of four stimuli from total set in Fig. 5.4. The subset presented led to the classifications with the percent used indicated in parentheses. (Data from Imai and Garner, 1968.)

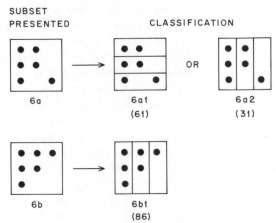

FIG. 5.8. Free classification of subsets of six stimuli from the total set in Fig. 5.4. Interpretation is as in Fig. 5.7. (Data from Imai and Garner, 1968.)

do was to split the stimuli into two classes of two members each, with one class containing two levels of the dimension that is also used to differentiate the classes.

In similar fashion, for presented stimulus 4b, three classes were used—one for each level on one of the two dimensions. Again, it is important that the subjects did not use the easily formed two subsets of two members each.

Before commenting on these results, let us look at some free classifications of subsets of six stimuli, as shown in Fig. 5.8. Here again three classes were used for both subsets 6a and 6b, even though it would have been very easy in each case to form two classes of three members each, simply by combining two levels on one of the dimensions, although such a combination would have meant confusing the role of the differentiating dimension.

These results, which have been confirmed by Handel and Imai (1972), indicate that the dimensional structure of these stimuli is of very great importance and that similarity relations that ignore the dimensional structure have little to do with the classifications produced. If only similarity relations were important, it would not cause that much difficulty for the subjects to have combined the two smaller classes to produce two classes of an equal number of members. Actually, in terms of some of the introductory remarks I made about the need for stimuli to be alike in some way and also different in some way, these data on classifications show that subjects keep the functions of the two dimensions quite straight: They consistently use the levels on a single dimension as the basis of differentiation between classes, but once that has been done, then all stimuli that are alike by virtue of sharing the level are included in the class. To illustrate with anthropocentric language and cognitions, if I am presented with a subset of stimuli, I decide that color will differentiate the classes, regardless of numerical distributions. This means that two different colors can never be placed in the same class. However, once that has been decided, then all stimuli having the same color are considered to be alike, regardless of their form. So as many of each color as are available to me I will place in the same class. I have in effect decided that different colors will differentiate classes, that a single color means that all stimuli having it are the same, and that form is an irrelevant dimension for this classification.

Certainly such a use of dimensions suggests that the perceived structure of these stimuli is that based on dimensions, not that based on similarities. And as we saw earlier, the data from the experiment by Handel and Imai indicated that form and color are separable dimensions, because in similarity judgments the city-block metric is more appropriate than the Euclidean metric. Imai and Handel (1971) have argued even further that with nominal dimensions only a dimensional structure can be meaningful, since to state that the levels on a dimension are purely nominal is to state that distance relations are not specifiable. But if distance relations do not exist with nominal dimensions, then we would expect that stimuli defined by two such dimensions would produce classifications that maintain the dimensional structure but that show little evidence of the existence of a similarity structure. This is what we have seen.

Scalable Dimensions

So in order to carry out classification experiments that can meaningfully distinguish between integral and separable dimensions, we must use scalable dimensions, those on which the levels can at least be ordered. For this purpose, I will return to the experiments of Handel and Imai (1972), who carried out classification experiments in addition to the experiments involving direct judgments of similarity.

As we saw earlier, these authors used two pairs of scalable dimensions: dimensions of size and lightness, shown to be separable by the criterion of their producing

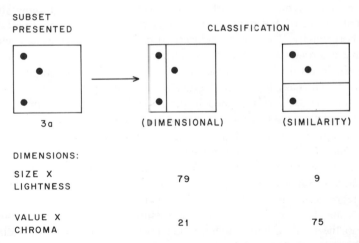

FIG. 5.9. Percent use of two types of restricted classification for two subsets of three stimuli generated from two scalable dimensions. The types of classification emphasize dimensional or similarity structure. (Data from Handel and Imai, 1972.)

the city-block metric in direct similarity-scaling experiments; and dimensions of Munsell value and chroma, shown to be integral by the criterion of their producing the Euclidean metric in similarity-scaling experiments. Other aspects of their classification experiments can best be shown with the help of Fig. 5.9.

The total set of stimuli, for each pair of dimensions, was formed by the orthogonal combination of four levels on each dimension. Any subset from this total set can be diagrammed as indicated in Fig. 5.9. In this figure a subset of three stimuli is presented from the total set of 16. We have been using such schematic diagrams all along, but the important point to remember now is that the ordering of the stimuli matters, although it did not with nominal dimensions. This ordering of stimuli makes possible the manipulation of distances between stimuli in a subset both within and between dimensions, and these manipulations in turn mean that we can select subsets that put dimensional and similarity classifications in direct conflict if in fact similarities are a pertinent factor in perceptual classification.

The general procedure was to present subsets of stimuli to subjects and to require some form of classification. In all cases that I will report, two classes were required; thus the task is what we call restricted classification. The two dimensions are represented horizontally and vertically in the diagram, and all data reported for the moment are summary data for each of the real dimensions being used as the horizontal and vertical dimensions. Later I will discuss some problems concerning differences between the dimensions within a pair.

But now let us return to the data shown in Fig. 5.9. On the lower part cf the figure are shown the percentages of two different classifications for the dimensions of size and lightness (presumably separable) and the dimensions of value and chroma (presumably integral). A word or two about the nature of the presented subset and its relation to the issue of similarity versus dimensional structure is in order. Notice that the stimuli differ on three levels with respect to the dimension represented vertically, but only on two levels with respect to the dimension represented horizontally. As we saw, subjects, if using dimensions in their classifications, have a strong preference to form classes such that all stimuli in a class are on a single level of one dimension. The only way the required two classes can be formed with these three stimuli is to classify by using the horizontal dimension to differentiate classes, as indicated in the classificiation called dimensional. As the data show, this classification was used to a great extent for the dimensions of size and lightness but much less frequently for the dimensions of value and chroma. Thus the use of dimensional classification does go with the separable dimensions, those giving the city-block metric in similarity scaling.

Alternatively, suppose that similarity is the basis of classification. The top two stimuli, representing levels one and two on the vertical dimension, as well as levels one and two on the horizontal dimension, are closer to each other than either is to the third stimulus, representing level four on the vertical dimension and level one on the horizontal dimension. The classification shown on the right and indicated as a similarity classification is that which should be used if similarity is the basis of the classification. The data indicate that this classification was

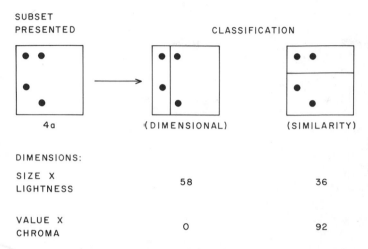

CLASSIFICATION

4a   (DIMENSIONAL)   (SIMILARITY)

DIMENSIONS:

SIZE X LIGHTNESS	58	36
VALUE X CHROMA	0	92

FIG. 5.10. Percent use of two types of restricted classification for two subsets of four stimuli, as in Fig. 5.9. (Data from Handel and Imai, 1972.)

rarely used for the separable dimensions of size and lightness and very frequently used for the integral dimensions of value and chroma. So for these subsets of three stimuli, it is very clear that different classifications are used for the two types of stimulus dimensions, and that the classifications used are consistent with the idea that dimensional structure is important for separable dimensions and similarity structure is important for integral dimensions.

Figure 5.10 shows some data for classifications of four stimuli. Once again the subset of four stimuli was selected so as to put a dimensional and a similarity classification into conflict with each other. Three levels of the vertical dimension are represented in the subset, and two levels of the horizontal dimension. Thus the stimuli could satisfy the requirements that each class represent a single level on one dimension only if the horizontal dimension is used as the basis of classification. However, because level two of the vertical dimension was not used, the top two stimuli easily segregate from the bottom two on the basis of providing maximum intraclass similarity along with maximum interclass difference. Thus there are two major classifications, one easily characterized as dimensional and the other just as easily characterized as similarity.

The data show a considerable difference in the classification of the two kinds of dimensions. The separable dimensions of size and lightness lead to a dimensional classification a good majority of the time, while the integral dimensions of value and chroma lead to a similarity classification nearly all the time. So once again the differences between these pairs of dimensions shown with similarity scaling are reflected in classification behavior in a logically consistent fashion.

Let us look at one last illustrative case in Fig. 5.11. Here the subset of four stimuli represents all four levels on the vertical dimension and two levels only

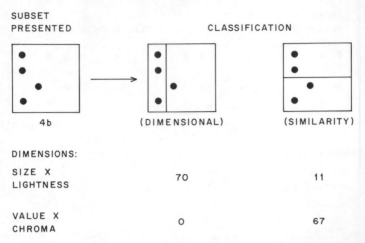

SUBSET
PRESENTED   CLASSIFICATION

4b   (DIMENSIONAL)   (SIMILARITY)

DIMENSIONS:

SIZE X
LIGHTNESS   70   11

VALUE X
CHROMA   0   67

FIG. 5.11. Percent use of two types of restricted classification for two subsets of four stimuli, as in Fig. 5.9. (Data from Handel and Imai, 1972.)

on the horizontal dimension. As before, this arrangement means that only the horizontal dimension can be used to differentiate two classes if dimensional classification is desired. This classification, however, shown in the middle, provides an extra difficulty for the subject wanting to use dimensional classification, because its use requires that he divide the stimuli three to one, and we saw before that the balanced two-two distribution is preferred. Despite this additional obstacle, 70 percent of the classifications of stimuli defined by the separable dimensions of size and lightness were dimensional, and none of the classifications of the stimuli defined by value and chroma were.

The available similarity classification, requiring only that the stimuli be split two-two on the basis of the four ordered levels of the vertical dimension, not only provided a good similarity classification but a balanced distribution. Yet it was rarely used for the dimensions of size and lightness, although predominantly used for the dimensions of value and chroma.

To summarize these data from the experiments of Handel and Imai, there clearly are two different modes of classification of stimuli used by subjects. One of these modes depends on the dimensional structure of the total set and subset of stimuli; and for the dimensions of size and lightness, such dimensional classification is used even when it requires that similarity relations be ignored and that unbalanced distributions be used. Since these are the dimensions that produced the city-block metric in direct similarity scaling, it is clear that the dimensional structure of a set of stimuli dominates the perceived structure when the city-block metric is obtained. However, when the Euclidean metric is obtained in direct similarity scaling, as with value and chroma, then classification depends almost completely on similarities and differences between stimuli, and the classifications show little sensitivity to the dimensional structure at all.

DIMENSIONAL PREFERENCES

Let us consider now the relations between the pair of dimensions defining a set of stimuli, a problem I have so far avoided in this discussion. Suppose we present a subject with a simple set of four stimuli generated from the orthogonal combinations of two dichotomous dimensions, just as illustrated in Fig. 5.1. We ask him to form two classes of two members each, an easy task, since that is what he would do anyway in a completely free classification task. We know that he will form two classes specified by the two levels of one of the two dimensions. He will, in other words, use one of the two dimensions as the basis of his classification, and the other dimension becomes, in effect, irrelevant to the classification. Is there any reason to expect such classifications to be based on one of a particular pair of dimensions more often than the other? Are there, in other words, dimensional preferences?

If the dimensions are integral, we know that classification is based on similarity rather than on dimensional structure. So with integral dimensions we have every reason to expect that which dimension is used as the basis of classification would depend entirely on the relative similarity or discriminability of the two levels on one dimension compared to the similarity of the two levels on the other dimension. To simplify our language, we can state that one dimension is more discriminable than the other, and that the more discriminable dimension will be used as the basis of classification. It will be used because its use will provide the maximum interclass difference along with the maximum intraclass similarity.

Actually, it is almost meaningless to ask whether there are dimensional preferences with integral dimensions, since with integral dimensions classification does not really depend on dimensions at all, but on similarities. The fact that we as experimenters can manipulate the discriminability of dimensions does not mean that the subject perceives a manipulation of dimensions. He only perceives differences. Clearly the concept of dimensional preferences must imply first that dimensions are the basis of classification, not just the means to produce stimuli that differ. And if one dimension is used more often than another as the basis of classification, we should not use the concept of a dimensional preference if the difference in frequency of classification is due entirely to differences in similarity.

But what kind of rationale holds for separable dimensions? Clearly if classification is based upon dimensions rather than upon similarities, it is the dimensions to which the subject attends primarily. In fact, the idea of selective attention based upon dimensions can only be meaningful when we know that dimensions rather than similarities are the basis of stimulus structure. However, a subject might perfectly well have a preference for one dimension rather than the other, without regard to the similarity considerations which are relatively unimportant with separable dimensions anyway. At least the concept of dimensional preference (or salience, if you like) is potentially meaningful with separable dimensions.

However, to state that the concept is meaningful because dimensions rather than similarities are attended to does not mean that differences in similarities between

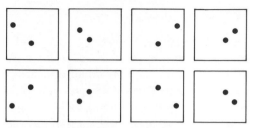

FIG. 5.12. A total set of stimuli, with dichotomized dimensions of lateral Position (P), Orientation (O), and Distance (D) between a pair of dots, used by Imai and Garner (1965). Each dimension was used with four degrees of discriminability between the dimensional levels.

levels on two dimensions will not affect the preference. It is quite possible that a dimensional classification will be used, and that the dimensions are in no sense integral, but that which dimension will serve as the basis of classification will be influenced by discriminability. The way first to determine whether dimensional preferences exist is to use dimensions that are known to be equally discriminable or similar by some experimental operation other than classification, and then to see whether dimensional preferences still exist. Imai and Garner (1965) carried out such an experiment, with stimuli shown in Fig. 5.12.

Our stimuli were pairs of dots whose positions on a card were defined by three dichotomous dimensions: the lateral Position (P) of the dots, the angular Orientation (O) of the dots, and the Distance (D) between the dots. Since we used three dichotomous dimensions, the total set of stimuli was eight. In the actual experiments, classifications of subsets of four stimuli defined by pairs of the dimensions were used, as well as the total set of all eight stimuli.

One part of the experiment was concerned with establishing that each of the three dimensions had levels that were equally discriminable. This was accomplished by using a constrained classification task in which decks of 32 cards were sorted as fast as possible into two piles specified by the levels of one of the dimensions. Equal sorting speeds were taken as evidence of equal discriminability. This sorting task was used to establish four different degrees of discriminability for each of the stimulus dimensions, so that we could investigate the effects on classification of changing the discriminability of one dimension relative to the others. But for our immediate purposes, it is only necessary to feel assured that we had a set of three dimensions to use in a classification experiment which had levels equally discriminable, so that any differences found in frequency of use of different dimensions could not be readily attributable to differences in discriminability.

The experimental task was free classification, and we used all three of the pairs of dimensions to form orthogonal subsets of four stimuli as well as the total set itself. Practically all classifications, whether of two- or three-dimensional sets, used a single dimension as the basis of the classification, so that we can describe each classification simply in terms of which dimensions the subject used.

Our overall results are shown in Table 5.2. At the bottom are shown the percent use of each of the three dimensions for all of the 24 subjects, and you can see

TABLE 5.2

Percent Use of Each of Three Dimensions in Free Classification[a]

Subject type	Dimensions used		
	Distance	Orientation	Position
D preferring (12)	69	22	5
O preferring (8)	23	62	12
Other (4)	40	40	19
Total	49	38	10

[a]Figures in parentheses indicate the number of subjects in each of three categories (Distance, D; Orientation, O; or neither) that these subjects preferred to use in classifying. (Data from Imai and Garner, 1965.)

that there was a slight preference for the dimension of Distance over Orientation, but that lateral Position was rarely used as the basis of classification. If we look at data for individual subjects, however, the evidence for dimensional preference is much greater still. We noted, for each subject, how often he used each of the dimensions as the basis of classification, and if he used one dimension at least 50 percent of the time (33 percent being chance), then we labeled him as preferring that dimension. As you can see, 12 of the subjects preferred the dimension of Distance, 8 preferred the dimension of Orientation, and 4 had no real preference between Distance and Orientation. No subject preferred the dimension of lateral Position.

These preferences are very strong for each individual and are in fact even stronger than is suggested by these summary numbers. The experimental design used was quite complicated, and its details are not important for our present overview. However, as I mentioned earlier, different degrees of discriminability were used for each dimension, and different classification sets involved cases where one dimension was more discriminable than the other. The design prevented there being any overall advantage of one dimension over the others in terms of discriminability, but the counterbalancing arrangement should have minimized overall greater use of any single dimension, because in most cases one dimension was clearly more discriminable than the other. Thus these dimensional preferences were strong enough to overcome an inherent factor in the experimental design that tended to produce equal use of the dimensions.

We have established that dimensional preferences exist for these dimensions. Are these integral or separable dimensions? I would like to argue that the very fact of dimensional preference is sufficient evidence that the dimensions are separable, but there is more evidence that they are in fact separable. This evidence is more appropriate to the next lecture than to this, but briefly, it is that no interference occurs when one or two of the dimensions are varied orthogonally to the dimension that is relevant in the constrained classification task. Still further, when pairs of the dimensions are used in a correlated (i.e., redundant) fashion, there is little improvement in sorting speed (Garner, 1969). But more of this in the next lecture.

Additional confirming evidence that dimensional preferences exist only with separable dimensions comes from the experiments by Handel and Imai, who found individual preferences for the dimensions of color and form as well as lightness and size, but no such individual preferences for value and chroma. The latter two dimensions are, of course, integral, and as I argued earlier, there is sound reason for believing that dimensional preferences should not exist for integral dimensions.

Relative Discriminability and Preferences

I have argued, and data from Handel and Imai have shown, that when two dimensions are integral, dimensional preferences do not exist. If preferences exist with separable dimensions because stimulus similarity is unimportant in the perceived structure, and if they do not exist with integral dimensions because dimensions are not really perceived, but only similarities, then we have some further expectations concerning the effectiveness of manipulations of dimensional similarities or discriminabilities on the use of specific dimensions in classification.

We need not believe that the relative discriminability of one dimension compared to the other, even when the dimensions are separable, should have no effect on the choice of dimension in classification. Discriminability may well affect the salience of the dimension, and in the limiting case where the subject can perceive

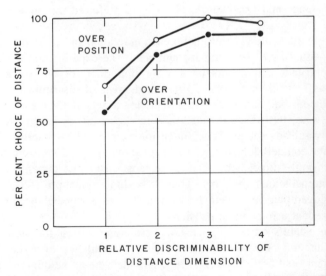

FIG. 5.13. Effect of discriminability of the Distance dimension on its use in classification when contrasted with dimensions of Orientation and Position. Data are for D-preferring subjects only, as in Table 5.2. (Data from Imai and Garner, 1965.)

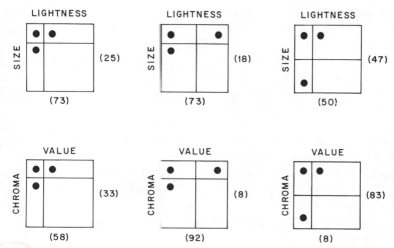

FIG. 5.14. Percent use of two alternative restricted classifications of three stimuli defined by two pairs of scalable dimensions. Percentage used of each classification is shown in parentheses. The subsets vary on relative discriminability of the two dimensions. (Data from Handel and Imai, 1972.)

no difference between the two levels on one dimension, clearly the classification must be made on the basis of the more discriminable dimension. However, if the dimensions are separable, and the perceived structure is based primarily on dimensional rather than similarity properties of stimuli, such effects should be small.

Figure 5.13 presents some data from the experiment by Imai and Garner (1965) we have been discussing. You may recall that I said that we varied the relative discriminability of the different dimensions, and in Table 5.2 we examined overall preferences for all combinations of relative discriminability. The data in Fig. 5.13 are for those subjects who had a dimensional preference for the Distance dimension. The data show how the use of that dimension when paired with Position or with Orientation is affected by the discriminability of the Distance dimension itself. Four levels of discriminability were used. The two curves shown are for all discriminabilities of the nonpreferred dimension. Notice that the preferred dimension is used practically all of the time when it has a high level of discriminability (3 or 4), but it is used less frequently when it has a lower discriminability. However, the percent choice or use of the preferred dimension does not go below 50 even at its lowest discriminability, and this level was close to the limit of discriminability. The dimensional preference is very strong and resists striking changes in stimulus discriminability.

A return again to the Handel and Imai data will make the point even more strongly. In Fig. 5.14 are some classification data for subsets of three stimuli, for the dimensions of size and lightness and for the dimensions of value and chroma. The base sets of stimuli are shown on the left, where the stimuli differ on both dimensions equally (levels 1 and 2). The next two subsets of stimuli are changed by moving one stimulus so that it represents a level of 4 on first one and then the other dimension. What happens with each of these pairs of dimensions?

For the separable dimensions of size and lightness there is an overall preference to use the lightness dimension as the basis of classification, 73 percent of classifications being on the basis of that dimension when discriminabilities are presumed equal. When the lightness dimension is made more discriminable or dissimilar, there is no increased use of it as the basis of classification. When the size dimension is made more dissimilar, its use as the basis of classification increases but not enough for it to be used a majority of the time.

A quite different picture exists with the integral dimensions of value and chroma. In this case there is a slight preference (58 percent) for the use of value when the dimensions are equally dissimilar. If, however, value is made more dissimilar, its use jumps to 92 percent. And if chroma is made more dissimilar, its use jumps to 83 percent.

So once again we have confirmation of the fact that integral and separable dimensions function differently in classification. Dimensional preferences do exist with separable dimensions, and these preferences are fairly impervious to manipulations of discriminability or similarity of the levels on the two dimensions. With integral dimensions, however, there is little evidence for dimensional preferences, and the classifications are easily influenced by manipulations of the similarities of the levels on the two dimensions.

WHAT IS DIMENSIONAL INTEGRALITY?

I am fond of converging operations that provide us with unitary concepts having wide generality, and we certainly have many converging operations to help us differentiate integral from separable dimensions. Direct similarity scaling, free classification, the existence of dimensional preferences, and the effects of dimensional discriminability on these preferences all converge on the conception of a difference between integral and separable dimensions. Can we do more, however, in elucidating the nature of the integrality concept as it operates in perceptual and cognitive processes? I think we can.

Torgerson in 1958 made what I think is a very important point about the difference between the Euclidean and the city-block metrics, and it is illustrated in Fig. 5.15. We all remember from our course in analytic geometry that you can rotate axes, and that if you do so, all distance relations remain invariant. Thus in Fig. 5.15, we had an original right triangle with sides d_x and d_y and hypotenuse d_{xy}. The axes have been rotated so as to give us new dimensions X' and Y', but this rotation of axes does not change any of the three distances involved in the triangle.

Consider what happens to the city-block metric, however. If the distance d_{xy} with the original axes corresponded to the city-block rule, it was equal to the sum of $d_x + d_y$. The city-block rule for establishing the distance d_{xy}, after rotation

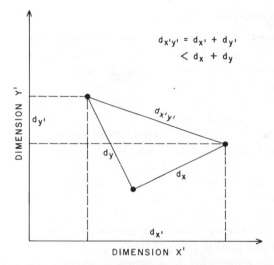

$$d_{x'y'} = d_{x'} + d_{y'}$$
$$< d_x + d_y$$

FIG. 5.15. Illustration of the lack of invariance of the city-block metric with rotation of dimensional axes. The sum of the distances on the new (primed) dimensions is not the same as it is on the original dimensions. (After Torgerson, 1958.)

of the axes, is to add the two projected distances on the new dimensions. The sum of these two distances $(d_{x'} + d_{y'})$ is, however, no longer the same as it was with the original dimensions and is in fact less than the original distance.

Thus only with a Euclidean metric is there any meaningful invariance to distances, or similarities, or differences, or dissimilarities. The idea of distance, however, is the crucial one. Distance in its ordinary sense is a meaningful concept for the integral dimensions that correspond to the Euclidean geometry. But distance is really not a meaningful concept when the city-block metric is appropriate, as with separable dimensions.

On the other hand, the idea of dimensions is really not very meaningful with the Euclidean metric, since the axes specifying the dimensions can be rotated with no loss of meaning relative to distance relations. With separable dimensions, however, and their city-block metric, the idea of dimensions is everything, and they must remain invariant to preserve the perceptual structure of a set of stimuli.

Psychologically, if dimensions are integral, they are not really perceived as dimensions at all. Dimensions exist for the experimenter, and they may even exist in elaborately calculated multidimensional solutions for data from similarity scaling experiments. But these are constructs that are highly derived and do not reflect the immediate perceptual experience of the subject in such experiments, or in classification experiments either.

On the other hand, if the dimensions are separable, distances do not really exist for the subject. What he perceives are dimensions, and we have seen that relative distances on each of two or more dimensions have little to do with how the subject perceives and classifies a set of stimuli.

Primary and Secondary Process

At the same time we must remember that subjects can differentiate integral dimensions, since that is how, after all, the Munsell color system was developed. And they can produce numbers that reflect similarities in some coherent fashion with separable dimensions. Perhaps the best way of considering the difference between integral and separable dimensions is to ask what is the primary process for each, and what is the more derived or cognitive process. Put this way, it is clear that both dimensions and similarities are in some sense perceived both for integral and separable dimensions, but that which is the primary and which the secondary is different in each case. For integral dimensions, similarity, with properties of ordinary distance, is the primary process, and sets of stimuli are perceived in terms of similarities. However, a dimensional structure can be extracted, certainly by a sophisticated experimenter, and probably by a less sophisticated subject. It will, however, not destroy the primary similarity or distance structure, with its Euclidean properties.

For separable dimensions the situation is reversed. The dimensional structure is the directly perceived structure of a set of stimuli. But a similarity structure does exist. Its structure, however, as with the city-block metric, requires the maintenance of the primary dimensional structure.

SUMMARY

In summary:

1. The structure of stimulus sets may be based upon similarity relations between stimuli, or it may be based upon dimensional relations between stimuli.

2. Stimulus dimensions that produce sets in which similarity is important are termed integral. Those that produce sets in which dimensional structure is important are termed separable.

3. In direct similarity scaling, integral dimensions produce interstimulus relations with a Euclidean metric; separable dimensions produce interstimulus relations with a city-block metric.

4. In perceptual classification, stimulus sets defined by integral dimensions are classified primarily in relation to similarities; sets defined by separable dimensions are classified in relation to dimensional structure.

5. In perceptual classification, dimensional preferences or saliences exist only for separable dimensions.

6. Manipulation of relative discriminabilities of dimensions has little effect on the dimensional preferences exhibited with separable dimensions, while almost completely determining classification with integral dimensions.

7. Both similarity and dimensional structure of sets of stimuli exist for both integral and separable dimensions. However, with integral dimensions, the primary structure is similarity in the sense of distance, while the dimensional structure is based upon a more derived, cognitive process. On the other hand, with separable dimensions, the primary structure is dimensional, and the similarity structure is based upon a more derived, cognitive process.

REFERENCES

Attneave, F. Dimensions of similarity. *American Journal of Psychology,* 1950, **63**, 516–556.

Coombs, C. H., Dawes, R. M., & Tversky, A. *Mathematical psychology.* Englewood Cliffs, New Jersey: Prentice-Hall, 1970.

Garner, W. R. Speed of discrimination with redundant stimulus attributes. *Perception & Psychophysics,* 1969, **6**, 221–224.

Handel, S., & Imai, S. The free classification of analyzable and unanalyzable stimuli. *Perception & Psychophysics,* 1972, **12**, 108–116.

Hyman, R., & Well, A. Judgments of similarity and spatial models. *Perception & Psychophysics,* 1967, **2**, 233–248.

Hyman, R., & Well, A. Perceptual separability and spatial models. *Perception & Psychophysics,* 1968, **3**, 161–165.

Imai, S. Classification of sets of stimuli with different stimulus characteristics and numerical properties. *Perception & Psychophysics,* 1966, **1**, 48–54.

Imai, S., & Garner, W. R. Discriminability and preference for attributes in free and constrained classification. *Journal of Experimental Psychology,* 1965, **69**, 596–608.

Imai, S., & Garner, W. R. Structure in perceptual classification. *Psychonomic Monograph Supplements,* 1968, **2**, (9, Whole No. 25).

Imai, S., & Handel, S. Hierarchical stimulus and preference structures in the classification of one-dimensional stimuli. *Japanese Psychological Research,* 1971, **13**, 192–206.

Lockhead, G. R. Effects of dimensional redundancy on visual discrimination. *Journal of Experimental Psychology,* 1966, **72**, 95–104.

Mavrides, C. M. Selective attention and individual preferences in judgmental responses to multifeature patterns. *Psychonomic Science,* 1970, **21**, 67–68.

Shepard, R. N. Attention and the metric structure of the stimulus space. *Journal of Mathematical Psychology,* 1964, **1**, 54–87.

Torgerson, W. S. *Theory and methods of scaling.* New York: Wiley, 1958.

Torgerson, W. S. Multidimensional scaling of similarity. *Psychometrika,* 1965, **30**, 379–393.

LECTURE 6
DIMENSIONAL INTEGRALITY
AND INFORMATION PROCESSING

In the last lecture we were concerned with the structure of stimulus sets, both as produced by the experimenter and as perceived by the experimental subject. In a sense we were looking for perceived relations between stimuli which were independent of what the subject had to do about them. While the experimental procedure of direct similarity scaling provided us with some evidence about stimulus structure, our primary concern was with classification techniques that were as free as possible of constraints imposed by the experimenter.

I mentioned that the second lecture might have been titled "What good is goodness?" because I wanted to discuss the processing consequences of goodness, in the Gestalt sense. This lecture has a similar function in that I want to talk about some processing consequences of the differentiation between integral and separable dimensions. However, research on information processing of different kinds of stimulus dimensions will also further clarify the nature of dimensional integrality.

Our primary concern in this lecture is with tasks involving a measure of time, and for this type of measurement we shift to the paradigm of constrained classification, in which the experimenter defines the subsets of stimuli to be used by the subject and then measures with either a continuous or discrete reaction-time procedure how long it takes the subject to carry out different constrained-classification tasks. Errors in performance constitute, of course, a common alternative to the measurement of time.

Figure 6.1 illustrates the kind of task we will be talking about. Four stimuli are defined by the orthogonal combination of levels on two dichotomous dimensions, X and Y. This is the minimal orthogonal set possible, so I use it to illustrate. There are three basic or primary classification tasks based on a single dimension

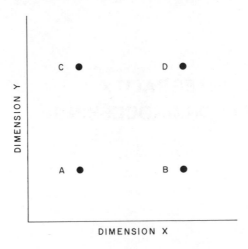

ONE DIMENSION: A *vs* B or C *vs* D
CORRELATED DIMENSIONS: A *vs* D or B *vs* C
ORTHOGONAL DIMENSIONS: (A & C) *vs* (B & D)

FIG. 6.1. Three types of stimulus set for classification by dimension X of stimuli generated by dichotomous dimensions, X and Y.

that can be carried out with such stimuli, and these are defined by the subsets used in classification, as follows:

A subset varying on *one dimension* only may be used, and if classification is by dimension X, as in this illustration, then the classification task can require the discrimination of A from B or C from D. Two other subsets of just two stimuli can be used, but these involve *correlated dimensions*. In this case the task can require discrimination of A from D or B from C. Even though the two dimensions are correlated we can still ask our subject to classify by dimension X or alternatively by dimension Y. What the subject does in these circumstances is of interest to us. A third basic classification task involves the total or *orthogonal set* divided into two subsets defined by one of the two dimensions. If classification by dimension X is required, then the subject is instructed to give one response to stimuli A and C and another response to B and D. Dimension Y is irrelevant in this task.

FACILITATION AND INTERFERENCE

Our interest in these three constrained-classification tasks is to provide a greater understanding of the difference between integral and separable dimensions. What is the function of each of these tasks in providing this understanding? First, the one-dimension tasks are the *control* conditions. These provide the base levels of performance when stimuli differ on only a single dimension so that we can establish the consequences of using stimuli varying on two dimensions.

The task with correlated dimensions addresses itself to the role of *redundancy* in perceptual discrimination. The normal expectation is that discrimination will be improved with subsets of stimuli varying simultaneously on more than one dimension, because the stimuli differ in more ways, or are somehow more different. The literature on whether such improvement occurs is most erratic and confusing (see Garner, 1972), and the intent in this discussion is to help bring order to the topic by considering the nature of the stimulus dimensions that are made redundant in these experiments.

The task with orthogonal dimensions is concerned with the role of *irrelevant dimensions* in constrained classification. In this case the normal expectation is that classification will be more difficult if irrelevant dimensions are added because the intraclass variability will be greater. Here again the literature is not terribly consistent (see Egeth, 1967), and our intent is to investigate the role of dimensional integrality in determining whether irrelevant stimulus dimensions produce interference in constrained classification.

More Converging Operations

These two problem areas have been investigated almost independently of each other, and there has been very little cross referencing of literature from those doing research on stimulus redundancy and those doing research on the role of irrelevant stimulus dimensions, this latter topic occurring almost exclusively within the context of the problem of selective attention. However, it has seemed to me almost axiomatic that there be some reasonable consistency between results obtained on these two problems. Certainly the research that I began with Gary Felfoldy (Garner and Felfoldy, 1970) was undertaken with the idea that these two problem areas would provide some more converging operations to help clarify the distinction between integral and separable dimensions, a distinction already conceptually strong by virtue of the several experimental operations shown in the last lecture to converge on the concept of integrality.

Integral Dimensions

Felfoldy and I carried out several experiments using stimuli defined by two dichotomous dimensions and with these three primary classification tasks all used within the same experiment. Data for the first of these are shown in Table 6.1. The stimulus dimensions for this experiment were value and chroma varying in a single stimulus chip centered on a card. These dimensions showed clear integrality in several experiments discussed in the last lecture. We used sets of stimuli defined by one dimension, correlated dimensions, and orthogonal dimensions. In each case we asked the subjects to classify or sort a deck of 32 stimulus cards into two piles as rapidly as possible. Total time per deck was measured, and it is the value shown in the table. Note that even when we used correlated dimensions

TABLE 6.1

Time (sec) for Sorting Stimulus Cards with Three Types of Stimulus Set
Dimensions: Value and Chroma in a Single Stimulus Chip (Data from Garner and Felfoldy, 1970)

	Type of stimulus set		
Relevant dimension	One dimension	Correlated dimensions	Orthogonal dimensions
Value	15.1	13.7	18.6
Chroma	14.2	13.2	17.4

we asked the subject to classify by each dimension. (This instruction did not seem to cause confusion, although Felfoldy and Garner, 1971, showed that the instruction is violated if one dimension is more discriminable than the other; or, if the subject is never required to sort stimuli formed from orthogonal dimensions.) We had, on the basis of preliminary work, tried to use dimensions with equally discriminable levels, and we succeeded reasonably well, as you can see. Value and chroma were approximately equally discriminable when used alone. When used as correlated dimensions, speed of discrimination improved. We have no meaningful formal model to indicate whether this much improvement in time per deck of 32 cards is a lot or a little. However, in the context of many such experiments we know that this is about as much improvement in speed as ever occurs, so we can state that it is a lot. When these two dimensions were made orthogonal, so that each acted as an irrelevant variable when sorting was carried out with the other dimension as the relevant one, then there was an intereference effect. Once again, in the context of many such experiments, we know that this is a great deal of interference.

So as a start we know that with dimensions known to be integral by other experimental operations, there is a gain in discrimination speed when the dimensions are used redundantly, and a loss when they are used orthogonally. There is more convergence on the concept of integrality.

Separable Dimensions

It should be obvious now what our second experiment was, with data shown in Table 6.2, again for sorting 32 stimulus cards. We used these same two dimensions but varied each separately in two stimulus chips. This procedure had produced clear evidence of separable dimensions with other experimental operations, as discussed in the fifth lecture. This change to two chips did not alter the relative discriminability of the two dimensions when used singly. (A different group of subjects was used for each of the experiments, so that direct comparisons of times from one experiment to another are not valid; comparisons within each experiment are, however.) With correlated dimensions there was a slight improvement in sorting

TABLE 6.2

Time (sec) for Sorting Stimulus Cards with Three Types of Stimulus Set
Dimensions: Value and Chroma in Two Stimulus Chips (Data from Garner and Felfoldy, 1970)

Relevant dimension	Type of stimulus set		
	One dimension	Correlated dimensions	Orthogonal dimensions
Value	15.9	15.7	15.8
Chroma	15.6	15.1	15.1

speed, but it was not statistically significant. And with orthogonal dimensions, there was no interference effect whatsoever; in fact, numerically there was a slight improvement. The best summary for these data is that all numbers are the same.

So again we have reasonable convergence: With dimensions known to be separable by other experimental operations, there is no improvement in sorting speed when the dimensions are used redundantly and no interference when they are used orthogonally.

Integrality as a Continuum

Both in the last lecture and so far in this one I have talked as though the concept we are trying to understand is a simple dichotomy: There are integral dimensions and there are separable dimensions. We need to begin to clarify, and unfortunately complicate, the concept. As a beginning, we need to consider the possibility that integrality is itself a continuum, that there are degrees of integrality. The data shown in Table 6.3 will indicate the need for this idea.

The stimuli for this experiment were single black dots placed in the middle of an outline square drawn on each stimulus card. The dimensions were the horizontal and vertical positions of the dot We used these dimensions because it seemed to us that such stimuli would most likely satisfy the requirements of a distance metric, that is, of a true Euclidean metric, and so these dimensions ought to

TABLE 6.3

Time (sec) for Sorting Stimulus Cards with Three Types of Stimulus Set
Dimensions: Horizontal and Vertical Position of a Dot (Data from Garner and Felfoldy, 1970)

Relevant dimension	Type of stimulus set		
	One dimension	Correlated dimensions	Orthogonal dimensions
Horizontal	18.3	16.9	19.4
Vertical	17.5	16.2	18.0

be about as integral as any two dimensions can be. The results of the experiment required us to be a little more cautious about *a priori* assumptions of this sort.

The results show that sorting by the vertical dimension was a bit easier than sorting by the horizontal dimension, but that in either case there was a substantial gain in sorting speed when the two dimensions were used redundantly. In fact, the amount of gain was about as great as that obtained with the dimensions of value and chroma in the single color chip. So far, so good, because this result fits nicely with the integrality idea.

When the dimensions were used orthogonally, there was interference with each dimension. So the overall result gives the same convergent result for integral dimensions that we had found before. However, the reason for considering the idea of integrality as a continuum is that the amount of interference obtained with the stimulus dot was much less than that obtained with value and chroma.

Some other evidence suggesting the greater complexity of the concept comes from an experiment by Egeth and Pachella (1969). They used 15 vertical and 15 horizontal positions of a dot, with an absolute-judgment technique requiring the subjects to identify one or the other of the two-dimensional positions. They did not use correlated stimulus dimensions, but did use the orthogonal dimensions as well as single dimensions, and found no loss in accuracy of judgment of a single dimension when the other dimension was varied as an irrelevant dimension. Still further, Morgan and Alluisi (1967) found that interference was produced by the irrelevant dimension of color only if the relevant dimension of size had very low discriminability. Again, the experimental paradigm was absolute judgment.

I do not want to pursue the issue further at this point, but I did want to introduce the idea that integrality is not quite as simple a concept as we might like, and that we need to look for various additional concepts in trying to understand results with information-processing experiments.

INTEGRALITY OF AUDITORY DIMENSIONS

So far all of the stimuli I have discussed have been visual, and we could easily get the idea that the integrality concept is pertinent only for the visual modality. Fortunately, there is now some evidence from the realm of audition, evidence that allows us to generalize across modalities, but evidence that also further elaborates the concept of integrality itself.

Certainly if we were to make a reasonable extrapolation from what we know about the nature of integral visual dimensions, we would expect pitch and loudness to be integral. Table 6.4 shows some data (provided by Wood, 1973) for these two dimensions. Wood used a single syllable, /bae/, which varied in pitch and loudness. Instead of the card sorting procedure, he used a discrete reaction-time technique, so the data in Table 6.4 are individual reaction times in milliseconds. He used stimuli varying in one dimension only and also varying orthogonally; thus he used the control task plus the classification task that could show interference.

TABLE 6.4

Mean Discrete Reaction Time (msec) for Two Types of Stimulus Set
Dimensions: Pitch and Loudness of the Syllable /bae/ (Data from Wood, 1973)

| | Type of stimulus set | |
Relevant dimension	One dimension	Orthogonal dimensions
Pitch	411	455
Loudness	408	446

Discrimination times for both dimensions showed a substantial increase when the
second dimension varied as an irrelevant dimension, the result we now know indicates integrality of dimensions. *has anyone done this w/ correlated
dimensions?*

Linguistic Dimensions

Are there other auditory dimensions which can be shown to be integral? The
most important aspect of the auditory system from the point of view of human
information processing is that it is the primary means by which we understand
speech. Thus some investigation of the dimensions that define basic linguistic
units such as phonemes is certainly called for, and it has been provided by Day
and Wood (1972b), with data shown in Table 6.5. Once again they used a discrete
reaction-time procedure, so these data show individual reaction times in milliseconds.
The stimuli were nonsense syllables of the consonant-vowel form, produced with
precision by simulation equipment at the Haskins Laboratories in New Haven,
as were the stimuli used by Wood in the pitch-loudness experiment.

The two dimensions used were vowels (/a/ or /ae/) and initial stop consonants
(/b/ or /d/). For the one-dimension conditions, each of the vowel pairs was used
with each consonant. Thus /ba/ was discriminated from /bae/ and /da/ from /dae/
in separate tasks. And each of the consonant pairs was used with each vowel,

TABLE 6.5

Mean Discrete Reaction Time (msec) for Two Types of Stimulus Set
Dimensions: Vowel (/a/ or /ae/) and Stop Consonant (/b/ or /d/) of Consonant-Vowel Syllables
(Data from Day and Wood, 1972b)

| | Type of stimulus set | |
Relevant dimension	One dimension	Orthogonal dimensions
Vowel	348	414
Consonant	400	450

so that /ba/ was discriminated from /da/, and /bae/ from /dae/. The data in Table 6.5, the average for each contrast, show that vowels were considerably easier to discriminate than consonants, as indicated by a reaction time 52 milliseconds faster on the average. Generally speaking, these experiments are easier to interpret when each dimension has levels equally discriminable, because interference may not occur with orthogonal dimensions if the irrelevant dimension is considerably less discriminable than the relevant dimension. Fortunately, in the present case this danger caused no problem, since reaction times increased considerably when orthogonal dimensions were used, and for both dimensions. Thus when /ba/ and /bae/ were discriminated from /da/ and /dae/, or when /ba/ and /da/ were discriminated from /bae/ and /dae/, reaction times were slower than when there was no irrelevant dimension.

Integrality, then, is not limited to the simplest auditory dimensions but may exist for more complex dimensions such as those defining vowels and consonants. The next obvious question is: What happens if a linguistic and a nonlinguistic dimension are used together? Day and Wood (1972a) first showed that in this case the interference is asymmetric, with a nonlinguistic dimension producing interference when it is irrelevant to a judgment requiring differentiation of a linguistic dimension, but with the converse interference not occurring.

I shall once again use some data from Wood (1973) on this particular problem, as displayed in Table 6.6. He used consonant-vowel syllables, but the vowel sound, /ae/, was the same for all stimuli. The dimensions that varied were the initial stop consonant (/b/ or /g/), and the fundamental pitch of the vowel phoneme, low or high. Thus the four stimuli were /bae/–high pitch, /bae/–low pitch, /gae/–high pitch, and /gae/–low pitch. These stimuli were also produced with the simulation equipment at Haskins Laboratories. The same experimental paradigm was used as before, with comparison of stimulus sets formed from one dimension to those formed from orthogonal dimensions, for discrimination on each of the two dimensions.

The results of the experiment are quite straightforward. When pitch was the dimension relevant for discrimination, essentially no interference occurred when the stop consonant became an irrelevant dimension. When, however, the stop

TABLE 6.6

Mean Discrete Reaction Time (msec) for Two Types of Stimulus Set
Dimensions: Pitch and Stop Consonant (/b/ or /g/) of Consonant-Vowel Syllables
(Data from Wood, 1973)

Relevant dimension	Type of stimulus set	
	One dimension	Orthogonal dimensions
Pitch	411	413
Consonant	416	467

consonant was itself the relevant dimension, then considerable interference occurred when the fundamental pitch of the phoneme was varied as an irrelevant dimension.

The auditory studies cited so far did not use the condition with correlated dimensions, and in those cases where interference was mutual, or symmetric, we would assume that there would have been facilitation of discrimination when the dimensions were used redundantly. There is more question about what would happen, however, when the linguistic and nonlinguistic dimension are used together. C. C. Wood now has some unpublished data on this problem, using exactly the same stimulus dimensions as he used in the study already cited. The results were, fortunately, unequivocal: Considerable facilitation was obtained with correlated dimensions, when the subjects were discriminating either on the basis of pitch or on the basis of consonant. So the integral nature of the dimensions is controlling when redundancy is used. Or to summarize another way, there is improvement in performance when the subject needs it, as with correlated dimensions. There is, however, avoidance of interference only when the subject is judging the nonlinguistic dimension; the subject cannot avoid interference when judging the linguistic dimension.

Levels of Processing *as explanation of Wood (1973) - Table 6.6*

This result is quite clear-cut: Interference is produced asymmetrically, and if we are to stay with the concept of integrality, we are then forced to state that integrality, or separability, is an asymmetric relation, and only in some cases is it fully symmetric. Described in these terms, this result is that the stop consonant is separable from the fundamental pitch; but the fundamental pitch is not separable from, and is thus integral with, the stop consonant.

Such a situation makes sense, as the authors of these studies suggest, if we consider that pitch, as a nonlinguistic dimension of a phoneme, is processed at a lower level than the linguistic dimension of stop consonant. Thus pitch is processed prior to processing of any linguistic properties and can be discriminated without interference from irrelevant variation in the linguistic property. If the linguistic dimension is itself the relevant dimension, then pitch variation will interfere with discrimination of the linguistic dimension, because processing of it is required before the linguistic properties are perceived. Certainly this seems like a reasonable explanation of the asymmetric interference, and if the logic of the explanation is sound, we have a valuable tool in separating process levels.

OPTIONAL PROCESSING MECHANISMS

The simple picture is of a dichotomy between integral dimensions and separable dimensions. Integral dimensions are those that produce (*a*) an Euclidean metric in direct similarity scaling, (*b*) free and restricted classifications based upon a similarity structure, (*c*) facilitation when used redundantly in a constrained classification task, and (*d*) interference when one is used as an irrelevant dimension and classification is required by the other, the relevant, dimension. Separable dimensions are those that produce (*a*) a city-block metric in direct distance scaling, (*b*) classifications based upon a dimensional structure, (c) no facilitation when used redundantly in a constrained-classification task, and (d) no interference when one is an irrelevant dimension in a classification task.

We have now seen two types of evidence which require us to modify this simple picture. When linguistic and nonlinguistic dimensions of phonemes were used, the relationship between dimensions was asymmetric in that interference was produced in one direction only. Still further, when the horizontal and vertical positions of the single dot were dimensions, there was considerable facilitation but very little interference in constrained classification. I suggested then that possibly we need to consider the idea of degrees of integrality. That result can be considered in another way, however, namely, that the organism has some option in how it uses properties of stimulus dimensions. In the constrained-classification tasks, which are the primary concern of this lecture, if the organism had complete option, it would use correlated dimensions to facilitate discrimination but would selectively attend to these dimensions, if used orthogonally, to prevent interference in that classification task. So if the human information processor has some option, ordinarily it will appear as an experimental result showing facilitation with correlated dimensions when other evidence shows that the dimensions are separable because of a lack of interference when one dimension is irrelevant. For a moment I want to discuss some optional mechanisms that might lead to an improvement with correlated dimensions, although I would argue that in these cases we should not conclude that dimensions are integral. Rather, we should conclude that the human is a highly flexible information processor who will usually manage to find any available technique for improving his processing, and that he can do so even with separable dimensions.

Selective Serial Processing

One such mechanism available with separable dimensions is selective serial processing, a term meaning simply that the organism processes one dimension before the other, but does so selectively so as to maximize performance. Figure 6.2 provides us with an experimental illustration of this point. The stimuli we (Felfoldy and Garner, 1971) used were circles that varied in size and an internal diameter that varied in angle; the task being to sort 32 stimulus cards. You may recognize that these stimuli were similar to those we discussed in the last lecture, with evidence that the dimensions are separable. Garner and Felfoldy (1970) had used these stimuli, with the two dimensions being approximately equal in discriminability, and had found the processing result we now know to be consistent with separability—no facilitation and no interference.

Under one circumstance, however, it does not seem reasonable to obtain no facilitation on the average with separable dimensions, and that is when the two dimensions are unequally discriminable. In such a case, and if the dimensions can be selectively attended to, the discrimination ought to be carried out entirely on the basis of the easier of the two dimensions, so that there appears to be improvement with respect to the poorer of the dimensions. We had found little

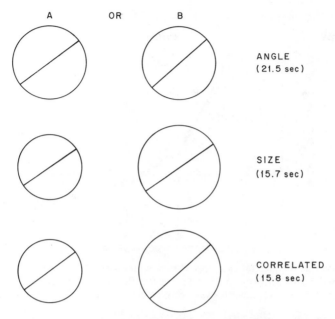

FIG. 6.2. Card sorting time with dimensions of size of circle and angle of diameter, used singly and correlated. These data show selective serial processing. (Data from Felfoldy and Garner, 1971.)

evidence of such a processing technique in our first experiments, so we ran this one to check on the point. We simply made the two dimensions unequal in discriminability to see if selective serial processing would occur.

Angle of the diameter was the poorer of the two dimensions, and when it varied alone, average sorting time was over 21 sec. Size of the circle was the more discriminable of the two, and when used alone, average sorting time was under 16 sec. When the two were used redundantly, sorting speed was the same as it was with the better of the two dimensions used alone—the result we would expect if the size dimension were processed first and a decision made on that basis as soon as possible. So the fact that dimensions are separable does not mean that an average facilitation with correlated dimensions cannot occur. If selective serial processing is used, there will be a gain, but it will not be a performance level beyond that provided by the better of the two dimensions alone.

Stimulus Redefinition

Another optional processing mechanism the human information processor may use is to redefine the stimuli so that a new dimension, which is more discriminable than either dimension alone, is provided. In some cases, the experimental subject may in effect change the two dimensions so that they are integral. Figure 6.3 shows some data from the experiment I discussed primarily in the last lecture. The stimuli were two pairs of dots, and these could vary in Distance between the dots, angular Orientation of the dots, and the lateral Position of the dots.

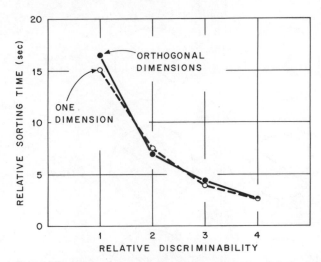

FIG. 6.3. Card sorting time for two types of stimulus set with pairs of dots varying in Distance, Orientation, and Position, as shown in Fig. 5.12. Relative discriminability is of the relevant dimension, paired with all degrees of discriminability of the irrelevant dimension. (Data from Imai and Garner, 1965.)

Imai and Garner (1965) were concerned with the question of dimensional preferences in this experiment, and it was in that context that I discussed this experiment. I also mentioned, however, that these three dimensions were separable, regardless of the relative discriminability of the dimensions that were paired, and the evidence for that statement is in Fig. 6.3. We have two curves, each showing sorting times (relative to a highly discriminable control condition) for all conditions in which stimuli either varied on one dimension or varied in two or three dimensions, with only one dimension being relevant for sorting. The data shown are for all degrees of relative discriminability of the irrelevant dimensions for each level of discriminability of the relevant dimension. There is no real difference between these two curves, so we conclude that all three dimensions are separable.

Later, however, Garner (1969) did the experiment involving correlated dimensions and found an overall improvement in sorting speeds when the dimensions were used redundantly. Figure 6.4 illustrates the stimuli and results for the dimensions of Distance and Position. This improvement with correlated dimensions at first glance argues for integrality of the dimensions, but I felt that this conclusion was not valid. First, there were individual differences in the speed of discrimination with these dimensions so that each subject could have been using selective serial processing. After correction was made for this factor, however, there still remained some improvement. My feeling is that this improvement did not occur because of integrality of the dimensions as defined by me, the experimenter, but rather because the subject was able to redefine the dimensions so that in effect they became integral for him.

These illustrations will help me to explain. If the *pair* of dots is considered to be the stimulus, then the dimensions are separable. Furthermore, the internal

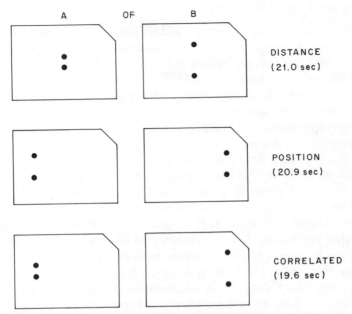

FIG. 6.4. Card sorting time for dimensions of Distance and Position of a pair of dots, used singly and correlated. (Data from Garner, 1969.)

evidence is that the pair of dots was usually the stimulus, not just, for example, the lower dots in these illustrations. Notice that sorting time obtained for Distance alone is as good as that obtained for Position alone. Yet if the subject attended to only the lower dot in the upper illustrations he would have a much more difficult discrimination task. So we can assume he in fact made his discrimination on the basis of the distance between the pair, and not on the basis of the distance of the bottom dot from the center line, or from the edge of the card, or whatever.

However, when these two dimensions are correlated, it now becomes worth his while to attend to only the lower dot and discriminate on the basis of the total distance between positions of these single dots. As we saw in the Garner and Felfoldy (1970) experiment, the correlated dimensions of horizontal and vertical positions of a single dot did facilitate discrimination. The facilitation obtained in this experiment strongly suggests that the subjects did redefine the stimulus so as to have integral dimensions of the horizontal and vertical position of a single dot. Thus these dimensions were used as separable when it was to the subject's advantage to do so but were redefined as integral when it was to his advantage to do that.

MORE ON INTEGRALITY

I would like to pause here for a few moments now to summarize some things about dimensional integrality, adding to the comments made in the last lecture additional concepts which have come from the information-processing experiments.

Integrality and Logical Relations

As noted in the last lecture, most researchers concerned with this problem have tried to describe the properties of pairs of dimensions that make them integral. Lockhead (1966), for example, argued that integrality depends on the coexistence of the dimensions in the same place and time. Garner (1970) suggested only that a limiting definition is available, namely, that if in order for one dimension to exist the other must be specified, then the dimensions are integral. I would like to push this definition a little further in terms of the logical relations implied between pairs of dimensions.

Figure 6.5 illustrates three kinds of logical relation that can exist between a pair of dimensions X and Y. The diagrams each show the dimension as existing or not existing, and please keep clear than I am not referring to the existence of a level on a dimension but to the existence of the dimension itself. The filled parts of the diagrams are what exist as logical possibilities, and the empty cells are not logical possibilities. Diagram A shows the relation between integral dimensions. In logical form it is a biconditional relation, or double implication. This relation can be stated in this form: If X exists, then Y does also; and if X does not exist, then neither does Y. Or alternatively, X implies Y, and Y implies X. Essentially this is the definition of integrality I attempted earlier (Garner, 1970), based upon necessary coexistence of dimensions. It can be expanded, however.

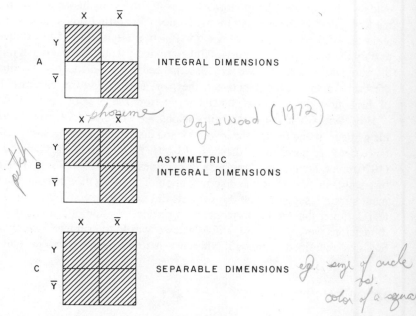

FIG. 6.5. Three logical relations between the existence and nonexistence of two dimensions and the concept of dimensional integrality.

Diagram C is at the other end of a continuum and is appropriate for separable dimensions. All combinations of existence and nonexistence of dimensions are possible. That is to say, there are no constraints between the dimensions in terms of their existence. If one dimension, to illustrate, is the size of a circle on the left, and the other dimension is the color of a square on the right, either dimension may be eliminated without in any way affecting the existence of the other. They are indeed separable.

The middle diagram, B, is the one which intrigues me because it clarifies that the relation between dimensions need not be symmetric at all. This relation, known as implication, states that if X exists then Y also exists, but if Y exists, X may or may not exist. In terms of an experimental outcome, this logical diagram satisfies the experimental results found by Day and Wood (1972a) that an irrelevant nonlinguistic dimension interferes with discrimination of a linguistic dimension, although the converse situation does not hold. We discussed this effect in terms of levels of processing, but that may not be necessary. It is possible that all that is involved is the asymmetry of the logical relation between the dimensions. That is, a phoneme cannot exist without a pitch, but pitch may exist as a dimension without any linguistic properties at all. So pitch truly is integral to the consonant, but the consonant is separable from the pitch.

We have little evidence of an asymmetric relation with other dimensions, but it seems likely that there are some. For example, consider the dimensions of color and form. Color can exist without a form, but a form must have a color. If these two dimensions were used orthogonally, it seems likely that irrelevant variation in color would interfere with discrimination of form, but not conversely, at least with large enough figures. Another example would be form and size, and it seems at least possible that two letters (as forms) would be difficult to discriminate with irrelevant variation in size, but that size could be judged easily with irrelevant variation in letter. Would such a result necessarily imply that discrimination of form is a higher-level process than discrimination of size?

This latter example is very similar to one used by Posner and Mitchell (1967). They used letters as stimuli, in either lower- or upper-case type, and required their subjects to state that two stimuli were either the SAME or DIFFERENT. Sometimes SAME meant the same name, even though the letters were in different cases, thus not physically identical. At other times, SAME meant physical identity. It took longer to respond when the names only were identical, and these authors interpreted this finding as indicating a difference in processing level. However, consider doing this experiment with the methods discussed in this lecture. We would use, say, two different letters orthogonally combined with two cases. The various control comparisons would be used, then classification of the orthogonal set would be carried out for both dimensions: letter and case. Would irrelevant variation in either lead to interference? As a guess, the result would be asymmetric, with case being easier to discriminate than letter, in each instance with irrelevant variation in the second dimension. That is to say, irrelevant variation in case would lead to interference in discrimination of letter. In effect, this is the result obtained by Posner and Mitchell, since the subjects were required to state that two letters were the same, even with irrelevant variation in case. They did not, however, carry out the equivalent experiment with irrelevant variation in letter.

There is little more I can or want to say now. Clearly the idea of processing levels is enticing, yet it may not really be a necessary concept if there are different logical relations between the stimulus dimensions. On the other hand, it is possible that the differences in processing levels produce the asymmetric interference itself. If ever there was a need for more converging operations to clarify these concepts, it is in this area.

A Stimulus or an Organismic Concept

Is integrality a concept pertinent to the stimulus or to the organism? My answer is that it is first and foremost a stimulus concept, but that important processing concepts are closely related to it and may modify it. In fact, that is what much of this lecture has been concerned about. Certainly these logical relations are entirely stimulus concepts. I am not saying that a tone has to have a pitch and a loudness in the head. Even though I have used terms for the psychological dimensions of pitch and loudness, the physical counterparts of intensity and frequency must coexist. Even when talking about the asymmetric integral dimensions, we are talking about constraints that exist within the domain of the physics of stimuli.

Nevertheless, the concept of integrality is a psychophysical one in the sense that we would not be concerned with it unless it had some processing consequences. Its status in this regard is much the same as that of light. Light is a physical thing, but the definition of light contains the psychological restriction that it is *visible* radiant energy. But that psychophysical implication of the concept does not mean that it is an organismic concept.

Actually, there are frequently parallel physical and psychological concepts, and because of that we often confuse the role of the two. Discriminability, for example, is a property of a stimulus; it is that property which makes it capable of the psychological process of discrimination. But we do need separate definitions for the physical thing and the psychological thing. If discriminability is increased by our increasing the physical separation between two levels on a continuum, we do not want that physical operation obscured by defining discriminability solely in terms of a processing outcome such as speed of discrimination. Two different experimental techniques can lead to different outcomes for the same stimulus manipulation, and we do not want to be forced to state that the same manipulation leads to two different concepts.

I would argue that the logical relations between dimensions constitute a definition of integrality, and even though we have to use psychological experiments to provide a set of converging operations to define integrality, it remains a stimulus concept. These converging operations help to establish that the concept is indeed independent of any single experimental outcome and thus has a status of its own.

However, as we have seen, with separable dimensions there are many processing mechanisms or strategies available to the subject, and these make it necessary for us to distinguish some processing concepts that are highly interactive with the stimulus concept. The best way to handle this problem is to use the ideas of mandatory and optional processes. Integral dimensions are mandatorily so—the organism can do nothing about it. But if the stimulus dimensions are separable, the evidence is clear that we need to distinguish between those cases in which option exists for the organism, and those in which it does not. I have elsewhere (1974) distinguished between three attentive concepts: mandatory distribution, optional selection, and mandatory selection. Mandatory distribution is the processing consequence of integral dimensions. Selection, however, may be either optional or mandatory, and it is what can happen with separable dimensions.

When I chose to use the words integral and separable as antonyms, many of you may have realized the connotative awkwardness of these terms. Integral connotes a mandatory process, two dimensions being integrated by their very nature. Separable clearly connotes an optional process, and perhaps that is how it should be. Alternatively, we could have three stimulus concepts paralleling the three attentive concepts: integral, separable, and separated. Language never seems to be adequate to our concepts, frequently because we have to start using terms for the concepts before we fully understand them.

The relation between mandatory and optional processing mechanisms is of special interest in relation to asymmetric integral dimensions. I pointed out earlier that selective serial processing is an optional process relevant only to separable dimensions, in which usually the better (easier to discriminate) dimension is processed first, and presumably no further processing takes place if a decision can be made on the basis of the first dimension. With asymmetric integral dimensions, however, there may be a natural or even mandatory ordering of the dimensions, based upon either the logical implications or the processing levels. However, it is quite possible that in this case the poorer of two dimensions would be processed first, if it is the one at the lower level. Thus serial processing mechanisms may be somewhat more complicated than they seem at first glance.

WHAT CAUSES INTERFERENCE?

I would like to turn now to a question of why. In particular, why do integral dimensions facilitate discrimination with correlated dimensions and interfere with orthogonal dimensions? The first part is, I think, fairly easy and almost a nonproblem. Since integral dimensions combine according to the rules of Euclidean geometry, and with similarity being the primary property of stimuli defined by integral dimensions, then when two stimuli differ on two dimensions simultaneously, they have an interstimulus difference which is greater than either dimension alone provides. Thus discriminability is greater for basically the same two-stimulus discrimination task.

But why should there be interference when classification of the orthogonal set of stimuli is required? With separable dimensions there is no interference, and our explanation in this case is that the human is able to attend selectively to one dimension and filter out or exclude the other. (See Garner, 1974; Treisman, 1969, for discussion of the types of selective attention possible.) Integral dimensions, then, are those to which we cannot selectively attend. But simply to state that the increased processing time obtained with irrelevant integral dimensions is due to a failure of selective attention is only to restate the experimental result. Presumably the cause, at a deeper level, lies in the fact that there is intraclass stimulus variability. But why should such variability cause interference? Perhaps this seems like something that is self evident, but I do not really think that it is. Consider the problem, with the aid of Fig. 6.6. This figure pertains to the next experiment we will discuss, but for the moment consider it only in terms of the several tasks involved. We want to consider only discrimination of items on the left from those on the right. There are four tasks which involve just two stimuli: Discriminate A from B, C from D, A from D, and C from B. The first two tasks involve one-dimensional stimuli, and the latter two tasks involve correlated dimensions. We know that these improve discrimination with integral dimensions. Now when we require classification of (C and A) against (D and B), we are simply pooling all of these two-stimulus discrimination tasks. Furthermore, we are adding the easier tasks with correlated dimensions to the control tasks with one dimension. If anything, the task should be easier because of this pooling, but it is not. It is more difficult.

Sequential Stimulus Effects

Felfoldy (1974), whose data we will now discuss, has suggested that the answer lies in our understanding the effects of sequential stimuli on the reaction-time

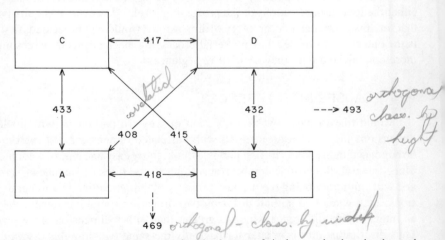

FIG. 6.6. Mean discrete reaction time (msec) for stimulus sets of single, correlated, and orthogonal dimensions: width and height of rectangles. The numbers inside are for various pairs of stimuli; the numbers outside are for classification of four orthogonal stimuli by height or width. Short interstimulus delay. (Data from Felfoldy, 1974.)

process and has carried out a fairly elaborate experiment to clarify the nature of these effects. His stimuli were the rectangles in Fig. 6.6 with the width and height of these rectangles constituting his stimulus dimensions. Four of his stimuli are shown here, with stimulus A differing from B, and C differing from D, in width only. Stimulus A differs from C, and B from D, in height only. Stimulus A differs from D in both width and height, but the shape (ratio of width to height) remains constant while area varies. Stimulus B differs from stimulus C in both width and height also, but area remains constant, with only shape varying.

A discrete reaction-time procedure was used, with the stimuli being projected onto a screen and the subject responding with one of two response keys. This technique was used to allow control of the rate of presentation of the stimuli and measurement of reaction time to each stimulus. The task was self-paced in that each stimulus occurred at some fixed time after each response to the preceding stimulus, but after each response and the termination of the stimulus, there was a fixed interstimulus delay of 42, 540, or 1040 msec.

The numbers shown here are the mean reaction times for eight different tasks, at the shortest interstimulus delay. Two contrasts required discrimination of height only, and the reaction times were 433 and 432 msec. Two contrasts required discrimination of width only, and the reaction times were 417 and 418 msec. Thus width was a bit easier to discriminate than height. Two contrasts required discrimination of height and width as correlated dimensions, and the mean reaction times were 408 and 415 msec. Thus processing was faster with redundant dimensions. At the lower edge of the figure is the reaction time when the orthogonal stimulus set was used for classification by width, and the value was 469 msec. At the right is the equivalent figure, 493 msec, for classification of the orthogonal set with height as the relevant dimension.

This pattern of results clearly establishes these two dimensions as integral, since facilitation was obtained with correlated stimulus dimensions and interference with orthogonal stimulus dimensions. So now we can proceed with the question of why the interference happens.

One point worth mentioning now is that amount of interference obtained with these dimensions was to some extent a function of the interstimulus delay, as shown in Fig. 6.7. Reaction time for one-dimensional and orthogonal-dimensional sets of stimuli decreases slightly as the interstimulus delay increases. Of further interest is the fact that the amount of interference, the difference between the two curves, decreases with an increased interstimulus delay. The interference effect does not disappear, however, even at the longest interstimulus interval, so we need not fear that the phenomenon we are trying to understand exists only with the card sorting task, or other very rapid discrimination tasks. This decrease in the magnitude of the interference effect will be paralleled by other effects of interstimulus delay, however.

Repetition effects. It has been known for many years that reaction time to a stimulus is faster if the stimulus is a repetition of the previous stimulus than

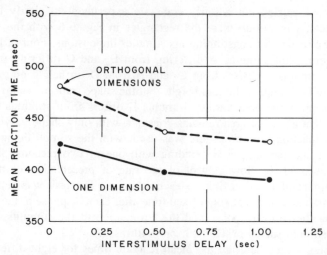

FIG. 6.7. Discrete reaction time for two types of stimulus set with dimensions of width and height of rectangles, at three interstimulus delays. (Data from Felfoldy, 1974.)

if the stimulus represents a change from the last trial. A review of this literature is not appropriate here, since our concern is not with that phenomenon *per se* but is rather with its relation to the interference found with classification of orthogonal integral dimensions. Figure 6.8 shows, for the stimuli used by Felfoldy, this effect. This particular pair of curves shows average reaction time for all of the two-stimulus comparisons, both those involving a single stimulus dimension and those involving two correlated dimensions. The two curves are for repetitions and changes of stimuli and responses.

Although this difference, with reaction times being faster for repetitions than for changes, has been called the repetition effect, the nature of the relation between interstimulus delay and the reaction times for the two cases suggests that the effect is more related to stimulus changes than to stimulus repetitions. In fact there is little effect of interstimulus delay on reaction times for repetitions but a considerable increase in reaction time for changes with shorter interstimulus delays. It is as though there is an interference effect when the stimulus changes, and this interference effect is greater at the shorter intervals. Is it possible that the interference effect found in the filtering task is related to the interference found in the change effect?

These two curves have been labeled as stimulus *and* response repeat or change to emphasize a point: When there are just two stimuli in a discrimination task, then if the stimulus remains the same, so also does the (correct) response. And when the stimulus changes, so also does the response. So we cannot really tell whether the interference is due to a change in the response or to a change in the stimulus.

When the filtering task is used, with orthogonal combinations of two stimulus dimensions, there are four stimuli in the set. There are still just two responses,

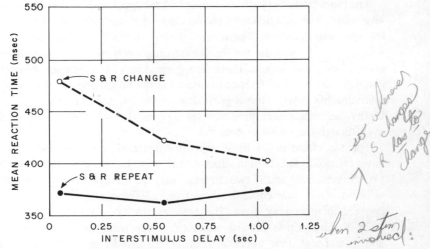

FIG. 6.8. Discrete reaction time for all sets of two stimuli, dimensions of width and height of rectangles, for successive repeating or changing stimuli and responses at three interstimulus delays. (Data from Felfoldy, 1974.)

but there are two stimuli per response. In terms of what can happen on successive trials, alternative possibilities and some data are illustrated in Fig. 6.9. At the bottom is the curve for those stimuli in which both the stimulus and the response repeat, and this curve is practically identical to the equivalent one in Fig. 6.8. Its shape is the same, but overall it runs about 12 msec higher; that is, when both the stimulus and response are repeated, reaction time is very slightly slower in the classification task than in the two-stimulus discrimination tasks.

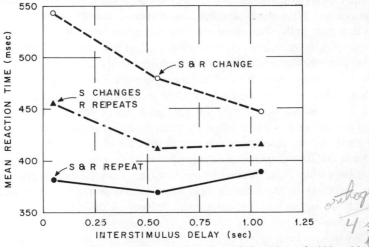

FIG. 6.9. Discrete reaction time for sets of four stimuli, orthogonal dimensions of width and height of rectangles, for successive repeating or changing stimuli and responses at three interstimulus delays. (Data from Felfoldy, 1974.)

The more interesting effects concern what happens when changes occur on successive trials. The middle curve shows data when the stimulus changes even though the response does not. The nature of this task is that intraclass variation occurs with respect to just the one irrelevant dimension, so these stimulus changes are always one-dimensional. There is a great deal of interference when the stimulus changes, and this interference is greatest at the fastest speeds, that is, at the shortest interstimulus delay. Thus a great deal of the interference effect can be accounted for by the interference produced on successive trials when the stimulus changes even though the response does not.

The top curve is for those stimuli when both the response and the stimulus have changed. When both change, the stimulus change may be either one- or two-dimensional, and if two-dimensional, the change may be one of area or one of form. Only one curve is shown for all these cases because the differences between them are very slight. These curves together make clear that there is interference in the reaction process when either the response or the stimulus changes, and as a rough first approximation, these effects are additive, being therefore greater when both stimulus and response change. *which is greater at shorter IS*

In terms of an understanding of the interference effect in the filtering or classification task, these data suggest the following picture: In speeded reaction-time tasks, the subject makes a quick first check to see if the stimulus is the same as the last one, and if it is, he responds the same as he did last time. This process is not affected to any great extent by the addition to the task of an irrelevant variable. However, with just two stimuli, on half the trials both the stimulus and the response are the same on successive trials. But with four stimuli, on only a quarter of the trials are both the stimulus and response the same. In another quarter of the trials the response is indeed the same, but the stimulus is not. The quick-check-for-sameness no longer works, and a substantial increase in reaction time occurs. When both stimulus and response change, there is interference in reaction time both when there are two and when there are four stimuli, but this interference is greater with the orthogonal set because it occurs in addition to an interference that exists for stimulus changes only.

In effect then, there are two factors contributing to the interference found with orthogonal dimensions, and which relate to the effects of sequential stimuli. The first factor is that opportunity for the quick check when successive stimuli are identical occurs less often when the orthogonal set of four stimuli is used. Thus the stimulus and response change more often with orthogonal sets. The second factor is that further interference is produced when the stimuli change on successive trials even when the response remains constant. Thus the overall effect that reaction time increases in the filtering task with integral stimulus dimensions is largely due to microprocesses occurring with respect to different sequences of stimuli and responses.

This quick check is very much like the reaction to a stimulus as a "blob," which Lockhead (1972) argues is the way all stimuli are reacted to initially, but that only stimuli generated from integral dimensions can be a single "blob."

An alternative term here could be "template," in which the stimulus is perceived as a holistic entity. But whatever the language used, it seems clear that only integral dimensions allow such perception of two-dimensional entities, and that separable dimensions are perceived as two (or more) distinct entities. We have no data for separable dimensions of the sort shown in Fig. 6.9, but such data would certainly be interesting. Would they show, for example, no interference effect when the stimulus changes but the response does not? There should be no such effect if complete filtering occurs, and such effective selective attention should occur since the subject always knows what is the relevant dimension for discrimination. So the middle curve in Fig. 6.9 should drop down to the lower curve, and the top curve would be the same as the top curve in Fig. 6.8. But this is only conjecture at this time.

OTHER INTERFERENCE EFFECTS

Let us consider, before closing, possible interference effects in classification other than those caused by the use of one dimension as relevant to classification and the other as irrelevant. I shall describe two other types of classification in which interference does occur.

Grouping with One-Dimensional Stimuli

One way of producing a classification task in which there is more than one stimulus per class is to use several stimuli that vary on a single dimension

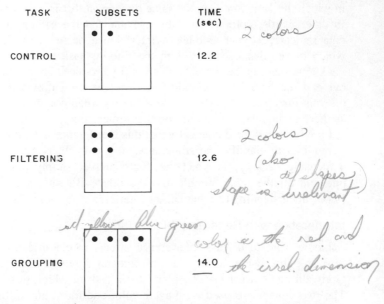

FIG. 6.10. Card sorting time for three types of constrained-classification task with dimensions of color and form, two or four stimuli. (Data from Gottwald and Garner, 1972.)

but to require the subject to group them into a smaller number of classes than stimuli. Figure 6.10 shows some data contrasting this procedure with a classification task of the sort we have just been discussing.

These are some data from a constrained-classification task used by Gottwald and Garner (1972). The total set of stimuli were the orthogonal combinations of four forms times four colors, and here are shown three different logical forms of two subsets used in the constrained-classification tasks. The task was classification, or sorting, of 32 stimulus cards, half of which were each of the two classes. The times are for sorting the entire deck. The data shown here are for classification by color, the four colors being red, yellow, blue, and green. For these particular tasks different forms were used only for the task labeled "filtering," and these were combinations of circles, squares, or triangles.

The task shown at the top is the control, in which two colors were discriminated from each other. The second task is called filtering, following the nomenclature of Posner (1964). While this nomenclature has become fairly common, and thus I use it, I want to point out that the term implies something about what the organism does, rather than being a description of the task itself. While filtering is logically possible with this task, it is an experimental question whether the human actually manages to filter, i.e., selectively exclude, a dimension. Our data for this task indicate very little interference effect, although the small increase in sorting times was statistically significant.

The critical task is one that we have called grouping, in which there are still two responses, one for each class, and in which there is intraclass variation, but in which the variation is on the same dimension that is also used for classification. In other words, color is both the relevant and the irrelevant dimension. As the data indicate, a great amount of interference occurs with this task, an amount which makes that occurring with the filtering task trivial by comparison. What we know, then, is that intraclass variability produces interference in classification, but that the intraclass variability need not be on a dimension orthogonal to the relevant dimension. Interference also occurs when one dimension is used, as long as there is intraclass variability on that dimension.

I might remark parenthetically that this interference does not occur if the subject is required to classify one stimulus against two others. In that case he shifts to a focusing strategy, in which he, for example, simply puts red stimuli in one pile and all the other stimuli into the other. But this strategy is not pertinent to our understanding of what causes interference in these classification tasks.

Interference with Separable Dimensions

I now want to discuss interference effects in classification which occur with separable dimensions as well as with integral dimensions. Figure 6.11, also from Gottwald and Garner (1972), illustrates a task in which this interference occurs. The two dimensions used were again color and form, and in this experiment both color and form were used as the relevant dimension, so data are shown as the average sorting times for the two dimensions. There is, of course, little difference between them or we would not pool the data this way. Also, the numerical values are slightly lower than in Fig. 6.10, but this is partly due to the fact that decks of 30 stimulus cards were used to allow an equal number of each of the six alternative stimuli used in these experiments.

In Fig. 6.10 there was some slight interference effect in the two by two orthogonal set of stimuli, but it was so slight that we can consider that these two dimensions more nearly satisfy the requirements of separable rather than integral dimensions. Certainly if brightness and size are separable, as we saw in the last lecture, color and form should be. Considering these two dimensions to be separable, the filtering-2 task (the "2" refers to the number of classes required) becomes a control experiment in which there are six stimuli classified into two classes on the basis of one dimension.

The critical comparison here is the task shown at the bottom and labeled "condensation." Once again, this is Posner's (1964) terminology, and a condensation task is any classification of dimensionally defined stimuli in which the logic of the task requires that both dimensions must be processed in order for the classification to be carried out. In this task, only one stimulus in each class shares no level on a dimension with stimuli in the other class. Two stimuli in each class do share levels, thus requiring that the subject determine both the color and the form of the stimulus before correct classification can occur. The subject simply cannot, in the condensation task, ignore either dimension as irrelevant.

The data are striking. This classification task requires nearly half again as long for the subject to sort the stimuli into two classes.

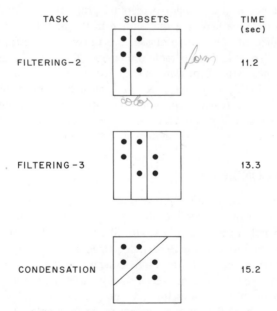

FIG. 6.11. Card sorting time for three types of constrained-classification task with dimensions of color and form, six stimuli. (Data from Gottwald and Garner, 1972.)

The task indicated in the middle, filtering-3, is sort of another control task. It involves exactly the same stimuli as those in the condensation task, but classification is made by the three levels of a single dimension. Even though this task requires more response categories than the condensation task, it is carried out considerably faster. The cost in processing time of the condensation task with separable dimensions is very great indeed.

There is strong supporting evidence for this result which I want to mention. Keele (1970) reports an experiment in which he used the discrete reaction-time procedure with some equivalent comparisons in it. His stimulus dimensions were also color and form, and he always used either two or four stimuli, never the six that Gottwald and I used in this experiment. His mean reaction time for the control conditions involving just two colors or two forms was 384 msec. He did not use a filtering task, but for the grouping task, with two forms or colors in each class, the mean reaction time went to 500 msec. For his condensation task, he used the diagonals of the two by two orthogonal set of forms and colors to construct each of the two classes. This is the simplest condensation task that can be generated, and with it the reaction time jumped to 620 msec. Forced processing of two dimensions does cause considerable interference in information processing.

Gottwald and I now have some unpublished data for a condensation task involving integral stimulus dimensions. As we expected, such a task is still difficult, but not as difficult as one with separable dimensions. The reason for the lowered difficulty of the condensation task with integral dimensions is that similarity in the sense of distance is the primary perceptual property of stimuli formed from integral dimensions, so a task like that shown in the bottom of Fig. 6.11 would not be all that difficult. These two classes are fairly easily differentiated on the basis of distance. No, it is the separable dimensions that give the greater difficulty with this task, since with them dimensional structure is primary and cannot be ignored. Thus the highly cognitive processing must be carried out, a processing in which the subject actually deals with each dimension separately, making a decision about each and then about the two in conjunction. He is unable to change his perceptual processes to suit the demands of the condensation task.

PROCESSING CONCEPTS

Much research on information processing with multidimensional stimuli has focused primarily on the processing alternatives, especially the two alternatives of serial versus parallel processing. I would like to comment briefly on this point and argue as I have before (Garner, 1970) that questions concerning the serial-parallel distinction must be secondary to questions concerning the nature of the stimulus dimensions themselves. The terms serial and parallel are both meaningful only if there are two or more of something to be processed, and there are two or more dimensions only if they can be shown to be separable. As I argued in the last lecture, it is not enough that we experimenters decide that there are two dimensions; we must also determine whether they are perceived as two dimensions by the subject. If they satisfy the requirements of integrality, then it is quite pointless to ask whether the two dimensions are processed in serial or parallel fashion.

The possibility of asymmetric integrality makes even more important the need to clarify the nature of dimensional structure before we undertake to ask the more specific processing questions. If dimension X is integral to dimension Y, but dimension Y is not integral to dimension X, what can it mean to ask whether these two dimensions are processed in parallel? To process in parallel connotes that the two dimensions have an equivalent status, whereas if integrality is asymmetric there is no such equivalent status. To process in serial fashion does not imply this equivalent status, especially with selective serial processing. But I still think it risky to attack the question of dimensional relations directly in terms of processing strategies rather than first asking about the nature of that which is to be processed.

SUMMARY

In summary:

1. In a constrained-classification task, when two dimensions are used in a correlated or redundant manner, discrimination performance is improved if the dimensions are integral, although no improvement occurs if they are separable.

2. If the constrained classification task involves orthogonal stimulus dimensions, so that one dimension is relevant and the other irrelevant, then interference in processing occurs if the dimensions are integral, although no interference occurs if they are separable.

3. Some auditory dimensions, either linguistic or nonlinguistic, are integral. If a linguistic dimension is paired with a nonlinguistic dimension, however, interference occurs only when the nonlinguistic dimension is irrelevant. This asymmetric integrality suggests a difference in processing level.

4. Optional processing mechanisms exist which can be used with separable dimensions to improve performance when the dimensions are correlated. Two of these mechanisms are selective serial processing and stimulus redefinition.

5. The concept of dimensional integrality is primarily a stimulus concept, although additional processing concepts pertinent to the optional processes are necessary for a full understanding of the differences between integral and separable dimensions.

6. The mechanism by which processing performance improves with redundant integral dimensions is that similarity, with an Euclidean distance metric, is a primary property of stimuli generated with such dimensions. Thus two correlated dimensions produce a greater interstimulus difference than either dimension alone, with a consequent improvement in speed of discrimination.

7. The loss that occurs when an integral dimension is irrelevant to the classification is due to intraclass variability. More particularly, this intraclass variability increases reaction time to successive stimuli, because there are more ways in which a stimulus can change, including changes in stimulus when the response remains constant.

The interference produced on reaction time by such changes thus operates more frequently, as well as being of greater magnitude.

8. Interference may also occur with separable dimensions if classification tasks require processing of both dimensions. In such condensation tasks interference is greater with separable than with integral dimensions.

REFERENCES

Day, R. S., & Wood, C. C. Interactions between linguistic and nonlinguistic processing. *Journal of the Acoustical Society of America,* 1972, **51**, 79. (a)

Day, R. S., & Wood, C. C. Mutual interference between two linguistic dimensions of the same stimuli. *Journal of the Acoustical Society of America,* 1972, **52**, 175. (b)

Egeth, H. Selective attention. *Psychological Bulletin,* 1967, **67**, 41–57.

Egeth, H., & Pachella, R. Multidimensional stimulus identification. *Perception & Psychophysics,* 1969, **5**, 341–346.

Felfoldy, G. L. Repetition effects in choice reaction time to multidimensional stimuli. *Perception & Psychophysics,* 1974, in press.

Felfoldy, G. L., & Garner, W. R. The effects on speeded classification of implicit and explicit instructions regarding redundant dimensions. *Perception & Psychophysics,* 1971, **9**, 289–292.

Garner, W. R. Speed of discrimination with redundant stimulus attributes. *Perception & Psychophysics,* 1969, **6**, 221–224.

Garner, W. R. The stimulus in information processing. *American Psychologist,* 1970, **25**, 350–358.

Garner, W. R. Information integration and form of encoding. In A. W. Melton & E. Martin (Eds.), *Coding processes in human memory.* Washington: V. H. Winston, 1972.

Garner, W. R. Attention and selection of stimuli and attributes. E. C. Carterette, & M. P. Friedman (Eds.), *Handbook of perception.* Vol. 2. New York: Academic Press, 1974.

Garner, W. R., & Felfoldy, G. L. Integrality of stimulus dimensions in various types of information processing. *Cognitive Psychology,* 1970, **1**, 225–241.

Gottwald, R. L., & Garner, W. R. Effects of focusing strategy on speeded classification with grouping, filtering, and condensation tasks. *Perception & Psychophysics,* 1972, **11**, 179–182.

Imai, S., & Garner, W. R. Discriminability and preference for attributes in free and constrained classification. *Journal of Experimental Psychology,* 1965, **69**, 596–608.

Keele, S. W. Effects of input and output modes on decision time. *Journal of Experimental Psychology,* 1970, **85**, 157–164.

Lockhead, G. R. Effects of dimensional redundancy on visual discrimination. *Journal of Experimental Psychology,* 1966, **72**, 95–104.

Lockhead, G. R. Processing dimensional stimuli: A note. *Psychological Review,* 1972, **79**, 410–419.

Morgan, B. B., & Alluisi, E. A. Effects of discriminability and irrelevant information on absolute judgments. *Perception & Psychophysics,* 1967, **2**, 54–58.

Posner, M. I. Information reduction in the analysis of sequential tasks. *Psychological Review,* 1964, **71**, 491–504.

Posner, M. I., & Mitchell, R. F. Chronometric analysis of classification. *Psychological Review,* 1967, **74**, 392–409.

Treisman, A. M. Strategies and models of selective attention. *Psychological Review,* 1969, **76**, 282–299.

Wood, C. C. Levels of processing in speech perception: Neurophysiological and information-processing analyses. Unpublished doctoral dissertation, Yale University, 1973.

LECTURE 7
INFORMATION INTEGRATION
WITH SEPARABLE DIMENSIONS

In this lecture I want to discuss information integration with dimensions that are for the most part separable. Before getting fully into this topic, however, I need to make some prefatory comments about the relation between the concepts developed in the last two lectures and the research I will describe here.

First, the topic of this lecture is integration of information. This fact means that we will be concerned primarily with the problem of redundancy, since if we want to understand integration of information there must be some information to integrate. This is what redundancy makes possible: the integration of two or more sources of information to provide better performance than can be provided with the information from either source alone. However, as we saw in the last lecture, we frequently can understand the nature of facilitation with dimensional redundancy better by also considering how and why interference occurs when there is additional irrelevant information.

Second, there are some semantic connotative problems. I have used the term integral to refer to dimensions for which a similarity or distance structure is the primary process, and for which there is facilitation in information processing when the dimensions are used redundantly, and interference when the dimensions are used orthogonally, in a classification task. Dimensional integrality, however, I consider to be primarily a stimulus concept. If we must use organismic concepts, then we must consider that integral dimensions are mandatorily so, that is, there is no option on the part of the processing organism. With such dimensions, I do not think that the idea of information integration is very meaningful. For the subject, the dimensions are not dimensions, so he does not integrate information with integral dimensions any more than he integrates information when the two levels on a single dimension are made more discriminable. The subject processes

151

information faster because of this increased discriminability, but there is no active integration of information. On the other hand, the term integration connotes an active organismic process; it is something the organism does, usually in a fairly deliberate fashion. It is a term that is meaningful for separable dimensions, where the subject does perceive dimensions, and usually has some option about his processing of them. So for me the concept of integral dimensions is a stimulus concept, while the concept of information integration is an organismic one.

Third, as I have remarked before, we must first ask whether a pair of dimensions is integral or separable before we ask questions concerning how multiple dimensions are processed. Integral dimensions are really not separate dimensions at all, so there is no point in asking whether the organism can integrate two sources of information in such cases. However, if we know that two dimensions, as sources of information, are separable, if not actually separated, then it becomes meaningful to ask whether the organism can integrate information. And the primary concern of this lecture is the understanding of how redundancy improves information processing when the dimensions do not satisfy the more rigorous criteria of being integral. And I hope it is clear from these comments that I do not feel that only integral dimensions can give improvement in information processing. Quite the contrary. There is this large set of converging operations to provide a definition of dimensional integrality, but that definition in no sense precludes the possibility of obtaining an improvement in information processing with redundant separable dimensions.

The Need for Redundancy

One further prefatory comment: If we want to investigate the circumstances under which redundant information will aid information processing, there must be some need for the redundancy for the problem to be experimentally meaningful. How can we improve performance by adding redundant information if performance is already at a maximum? We can't, and this point is commonly understood in work on redundancy; in fact, you can only do meaningless experiments if it is not understood.

There is a corollary to this problem, however, which is also crucial to understanding the role of redundancy in information processing. If performance is limited enough that improvement can occur with redundant information, there is some reason or cause for the inadequate performance. Furthermore, there are many different possible reasons for the inadequate performance, not just one. Still further, there are many different ways of producing redundancy experimentally, and we must remember that while redundancy is a single logical concept, it is not a single concept in use.

The problem, then, is to understand the reasons for inadequate performance, and to find those forms of redundancy that offset the particular factor that limits performance. It is not enough to know that performance is limited and that we provide redundancy. Improved performance may or may not occur, and whether it does depends on the factor that is limiting performance and whether the particular form of redundancy resolves that particular deficit problem. So our task in this lecture is to develop concepts that help us differentiate reasons for limited performance, and then to find the kinds of redundancy that improve it.

STATE AND PROCESS LIMITATION

One major distinction concerning inadequate performance is that between state and process limitation. Figure 7.1 will help to differentiate these two concepts. As this figure indicates, I find it convenient to think in terms of two orthogonal axes in differentiating factors that can limit information-processing performance. The axis of primary concern in information processing is what I have called the process axis. In any information-processing task there is a set of alternatives, here shown as the minimum of two. The experimenter sets a task for the subject, and he does so with respect to the process axis. He may tell the subject, for example, to identify each of 2, or 3, or 10 alternative stimuli, and to do so the subject must differentiate between them. If there are only two alternatives, these might be the two levels on a single dimension, the dimension that is pertinent to the processing task.

Clearly one general class of limitation has to do with this process dimension or axis. If the subject cannot discriminate stimulus A from stimulus B with 100 percent accuracy, and if the failure is due to the fact that the stimuli do not differ from each other enough, then the inadequate performance is due to a process limitation.

The other axis is pertinent to state limitation. In this case, the inadequate performance is not due to differences between the alternative stimuli, but rather is due to the fact that each stimulus is inadequately represented in the organism. It may be that the organism's alertness level is too low, or even that the organism is

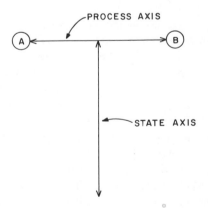

FIG. 7.1. Two axes that differentiate factors limiting information-processing performance. The process axis is directly pertinent to the information being processed. The state axis is pertinent to the adequacy of information representation in the organism.

asleep. It may be that the organism's sensitivity is too poor, so that it cannot get a full representation of the input with the energy available.

As a simple example, to differentiate state from process, consider the task in which a subject is required to identify one of two letters on single presentations, for example, the letters A and B used in Fig. 7.1 to represent two stimuli. He makes mistakes in his identification. Why? It may be that whoever wrote the letters did so sloppily, so that even the best of us is not sure what each letter is. Failure of perfect discrimination for such a reason is due to process limitation. Alternatively, suppose two beautifully and clearly inscribed letters are the stimuli, so well written that anybody can identify each of them perfectly as long as each is presented at a sufficiently high contrast and a long enough duration that it can be seen. But now suppose that we decrease the contrast and the duration until finally the subject cooperates by making errors. Such errors are due to a state limitation, not to a process limitation.

In either case we might end up with 75 percent correct identification. So we know that improvement can occur, and thus might occur if redundant information is presented. But the causes for the limited performance are entirely different in the two cases, and as we shall see, different kinds of redundancy are necessary in each case in order to obtain a gain with redundancy and thus to demonstrate that the processing organism can integrate information.

The important point differentiating state and process lies in how the task is specified—the task requirement being related to the process axis. Parenthetically, I might mention that in some tasks the process and the state axes are the same, as for example in the measurement of an absolute threshold, in which the subject is required to differentiate energy from no energy. Our concern will not be with such tasks, but with tasks in which the state and process aspects are fairly easily distinguished.

Organismic and Stimulus Concepts

Once again we run into the problem of deciding whether organismic or stimulus concepts are more valuable. For example, we can (Garner, 1965) differentiate between energic and dimensional, or even informational, aspects of the stimulus. Energic variables, of course, correspond to the state axis, and the informational variables correspond to the process axis. If the difference between two levels on the process dimension is too small, this can be considered either a limit to the discriminability of the stimuli (a stimulus concept) or a limit to the ability of the organism to discriminate the two levels. Or if the energy level is too low (a stimulus concept), we might just as well have said that the organism was too insensitive. Fortunately, the difference between stimulus and organismic concepts has not proven to be too awkward an issue in this area because it is fairly easy, usually, to relate some kinds of stimulus variables to process limitations and other kinds of stimulus variables to state limitations. This ability to have accurate *a priori* judgments about the functions of variables simplifies our experimental lives considerably.

State and Process Differentiation

How do we know when inadequate performance in a task is due to a state limitation or to a process limitation? The experimental operations required are illustrated in Fig. 7.2. We have some measure of performance, and also knowledge of the best performance that can be obtained, so that we can know when there is no limitation on performance. In this illustration I have used a measure of percent correct, and 100 percent correct is a nonlimited performance. We then find a stimulus variable that is reasonably likely to be related to a process limitation, and we systematically vary the levels on it. If, as in the top function, performance continues to improve up to 100 percent, then clearly there has been no state limitation, and at all levels of performance less than the maximum, only process factors have limited performance.

Consider the bottom curve now. As we increase the process units, which might be simple discriminability, performance improves but reaches an effective asymptote with performance less than 100 percent. Since we cannot improve performance any further by the addition of process units, we conclude that performance is state limited.

Notice that at all levels of performance below this asymptote we must conclude that there was process limitation as well as state limitation, since adding of process units does improve performance. There is, of course, no reason why performance

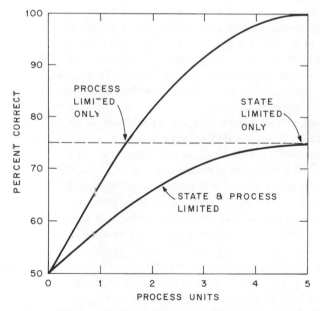

FIG. 7.2. Idealized functions relating performance to increase in a process-related variable with performance either state or process limited. (After Garner, 1970.)

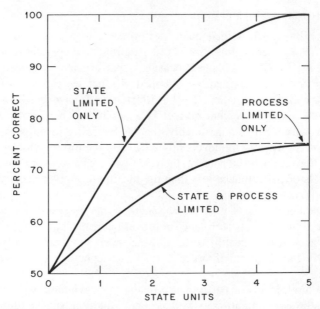

FIG. 7.3. Idealized functions relating performance to increases in a state-related variable with performance either state or process limited.

must be limited to just state or just process. Both limitations can and frequently do coexist to complicate our experimental lives.

To emphasize the need to differentiate state and process limitations, notice the dashed line at a performance level of 75 percent. On each of the curves there exists a condition at which 75 percent performance occurs. But notice also that on only one of the curves—the one for process limit—does improvement occur with an increase in process units. Identical performance does not guarantee identical mechanisms.

We can, of course, handle this logical problem in reverse, as shown in Fig. 7.3. In this case we manipulate state units, ordinarily some energy variable pertinent to the stimulus, such as duration, energy, or contrast. Now the curve that continues to rise until 100 percent performance is reached is identified as having only state limitation. The lower curve, which reaches an asymptotic value at less than full performance, has reached a condition of pure process limitation. Lower points on that curve indicate that state limitation is operating as well as process limitation.

A real experiment differentiating state and process limitation is illustrated in Fig. 7.4. Garner, Kaplan, and Creelman (1966) used an absolute-judgment task requiring identification of 20 alternative sizes of squares. Thus size was the process variable, the one pertinent to the demands of the task. The stimuli were presented as dark squares against a lighter background, and both contrast and stimulus duration were used in the experiment as state variables. The results shown in this figure are for high contrast stimuli only, with information transmission plotted as a function

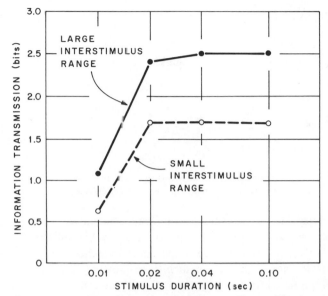

FIG. 7.4. Information transmission as a function of a state variable (duration) for two levels of process limitation (interstimulus range). (After Garner et al., 1966.)

of the other state variable—stimulus duration. There are two different ranges of stimulus size, the process variable.

The results for the small interstimulus range show an increase in information transmission for the two lowest values of duration, and then no further increase. So beyond 0.02 sec there is no more state limitation, but only process limitation. The same general picture exists for the large interstimulus range. So for each curve there is no state limitation at the upper end. There is, however, process limitation. This fact means that performance can be improved with an improvement in process factors, as indeed happens as the interstimulus range is increased. It should be possible for it to increase still further because even with the large interstimulus range, information transmission is not as great as it could be with 20 alternative stimulus sizes.

Redundancy Gain with State Limitation

This is fine to differentiate state and process limitation, but our special concern is redundancy and how and under what circumstances it can lead to improvement in performance. We already know that a process limitation, which is essentially a limitation of discriminability, can be offset with redundancy which increases interstimulus difference; for this, integral dimensions are required if the redundancy is to be effective. What kind of redundancy can offset state limitation? Certainly what we need to look for is the kind of redundancy that increases the probability of getting the stimulus into the organism. Simple element repetition is one such possibility.

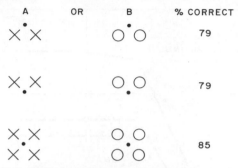

FIG. 7.5. Accuracy of discrimination with two or four identical stimulus elements. Stimuli were state limited by use of low contrast and short duration. (Data from Garner and Flowers, 1969.)

Figure 7.5 presents some data showing that element repetition or redundancy does improve information-processing performance if the limitation is one of state. Garner and Fowers (1969) used three experimental conditions requiring discrimination of two alternatives perceived tachistoscopically. The first two conditions required differentiation of two X's from two O's, in one case above the fixation point, and in the other below the fixation point. Average correct identification was 79 percent for each of these cases. The third condition required differentiation of four X's from four O's, located both above and below the fixation point shown as the dot in all cases. Accuracy of identification improved to 85 percent with the increase in number of elements.

Was the inadequate performance due to a state limitation? We feel quite sure that it was. In the first place, if either an X or an O is presented under conditions of high contrast and long duration, nobody can fail to tell the difference. Nor did we deliberately blur them to make discrimination between them difficult. On the contrary, we made discrimination difficult not by manipulating the process variable but by manipulating the state variables: We decreased the contrast and the exposure duration in our tachistoscope until enough errors were made. Then we ran the experiment and found out that this state limitation could be offset, partially, at least, by increasing the number of elements—by increasing detection opportunity, in effect.

We did not manipulate a process variable to see if it failed to offset the state limitation in this experiment. In another experiment, however, we (Flowers & Garner, 1971) did, with speed of card sorting as our experimental measure. There were basically three different experimental comparisons, the first of which is illustrated in Fig. 7.6. At the top are shown two stimuli which differed by having a single dot located to the left or right of center. Thus lateral location was the process variable. The dot was black on a white stimulus card. Discrimination time was 21.3 sec for a deck of 32 cards. At the bottom are shown two stimulus alternatives on each of which there are two dots, both located the same distance to the right or left as the single dot at the top. Thus element redundancy was provided, and I might remark that in the actual experiment these two dots occurred

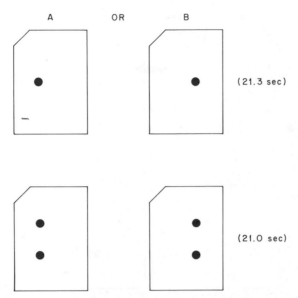

FIG. 7.6. The effect of element redundancy on speed of card sorting. Dots were high contrast and easily discriminated, so there was neither state nor process limitation. (Data from Flowers and Garner, 1971.)

at different vertical locations so as to prevent fixation on a single position. There was effectively no improvement in sorting speed with the addition of the second stimulus element. In a sense these two tasks are the control tasks, with little if any process or state limitation, and certainly showing no improvement with element repetition.

Figure 7.7 shows what happens if we introduce state limitation into the task. We did so by using light yellow dots instead of the black dots. That this manipulation was effective is shown by the more than 4.0 sec increase in sorting time for the single dot. (It is necessary, of course, to demonstrate this degradation in performance to be sure that there is room for improvement.) At the bottom we have once again the two-element stimuli, and now performance improved by 1.5 sec as a result of the addition of the second element. So we know that element redundancy facilitates performance in this task also, even when speed rather than accuracy is used as the dependent measure.

Figure 7.8 shows what happens if we introduce process limitation into the task. At the top are shown the two stimuli for the one-element task. These stimuli have been moved closer to the center line, thus producing a process limitation, although they are still black, with no resultant state limitation. We were, of course, trying to get as much process limitation in this case as state limitation in the last case, and we succeeded rather well. The sorting time was 25.0 sec, just slightly less than that we obtained with the state-limited comparison. In this case when element redundancy is added, there is virtually no improvement in perfor-

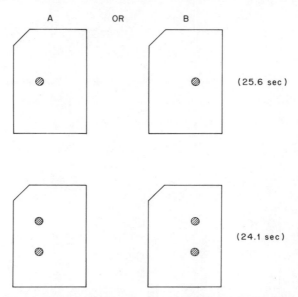

FIG. 7.7. The effect of element redundancy on speed of card sorting. The dots were low contrast yellow, so there was state limitation. (Data from Flowers and Garner, 1971.)

mance. (The slight improvement shown was not near statistical significance, with fewer than half the subjects showing any improvement at all.) Thus process-limited performance is not aided by element redundancy, although state-limited performance is.

Another experiment contrasting state and process limitations on performance was carried out by Pachella and Fisher (1969). They used an absolute-judgment task requiring subjects to identify one of ten lateral positions of the stimulus. In one condition they used a wide spacing of stimuli and high contrast. In a second condition they lowered only the contrast, and in a third condition they used a narrow range of stimulus alternatives, but at high contrast. They were specifically interested in the trade-off between speed and accuracy in such tasks and used different speed constraints on the subjects. Their results, in the present context, can be described fairly simply: When the stimuli were state limited by having low contrast, there was a loss of performance, but it was easily made up with a longer reaction time. When the stimuli were process limited by being close together, performance was again degraded, but compensation with longer reaction time was very slight. Thus increased time could compensate easily for state limitation, but not for process limitation; and time of course can be considered one particular form of redundancy, appropriate more to state than to process limitation.

In the experiments I have described here, we can feel fairly sure that the experimental conditions represent either state limitation or process limitation, but not both. If both types of limitation are involved in a given task, then improvement should

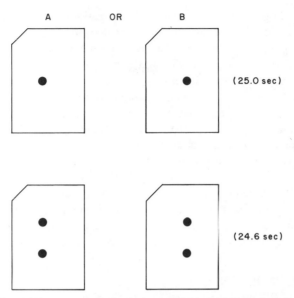

FIG. 7.8. The effect of element redundancy on speed of card sorting. The single dot locations were close together, so there was process limitation. (Data from Flowers and Garner, 1971.)

be obtained with redundancy appropriate to either limitation. Lockhead (1966a), for example, required his subjects to make absolute judgments of the length and vertical position of a line. With ten alternative levels for each dimension, tasks with single dimensions were almost certainly process limited, since rarely can subjects identify 10 alternative levels of a single dimension. In addition, however, low contrast and short duration exposures were used, and these stimulus conditions provided state limitation. Lockhead obtained improvement in performance when the two dimensions were used redundantly, and these dimensions were almost certainly integral and thus provided redundancy appropriate to process limitation. Thus the fact that state limitation exists does not prevent a redundancy gain which offsets a process limitation, or vice versa. The gain will occur as long as there is some limitation appropriate to the kind of redundancy used. In fact, we would have to conjecture that this experimental task would have shown a redundancy gain with element repetition as well as with dimensional redundancy.

What Is a Dimension?

A brief comment is in order at this point about what constitutes a dimension. If we call this type of redundancy element redundancy, while calling others dimensional redundancy, do we have a sound logical basis for the difference? I think we do not, and that to call the present case one of element redundancy is simply a convenience, one that is useful in differentiating limiting cases. Two dots, each varying in right-left location, can easily be described as two variables that are correlated in the experiments of Flowers and Garner. Furthermore, we could have generated an orthogonal set and required classification of this orthogonal set by, for instance, the right-left location of the upper dot; or, alternatively, of the lower dot. In other words, there is nothing that we can do with any other two dimensions that we cannot do with these, so we need not differentiate this case from others if we consider only the logical structure.

However, it is useful to make these distinctions because they are meaningfully related to what we are trying to understand about human information processing. We might as easily argue that there is no need to distinguish between state and process limitation. After all, a simple (or naive) operational approach says that if we have a two-choice discrimination task, 75 percent correct is 75 percent correct, and there is no need to make any further differentiations. I hope I have made the inadequacy of such an attitude clear. We will not understand information processing unless and until we make as many differentiations as the processing organism requires us to make in order to understand it fully. We should never be constrained by overly simplistic logical or operational considerations.

PERCEPTUAL INDEPENDENCE

In dealing with the problem of redundancy in information processing, sooner or later the question of perceptual independence comes into the picture. Certainly in formal (usually mathematical) models that attempt to explain how redundancy aids in information processing, the concept must be brought in quite explicitly by dealing with the measurement of independence as zero correlation. Garner and Lee (1962), for example, used a model in which perceptual error variance was decreased with redundant stimulus dimensions, but such a decrease occurs

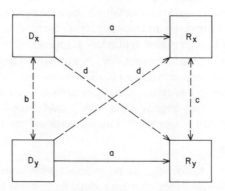

a: PROCESS INDEPENDENCE
b: INTERACTIVE INPUT PROCESS
c: INTERACTIVE RESPONSE PROCESS
d: CROSSED PERCEPTUAL PROCESS

FIG. 7.9. Process independence and three kinds of process correlation for two stimulus dimensions and their relevant response systems.

only if errors to the two or more dimensions are uncorrelated. If errors are correlated, then combining two or more dimensions does not produce a reduction in error variance, because in effect more of the same is simply being combined. Thus two processes must be independent if together they are to improve performance.

Somewhat later Garner and Morton (1969) elaborated this question and demonstrated that perceptual independence is not a unitary concept at all, but that there are many different kinds of correlation that can contribute to nonindependence in an information-processing task. One major distinction relates to the distinction we have been discussing here, that between state and process, since there can be either state independence or process independence, and their roles will be as different in understanding when and how redundancy improves performance as the basic difference between state and process limitation itself.

Process Correlation

First let us consider process correlation, with the aid of the diagram shown in Fig. 7.9. In this diagram, there are two inputs, the dimensions X and Y. And for each input there is an appropriate response or output. If the two dimensions themselves are uncorrelated, then there is at least the potential for independent processing. The lines connecting each dimensional input with its appropriate output, labeled "a," are the only connections that should exist, and if these are all that do exist, then we have perceptual independence of the kind appropriately called process independence. Notice, incidentally, that if there is such process independence, then we are in effect dealing with separable dimensions.

Consider, however, three different ways in which process correlation, or nonindependence, can occur. The dashed lines represent these correlations. For "b" there is an interaction between the dimensions themselves, between the input processes. This is the kind of interaction most appropriate to the concept of integral dimensions, in that the dimensions do not act as separate dimensions at all. They either interact in the physical stimuli or at the very least at an early stage in processing. For "c" there is an equivalent interaction between the two response systems so that they cannot operate independently. As an extreme illustration, consider that one finger is required to respond to both dimensions X and Y. Obviously it cannot do so simultaneously, and even if the dimensions are uncorrelated, the responses will be correlated. The third type of process correlation is that labeled "d," and it occurs when one response system crosses over and responds to the inappropriate dimension or input system. I suppose that this is the kind of interaction that most readily comes to mind when we speak about perceptual independence, but you can see that it is only one of several possibilities.

State Correlation

State correlation is quite a different thing from process correlation, and the diagram in Fig. 7.9 will, hopefully, continue to be useful in clarifying the distinction. The two lines labeled "a" are the only lines that should exist if there is process independence. These lines indicate that each response system deals just with its appropriate input system, but they do not indicate how well the two different processes are carried out. Suppose that each process, X and Y, is carried out inadequately because the state of the organism is poor. But suppose also that the state of the organism affects each process equally. Suppose still further that the state of the organism fluctuates or varies (and variation is, of course, a prerequisite for correlation). If this fluctuation in the state of the organism goes on equally for both processes, a correlation will be produced, but it is a state correlation and not a process correlation. What will happen is that each process goes on well or poorly, and in a correlated manner, but the specifics of what happens are not correlated at all. The X response system does not begin to react to dimension Y, nor do the two response systems interact, nor do the input systems. What is correlated is simply the adequacy of performance.

In a formal matrix required to show such a correlation, a state correlation appears as a correlation between the existence or nonexistence of errors on the two dimensions, but the direction or nature of the errors is not correlated. Such a correlation of direction of errors would indicate some kind of process correlation.

The point is simply that if performance is state limited and we try to improve it by providing redundant information, then the kind of perceptual independence required is state independence. If, however, performance is process limited, then we need process independence. While Garner and Morton do so, I do not want to pursue this topic further here, because these formal distinctions are limited to fairly formal models, and these are in turn limited to direct relations to data (in order to calculate correlations) more than I think advisable. Rather, we need to understand that many distinctions are required, both with respect to state and to process, but our real need is to find experimental operations that are appropriate to and help us delimit the causes of inadequate performance, and therefore indicate the kinds of redundant information whose integration can improve it.

REDUNDANCY THAT PRODUCES A NEW DIMENSION

One mechanism by which redundancy can improve information processing is that two dimensions when used in combination produce, in effect, a new dimension that is better for information processing than either dimension alone. I am now getting into a series of distinctions that I feel are quite real, although one mechanism easily shades or blurs into another (see Garner, 1972). We have already seen that integral dimensions improve discrimination performance when used redundantly; in fact, that is one of the several converging operations used to define dimensional integrality. But, as I have argued, I do not think that integral dimensions are really perceived as dimensions, at least for speeded processing, at all, so I do not consider this to be a case where two dimensions combine to produce a third. Integral dimensions are simply stimulus dimensions that combine according to an Euclidean metric. Thus redundant integral dimensions are simply dimensions that increase interstimulus differences.

be integral dimensions — see bottom of p. 167

to

Nominal Dimension Formed from Metric Dimensions

Let us consider the case where two dimensions combine to form a qualitatively new dimension which is simply an easier dimension to process. As an example, consider Felfoldy's (1974) experiment discussed in the last lecture. His dimensions were the width and height of rectangles. Each of these is a metric dimension, but when they are combined redundantly, they may form a new metric dimension of area; alternatively, they may form a new nominal dimension of form. Is it possible that form is a better dimension than either height or width, and even better than area, in the right experimental setting?

Figure 7.10 illustrates some stimuli and some data obtained by Weintraub (1971) concerning this question. His total set of stimuli was formed from 15 heights × 15 widths, and from this total set of 225 stimuli he selected various subsets of 15 stimuli for use in an absolute-judgment experiment. He used four different subsets which varied on only a single dimension (rows or columns from the matrix or stimuli), and the mean information transmission for these control conditions was 2.26 bits. He then used three conditions in which width and height were covaried redundantly. When the main diagonal was used, 15 squares varying in area were obtained, and for these, information transmission actually dropped from the control conditions to a value of 2.04 bits. Thus redundancy producing this new metric dimension did not facilitate information processing. When the secondary diagonal was used, 15 stimuli of approximately equal area but varying in form were obtained, and information transmission jumped to 2.65 bits. Thus the same

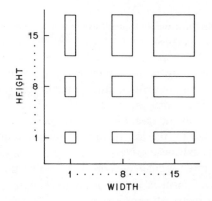

INFORMATION TRANSMISSIONS (BITS) FOR:
ROWS OR COLUMNS (AVERAGE): 2.26
REDUNDANT MAIN DIAGONAL (SQUARES): 2.04
REDUNDANT SECONDARY DIAGONAL
(EQUAL AREA): 2.65
REDUNDANT RANDOM RECTANGLES: 2.67

FIG. 7.10. Information transmissions in an absolute-judgment task, for four different methods of selecting 15 stimuli from 15 × 15 matrix of stimuli. (Data from Weintraub, 1971.)

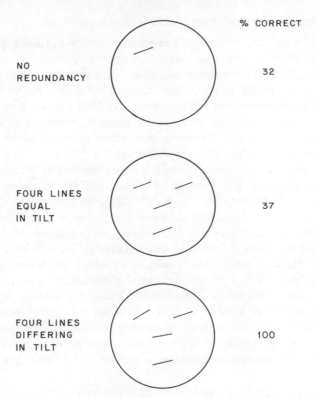

FIG. 7.11. Accuracy of identification of 20 alternative stimuli for nonredundant and two types of redundant stimuli. (Data from Lockhead, 1970.)

two dimensions which gave no improvement with one combination gave a great improvement when combined to provide the nominal dimension of form.

One can, of course, argue that these 15 stimuli selected this way gave a new metric dimension which was the ratio of height-to-width rather than the nonmetric dimension of form. However, the last redundant condition consisted of a random selection of rectangles, and these gave just as good information transmission as the forms varying in a more regular fashion. I think that the advantage is gained because the dimension of form is indeed a nominal dimension, and one that is easier to use than either metric dimension.

Figure 7.11 shows some stimuli and results from an experiment by Lockhead (1970) which, it seems to me, further strengthen the argument that form is an effective dimension in information-processing tasks. Lockhead generated 20 alternative stimuli in three different ways in this experiment. Each dimension was a line which could vary in angle of tilt (that being the process variable), and four different dimensions were four different locations within a circle, as shown. For the control condition, a single line was used, randomly presented at each of the four locations. With no redundancy, accuracy of correct identification was 32 percent and performance was almost certainly process limited.

For one redundant condition, the same tilt angle was simply repeated at each of the four locations. This is element redundancy, and it provided very little improvement in accuracy. This is the result we should expect, since in this experiment there was no stimulus degradation, or even time limitation, of the sort which would make us suspect a state limitation, and we know that repetition redundancy is not valuable when the need for redundancy is due to a process limitation.

The important condition, of course, is shown at the bottom of Fig. 7.11. Here there was redundancy again, but the line tilts were not simply repetitions of each other. They were selected so that each tilt at each position was used just once, but also so that each set of four tilts was a unique configuration. As you can see, accuracy of identification jumped to 100 percent, a truly remarkable improvement. Incidentally, Lockhead has pointed out to me that the illustrations in Fig. 7.11 are not as he used them. He had rotated the middle line 90 degrees, so that it would be like a nose on a face. He had done this with the idea that if the figures looked like faces they would be more easily identifiable. I did not correct the figures, however, because it seemed to me that the value of the uncorrelated line tilts does not depend on such a mnemonic device, and that the uniqueness of the configuration is alone sufficient to account for the excellent performance.

However, notice that in this experiment, as in Weintraub's, the forms are nominal representations generated from combinations of metric dimensions. What is the special role of nominal dimensions in information processing? I pointed out in the fifth lecture the argument made by Imai and Handel (1971) that nominal dimensions cannot be integral since with nominal dimensions the concept of distance, and therefore an Euclidean metric, is meaningless. But is it necessarily true, then, that nominal dimensions should be very good for information-processing tasks? Certainly nominal dimensions such as color and form usually do provide very good performance, and it may be that distance for such dimensions is meaningless, but in the sense that all levels are very far removed from each other. There does seem to be something special about nominal dimensions, but I am not certain what it is. In fact, I would even like to be certain how one defines a nominal dimension. Are all levels infinitely far apart—an idea that would certainly account for the easy processing—or is the very idea of a distance meaningless? I wish I understood this problem.

Interference with Nominal Dimensions

I used the experiment involving speed of classification of rectangles by Felfoldy (1974) to help understand why interference occurs with integral dimensions. Am I now arguing that these dimensions were not in fact integral? That is a complicated question, and we may have to accept the possibility that the dimensions of height and width are integral when combining to form a new dimension of area, but that they operate only to create a new nominal dimension when they combine to create changes in form. At least in the latter case it seems to me that integrality is not the best idea, and Weintraub's experiment is what makes me feel that way. I cannot be sure, however, and only a classification or direct similarity scaling experiment can further clarify the situation. But that is not important, because

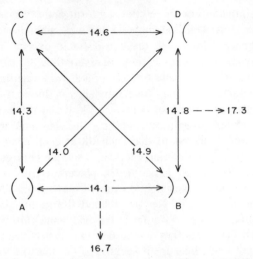

FIG. 7.12. Card sorting times (sec) for stimulus sets of single, correlated, and orthogonal dimensions which form nominal stimuli. The numbers inside are for each pair of stimuli. The numbers outside are for classification of the stimuli into two subsets vertically or horizontally. (Data from Pomerantz and Garner, 1973.)

the explanation for the interference effect itself did not depend on the metric properties of stimuli, but only on the fact that there were more alternative stimuli than response classes and that the subject could not effectively reduce the number of stimuli by selective attention or filtering of dimensions.

Further evidence concerning an interference effect with nominal dimensions is shown in Fig. 7.12. Pomerantz and I (1973) used a card sorting task, and the numbers shown here are the times to sort decks of 32 stimulus cards. Our two stimulus dimensions were simply right and left positions, and the levels on each dimension were the two different parentheses found on any typewriter. Four alternative stimuli can be formed from these two dimensions with their two levels, and they are shown in this figure. Discrimination was required of all six possible pairs of stimuli. Four of these pairs are control conditions involving variation on only a single dimension: The times for these contrasts ranged from 14.1 to 14.8 sec. The two diagonal contrasts are the redundant ones, and they give no evidence that these two dimensions lead to improved performance when used redundantly, since these two pairs lead to both the fastest and the slowest sorting times.

Actually, as mentioned briefly in the second lecture, the proper way to understand the results from all six possible pairs of stimuli is in terms of the number of alternatives which each has, as defined by rotations and reflections. Two of these stimuli come from R & R subsets of 2: They are () and)(, and discrimination between them is fastest of all. Two more of these stimuli come from the same R & R subset of 4 members: They are ((and)), and discrimination between them is slowest of all. So the most and least difficult pairs are the redundant ones, and all other pairs are intermediate in difficulty. It is clear that treating these results in terms of redundant dimensions simply is the wrong approach.

The numbers below and to the right in Figure 7.12 are the sorting times obtained when all four stimuli were used and classification was required by either a vertical or a horizontal grouping of the stimuli. These numbers (16.7 and 17.3 sec) are substantially greater than any obtained with the sorting of just two stimuli, so there is no question that interference did occur. But I would argue that this interference is due to stimulus grouping of the sort discussed in the sixth lecture and does not constitute evidence of integral dimensions.

REDUNDANCY THAT IMPROVES THE MEMORY PROCESS

Let me turn now to another problem in information processing. In many tasks, many stimulus alternatives must be kept in memory, and this memory requirement is probably the factor that limits performance. Such a limitation might be expected to occur with the usual absolute-judgment task or other multistimulus identification. If memory is the limiting factor, then in line with this general discussion, redundancy will be effective only if it improves the ability of an organism to maintain the items correctly in memory.

We have not really faced the question of why dimensions such as form provide better performance in information processing. We have simply been concerned with the kinds of redundancy that produce a dimension that is easier to use. It is very likely that the explanation lies in the effectiveness of form in providing a set of stimuli that is so easy to remember that the memory load is minimal. Weintraub (1971) suggested something close to this idea in his explanation of why rectangles varying in form give such better information transmission in the absolute-judgment task than did rectangles varying in size only. Rectangles varying in form in effect provide their own context in that one dimension can always be used as a reference for the other regardless of the absolute values involved. This is tantamount to saying that memory for the set of stimuli is less important for forms than for other stimuli; or, to paraphrase Weintraub, a series of stimuli varying in form minimizes the cognitive load on the subject.

In the first experiment to use redundancy in absolute judgment, Eriksen and Hake (1955) showed that the redundant use of size, hue, and brightness gave much better performance than did the use of any single dimension alone. We could argue that therefore these are integral dimensions. But even if hue and brightness are integral dimensions (which they probably are), I do not think that the gain obtained with this technique is due to that factor—i.e., to an increased interstimulus difference. With the absolute-judgment technique the limiting factor seems to involve such things as adaptation levels (in Helson's, 1964, sense), or frames of reference generally. The difficulty is in keeping track of which response number goes with which stimulus, and this is indeed very difficult with 20 stimuli varying on a single stimulus dimension. It seems to be easier with redundant dimensions, and these dimensions may be, but need not be, integral by other

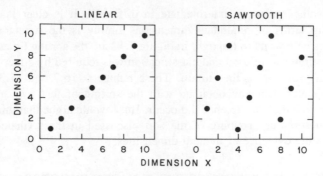

FIG. 7.13. Two types of dimensional pairings used in redundancy experiments by Lockhead (1970).

definitions. What I am really arguing here is that the memory factor is prepotent in tasks involving large numbers of alternative stimuli, and that even though performance is improved with redundant integral dimensions, it will occur just as well with separable dimensions.

Evidence on this point comes from further experiments by Lockhead (1970). Figure 7.13 shows two ways in which he generated redundant pairings of levels on two dimensions. On the left is what we usually do: If the dimensions are ordered, then we combine them so that the lowest value on dimension X goes with the lowest value on dimension Y, then the next lowest values are paired, and so on. This method is labeled linear pairing. On the right is an alternative method of pairing the values on the two dimensions. It is labeled sawtooth pairing because of its geometric configuration when plotted this way. In effect, successive values on X are paired with values three levels apart on Y, except that when there are no higher values on Y, a return is made to the lowest available value on Y. I think the diagram explains it better than my words. The advantage of this method of pairing is perhaps obvious—total interstimulus differences are maximized, so we might expect that information transmission in an absolute-judgment task will be improved more with the sawtooth rather than the linear pairing.

Table 7.1 shows what happens with three different pairs of dimensions Lockhead used. Hue and lightness showed a slight gain in information transmission when the linear pairing was used. Since these are certainly integral dimensions, it may be that some gain is obtained due to the integrality. There is, of course, plenty of evidence, including the evidence I showed earlier (Garner et al., 1966), that an increased interstimulus difference can increase information transmission. However, when the sawtooth pairing was used, information transmission jumped by a truly substantial amount. So it looks as though integrality may provide some improvement even with linear pairing, but that a much greater gain is obtained with the sawtooth pairing.

The second pair of dimensions is crucial. Lightness of a patch paired with loudness of a tone provide separable dimensions if ever there were such. When values on these two dimensions were paired in linear fashion, there was no gain.

TABLE 7.1

Information Transmissions (bits) for Three Pairs of Dimensions,
with Dimensions Used Alone or in Two Types of Redundant Pairing Shown in Fig. 7.13
Absolute Judgments of 10 Levels of Each Dimension (Data from Lockhead, 1970)

Dimension X	Dimension Y	X Alone	Y Alone	Linear pairing	Sawtooth pairing
Hue	Lightness	1.80	1.59	1.99	2.50
Lightness	Loudness	1.65	1.45	1.68	2.29
Roughness	Hue	2.15	2.31	2.65	3.05

That is what we would expect if only stimulus integrality were operative. However, when sawtooth pairing was used, information transmission again jumped dramatically. In fact, the gain in information transmission when sawtooth pairings were used was as great with the separable dimensions of lightness and loudness as with the integral dimensions of hue and lightness. Thus something other than simple interstimulus differences must be operating to produce the great gains found with the sawtooth pairing.

The third pair of dimensions used was roughness and hue, and I present these data less because I understand them than because they raise an intriguing question. A quick summary of the results shows the expected large gain with sawtooth pairings. However, there is also an unexpected gain with linear pairing, the kind of gain that makes us think of integrality again. But roughness and hue? Well, the stimuli were pieces of plastic that were rough on the top and transilluminated from below. Thus the subject saw the hue in the same stimulus that he was feeling to judge its roughness. To put it another way, the two dimensions were in fact in the same stimulus, even though two different sensory modalities were required to get the information into the organism. Perhaps integrality is in the distal stimulus rather than in the proximal stimulus, that which is defined in terms of the input modality. It is an intriguing question.

To summarize at this point is a bit difficult. I am arguing that in absolute-judgment experiments, or other experiments requiring a heavy memory load, some kinds of redundancy improve the ability of the organism to remember the different possible stimuli and their correct response designations. The problem is complicated by the fact that an increased interstimulus difference in a set of stimuli also produces some improvement in performance with absolute judgment. Thus improvement may occur if dimensional integrality increases the interstimulus differences, even when the inefficient linear pairing is used. However, if a sawtooth pairing is used, a substantial gain occurs even with clearly separable dimensions. This gain must be due to the improved ability for the subject to keep the alternative stimuli straightened out in his memory. Lockhead himself suggests that the improvement is due to the subject's ability to keep things better separated in a multidimensional memory space. In other words, the subject has a kind of cognitive memory space, and he locates objects in that space. Some spacings make it easier for the subject to keep things sorted out than others. Alternatively, as with the judgment of forms, the memory load may in fact be reduced because each stimulus provides a context for judgment. Whatever the exact mechanism, it is clear that memory factors play an important part in information transmission.

One last comment before leaving this problem concerns the relations between different kinds of experiments in trying to sort out the different factors involved in information integration. In the last two lectures, I based my argument concerning the distinction between integral and separable dimensions on experiments that have little or no memory factor. Direct similarity judgments do not require memory for the entire set of stimuli, although there is some problem of response context in such experiments. Free-classification experiments again put no load on the memory system, because all stimuli to be classified are right out there for the subject to see. Still further, experiments involving discrimination between two alternative stimuli put a minimum load on memory, as do those involving constrained classification of orthogonal sets of four stimuli.

The absolute-judgment experiments are the ones that are almost certainly limited by memory, or what Garner and Creelman (1964) called judgmental factors. That is, what gives the subject trouble in these experiments is not perceiving the stimulus accurately. Rather, it is in trying to remember and make a decision about which is the correct response label. But because the limitation in such tasks is due to a memory (or judgment) factor does not mean, as we have seen, that redundancy cannot improve performance. Information is indeed integrated, but for purposes not of improving interstimulus discriminability but of improving the internal representation of the entire set of stimuli and their responses.

REDUNDANCY THAT IMPROVES NUMERIC PROCESSING

There is one last type of processing in which information integration can and does occur, and that is numeric processing. In early models attempting to help us understand the role of redundancy in information processing, it was usually assumed that the underlying process was one involving numeric processing or

TABLE 7.2

Information Transmission (bits) for Absolute Judgments of One or Two Identical Stimuli, at Two Durations Per Stimulus, with Fifteen Levels of the Dimension of Brightness
(Data from Flowers, 1973)

| Duration | | Two repeated | |
(sec)	One	Simultaneously	Sequentially
0.1	2.31	2.31	2.48
2.0	2.48	2.52	2.63

TABLE 7.3

Information Transmission (bits) for Absolute Judgments of One or Two Identical Stimuli,
at Two Durations Per Stimulus, with Fifteen Levels of the Dimension of Hue
(Data from Flowers, 1973)

| Duration | | Two repeated | |
(sec)	One	Simultaneously	Sequentially
0.1	2.19	2.24	2.33
2.0	2.49	2.52	2.46

its equivalent. For such models, and such processing, the concept of perceptual independence is indeed crucial. Although I have been talking about mechanisms in information processing for which numeric models are not particularly pertinent in aiding our understanding, we must consider that under some circumstances exactly such a form of processing does occur.

Presumably, if numeric processing is used, information integration of two or more sources of information, usually dimensions, occurs by some sort of averaging process, and it is in this averaging process that the concept of perceptual independence, or zero correlation between the different information channels, is required. Such noncorrelation goes with, or even implies, separable dimensions. Certainly a numeric averaging process cannot occur with integral dimensions, since such dimensions cannot be processed separately enough for the averaging to occur, either actually or hypothetically.

Have we any evidence that redundancy can improve numeric information processing when the dimensions are separable? Lockhead (1966b), using absolute judgments, showed that when correlated dimensions of hue and brightness were presented as sequentially separate stimuli, there was some increase in information transmission, even though when these same dimensions were presented separately side by side there was no improvement. (Remember that these two dimensions in a single stimulus are integral, so an information gain is obtained with that condition. Here we are concerned with whether it can also be obtained when the dimensions are made separable in time and/or space.)

Flowers (1973) carried out experiments to clarify this finding more fully, with some results shown in Table 7.2. The numbers are information transmissions obtained from absolute judgments of 15 different stimuli. Brightness was the stimulus dimension, presented tachistoscopically in a single chip, in two chips side by side for simultaneous presentation, or in two chips presented in sequence. Two different exposure durations were used for each stimulus presentation, with a 0.5 sec delay between the end of the first stimulus and the beginning of the next for sequential presentation. Whenever two chips were used, they had the same brightness; that is, a linear pairing of the two dimensions was used. As the data in Table 7.2 show, there was no improvement in information transmission with simultaneous stimuli, at either short- or long-exposure duration, but there was

TABLE 7.4

Information Transmission (bits) for Absolute Judgments of the Better of Either Hue or Brightness, or Both, at Two Durations Per Stimulus, Fifteen Levels Per Dimension (Data from Flowers, 1973)

Duration	Better	Hue and Brightness	
(sec)	single	Simultaneously	Sequentially
0.1	2.33	2.37	2.46
2.0	2.52	2.69	2.86

a modest gain when the stimuli were presented sequentially. This gain would suggest that there is greater perceptual independence with the longer time of presentation with sequential presentation—a not unreasonable outcome. Thus even when the dimension is literally the same, differing only by being repeated, there can be an improvement in information processing with redundant dimensions.

Table 7.3 shows comparable data when hue was the stimulus dimension. Once again there was little improvement when the same stimulus was repeated simultaneously, but there was some improvement when it was repeated sequentially at the short duration. There was no improvement with sequential presentation at the longer duration, but Flowers attributes this to an offsetting color-adaptation effect, in which hues lose saturation on continued exposure.

Table 7.4 shows what happens when hue and brightness are used as the two dimensions. The control condition for such a comparison must be, for each individual subject, the better of the two dimensions used singly, and the averages of these are shown in the first column. At the short duration, there was still little improvement in performance with simultaneous presentation of hue and brightness, although once again the improvement with sequential presentation does occur. At the longer duration, there is improvement both with simultaneous and sequential presentation. This even greater improvement with hue and brightness used redundantly suggests that perceptual independence is greater if the dimensions are different than if they are the same except for being separated in space or time.

TABLE 7.5

Percent Accuracy of Identification of Letters (A, T, or U) and Landolt Rings (Four Orientations) with One or Four Identical Stimuli (Data from Keeley and Doherty, 1968)

Kind of stimuli	Number of identical stimuli		
	One	Four simultaneous	Four successive
Letters	51	68	70
Landolt rings	52	50	73

hue and brightness were used in separate stimuli

These results show that information can be integrated when the most likely process is one of numeric processing They also show, however, that the effectiveness of the integration is greater if it can be done over a longer time. And, of course, the need for the redundancy in this task was due primarily to a process limitation.

There is one last experiment I want to mention because I think that it demonstrates once again that the experimental result depends on the limitation that makes redundancy valuable. Table 7.5 shows some results of a pair of experiments carried out by Keeley and Doherty (1968). The task was one of identification, with brief tachistoscopic exposure of stimuli. In one experiment, the stimulus alternatives were the three letters A, T, or U. These stimuli were presented either singly or as four identical stimuli, and in the latter case, either simultaneously or successively. Considerable improvement in accuracy was obtained with either redundant condition. This result for simultaneous presentation is what we would expect, because of the high discriminability between the stimulus alternatives (thus no process limitation) and therefore the knowledge that errors were occurring because of a state limitation. (See also Eriksen and Lappin, 1965.) These data show that the same result occurs if the stimulus repetition is done over time, a very reasonable result indeed.

The important point to me is the entirely different result occurring in the second experiment, when the stimuli were the four alternative locations of a gap in Landolt rings (up, right, down, or left). With these stimuli, there is no improved performance when four identical stimuli are presented simultaneously. This failure to obtain a gain suggests that the need for redundancy was due to process limitations in this case, and the actual exposure durations used by the authors were considerably greater for the Landolt rings than for the letters. However, notice that with repetition over time, there once again is a gain, a result in line with those of Lockhead (1966b) and Flowers (1973) for process-limited conditions.

Thus once again we have evidence that information integration can occur over time with process-limited information sources. I do not care to speculate on the exact form in which the integration takes place, and Doherty and Keeley (1969) themselves argue for a form of Bayesian integration of information. I am content to have shown that we can separate out different reasons for inadequate performance and that different kinds of redundancy will be effective depending on the nature of the limitation.

SUMMARY

In summary:

1. Information integration can occur with separable redundant dimensions. However, in order for redundancy to improve performance, there must be a need for it. The nature of the need will itself determine what kind of redundancy will make information integration effective.

2. One major distinction concerning the need for redundancy is that between state and process. A process limitation occurs when some aspect of the processing task as defined cannot be handled. A state limitation occurs when the stimulus does not effectively get into the organism for processing. There are related distinctions concerning the nature of perceptual independence: There can be state correlation, which concerns only a correlation of level of performance. Alternatively, there can be several kinds of process correlation in which there is some form of interaction between two dimensions or channels of information.

3. If the need for redundancy is due to a state limitation, then redundancy that simply repeats the stimulus is effective in improving performance.

4. There are several ways other than dimensional integrality in which redundancy of dimensions can offset process limitation. One such way occurs when two redundant dimensions combine to form a new dimension that is easier to use than either dimension alone.

5. Another way is for the redundant dimensions to make it easier for the organism to handle a large set of alternatives in memory. In this case the particular pairings of levels on dimensions can be crucial.

6. A last way is for redundant dimensions to make possible integration of numeric information. Repetition of process-limited stimuli over time provides such improvement, although the improvement is greater if two different dimensions are presented in sequence.

REFERENCES

Doherty, M. E., & Keeley, S. M. A Bayesian prediction of four-look recognition performance from one-look data. *Perception & Psychophysics,* 1969, **5**, 362–364.

Eriksen, C. W., & Hake, H. W. Multidimensional stimulus differences and accuracy of discrimination. *Journal of Experimental Psychology,* 1955, **50**, 153–160.

Eriksen, C. W., & Lappin, J. S. Internal perceptual system noise and redundancy in simultaneous inputs in form identification. *Psychonomic Science,* 1965, **2**, 351–352.

Felfoldy, G. L. Repetition effects in choice reaction time to multidimensional stimuli. *Perception & Psychophysics,* 1974, in press.

Flowers, J. H. The effect of simultaneous and sequential presentation of stimulus dimensions on absolute judgment accuracy. *Perception & Psychophysics,* 1973, in press.

Flowers, J. H., & Garner, W. R. The effect of stimulus element redundancy on speed of discrimination as a function of state and process limitation. *Perception & Psychophysics,* 1971, **9**, 158–160.

Garner, W. R. Discussion on data presentation. In F. A. Geldard (Ed.), *Communication processes.* New York: Pergamon, 1965.

Garner, W. R. The stimulus in information processing. *American Psychologist,* 1970, **25**, 350–358.

Garner, W. R. Information integration and form of encoding. In A. W. Melton & E. Martin (Eds.), *Coding processes in human memory.* Washington: V. H. Winston, 1972.

Garner, W. R., & Creelman, C. D. Effect of redundancy and duration on absolute judgments of visual stimuli. *Journal of Experimental Psychology,* 1964, **67**, 168–172.

Garner, W. R., & Flowers, J. H. The effect of redundant stimulus elements on visual discrimination as a function of element heterogeneity, equal discriminability, and position uncertainty. *Perception & Psychophysics,* 1969, **6**, 216–220.

Garner, W. R., Kaplan, G., & Creelman, C. D. Effect of stimulus range, duration, and contrast on absolute judgments of visual size. *Perceptual and Motor Skills,* 1966, **22**, 635–644.

Garner, W. R., & Lee, W. An analysis of redundancy in perceptual discrimination. *Perceptual and Motor Skills,* 1962, **15**(4), 367–388.

Garner, W. R., & Morton, J. Perceptual independence: Definitions, models, and experimental paradigms. *Psychological Bulletin,* 1969, **72**, 233–259.

Helson, H. *Adaptation-level theory.* New York: Harper & Row, 1964.

Imai, S., & Handel, S. Hierarchical stimulus and preference structures in the classification of one-dimensional stimuli. *Japanese Psychological Research,* 1971, **13**, 192–206.

Keeley, S. M., & Doherty, M. E. Simultaneous and successive presentations of single-featured and multi-featured visual forms: Implications for the parallel processing hypothesis. *Perception & Psychophysics,* 1968, **4**, 296–298.

Lockhead, G. R. Effects of dimensional redundancy on visual discrimination. *Journal of Experimental Psychology,* 1966, **72**, 95–104. (a)

Lockhead, G. R. Visual discrimination and methods of presenting redundant stimuli. *Proceedings of the 74th Annual Convention of the American Psychological Association,* 1966, 67–68. (b)

Lockhead, G. R. Identification and the form of multidimensional discrimination space. *Journal of Experimental Psychology,* 1970, **85**, 1–10.

Pachella, R. G., & Fisher, D. F. Effect of stimulus degradation and similarity on the trade-off between speed and accuracy in absolute judgments. *Journal of Experimental Psychology,* 1969, **81**, 7–9.

Pomerantz, J. R., & Garner, W. R. Stimulus configuration in selective attention tasks. *Perception & Psychophysics,* 1973, in press.

Weintraub, D. J. Rectangle discriminability: Perceptual relativity and the law of Prägnanz. *Journal of Experimental Psychology,* 1971, **88**, 1–11.

LECTURE 8
SOME PERVASIVE PRINCIPLES

In this last lecture I will add no new substantive material. I think that you, and I too, for that matter, have had enough of experiments, results, and the concepts that have come from them. In this lecture I want to survey the entire research program of which I have been a part and which I have been reporting here. Are there any general principles, either about perception and information processing, or about the metascience which guides us in our research, which are truly pervasive? I think there are, and these are what I want to discuss in this lecture. Some of the ideas I will discuss were mentioned briefly in my first lecture in order to introduce the concept of structure. In this lecture I want to elaborate on these ideas and the issues behind them.

As I have thought about the principles that seem most pervasive throughout this research, it seems to me that nearly all of them can be encompassed in the epistemological position of critical realism. Epistemology is, of course, the philosopher's specialty concerned with the nature of knowing. It is not unlike the psychologist's specialty concerned with perception. The realist position, whether for the epistemologist or psychologist, is that there is a real world, one whose existence is quite independent of the existence of a knower or a perceiver. Or in today's terms, information exists whether or not an information processor is around to process it. The contrasting point of view is idealism, the view that reality is in the mind of the perceiver. In psychology, perhaps the term subjectivism would more readily connote the contrast; so I say I am a realist, not a subjectivist.

I am, however, a critical realist, not what is called a naive or simple realist. The naive realist believes that we perceive the real world in a fairly direct fashion. As a critical realist, I do not think we do, but feel rather that there is a considerable "critical" aspect to perception and information processing.

There is a dual theoretical or philosophical problem which exists for those of us working in information processing, perception, or just plain knowing. This dual problem is that we need to have a theoretical position about the perceiving organism itself and also about ourselves as scientists who are perceiving, through our experimental or other observations, what the organism who is the object of our study does. In other words, we as scientists are also trying to know, and what we are trying to know is how ordinary organisms know. It is, I think, permissible to have one epistemological position for the organisms we study and a different one for ourselves as studiers, on the grounds that the special techniques, rules, and paraphernalia, which we as scientists have, make possible some magical thing called the scientific method, and that by this method we come to know in ways fundamentally different from the ways in which ordinary mortals, i.e., the subjects in our experiments, come to know.

While this dual position can be defended, I do not choose to do so. I think that critical realism is the correct epistemological position both with respect to the information processors we study in our experiments and with respect to ourselves as scientists. I would like to elaborate on these two aspects of the role of critical realism as the pervasive principle throughout the research I have reported.

CRITICAL REALISM FOR THE PERCEIVER

First, let us consider critical realism for the perceiver, the information processor. I would like to separate the concept of critical realism into its two parts: that pertaining to realism and that pertaining to the modifier "critical." I consider the two words in the term to represent the contributions of the real world and of the processing organism to the total picture. Realism says there is an objectively verifiable world out there for the organism to know. But "critical" says that the organism who is trying to know or do something about that world enters into the picture as well. The organism is not simply a passive accepter of information, like the film in a camera. Quite the contrary. The organism actively engages in the knowledge process, by interacting with the real world.

The Real World

As I remarked in the first lecture, the concept of structure is a stimulus concept, one pertaining to the real world and not one subjectively created by an organism. We all find it easy to accept the fact that simple stimulus dimensions, such as energy, time, frequency, length, and other such, are dimensions of a physically real world. We also feel comfortable stating that these exist independently of a perceiver. At least I hope not many of us are concerned about that old saw so frequently used in introductory psychology textbooks, the one about the bell ringing in the desert with nobody to hear it, or is it the tree falling in the forest? At any rate, the question is whether sound exists. Of course physical sound exists, and we have available all sorts of physical operations to demonstrate its existence. There simply was no perception of the sound. The extreme subjectivistic idea that reality can only be in a perception and not in the world outside clearly is utterly untenable to a psychologist with an information-processing point of view: There must be information before we can ask how it is processed.

What seems to cause us more trouble is when higher-order properties are also ascribed to a real world which is objectively independent of a perceiver. James Gibson (e.g., 1966) has made the point many times that there is a true psychophysics of perception, based upon identifiable higher-order properties of a real physical world, such properties as textures and gradients. In the context of my research, I want to make the same argument. Structure is truly part of the physical world and can be defined independently of the perceiver of it. And concepts related to it are also part of the real world. Thus for me to talk about a dimensional structure is to talk about a property of the real world which does not depend on the processing of it by a human organism. When I say that two dimensions are correlated, I do not mean that they are perceived as one; I mean that they are correlated in objective fact. And when I manipulate sets of stimuli so that sometimes the set is orthogonal, and I arrange different classifications of it, these are all manipulations of properties of a real world.

I truly have difficulty on this point, because it is so patent to me that structure and related concepts are the properties of a real world that I cannot comprehend why anybody feels otherwise. Structure is what I manipulate in my experiments, and I arrange all these things long before bringing an experimental subject into the process. When the subject is brought in, it is for the express purpose of finding out what consequences my manipulations of structure have on the subject's performance. When people argue that structure is a subjective property, one only imputed to the world by the organism, I feel that a far greater degree of anthropocentrism (or perhaps egocentrism) remains in our objective discipline than most of us would otherwise want to admit. It is the child who thinks he creates what he perceives. But as the child grows up, he learns that things remain stable in a real world, even when his percepts of them change. I would hope that we adult psychologists can equally accept the fact that structure and related properties are external to the perceiving and processing organism and do not necessarily change when the organism's percepts change.

The Critical Perceiver

What then is the role of the perceiving organism? It is to add various rational processes, so that the organism can come to know the real world and to process information about it effectively. This is the "critical" part of critical realism, the part contributed by the organism. It is the addition of rationality to the perceptual process, and the organism does this in a number of ways.

One of the things the organism does is to seek information that is not immediately available. This is the process most emphasized by Gibson, and most appropriate to his particular interests. But it is also appropriate to such tasks as concept learning, in which the subject is required to learn a classification or structure specified by the experimenter. The subject will seek additional information to clarify the nature of the classification rule, and we saw in the fourth lecture that such information is used more effectively if the structure of the subsets forming the classes is made to be more easily perceivable.

Another rational function performed by the organism is to select structure from that available in the real world. This I consider to be an especially important function for the organism, and understanding what structure is selected has been a large part of the research described in several lectures. For example, we learned that the goodness of patterns is a function of the number of alternatives, and in the case of the visual patterns, this number of alternatives is meaningfully determined by the number of equivalent patterns formed from rotations and reflections. We had, however, no convincing *a priori* knowledge that these physical structural properties of rotation and reflection would be so pertinent to the rated goodness. It might have been that only rotations were important. Or possibly neither of these was important, and the number of equivalent patterns (as psychologically important) might have been based upon the number of alternative patterns that could be generated by moving one dot just one space vertically or horizontally. This operation too would be an objective one, pertinent to a real world, but not necessarily pertinent to any known perceptual process.

Consider another topic we discussed from the point of view of selection of structure. In the fifth lecture I described research that began to differentiate between integral and separable dimensions. With direct similarity scaling we found that some dimension pairs led to an Euclidean metric and others to a city-block metric. In either case, I would state that that was the metric structure as perceived. But surely you must understand that for any set of stimuli, at least those generated by metric dimensions, both metric structures exist in the stimuli. The psychological question is simply which one is perceived by the human organism. Or let us carry this illustration a little further. Remember my argument that when the city-block metric holds, the perception is really of a dimensional structure, and not of a distance structure at all. But once again, for any set of stimuli based on metric dimensions, there in fact is a distance structure, even one based on Euclidean geometry. There is also a dimensional structure which is independent of the distance structure. The psychological question is simply whether the dimensional or the similarity structure is pertinent to the organism. Such research does not ask which exists in the physical world, since both do. Thus the only meaningful psychological question concerns the choice or utilization of one structure rather than the other. You may recall my talking about this problem by saying that for integral dimensions, dimensions exist only for the experimenter and not for his subject. Translate this to mean that they exist in the real world, can therefore be measured and manipulated by the experimenter, but that such structure is irrelevant to the processing human.

A last example of information or structure selection is a fairly obvious one. When we use a concept of dimensional preference, we make the point about selection quite explicitly. A set of stimuli is structured with respect to several dimensions, but the dimensions may have different degrees of salience for the subject. Thus in many tasks it will appear that some dimensions are functional and others are not. But if, to illustrate, a subject did not pay attention to (i.e., use) a particular dimension in his classification, we do not conclude that the dimension does not exist in the real world. We correctly conclude only that it was of little or no importance to the subject.

In dealing with the real world, the subjects in our experiments act as though they expect the world to be structured, and that their task is to seek or select structure. When this assumption turns out to be incorrect, however, very inefficient performance may occur. In the fourth lecture I mentioned research done by Whitman and Garner (1963) on a concept task with a simple correlational structure and one with a complex structure composed of interactions. This latter type of structure (again a real-world concept) is not easily perceived, and in such cases the better learning technique would be for the subject to settle down to a sheer rote-learning procedure, dull as that might be. Our analyses showed that the subjects kept assuming that there was some fairly simple structure, and of course this assumption only led to trouble for them.

Subjects also assume that structure will be consistent, whatever it is. In the information-processing experiments that Garner and Felfoldy (1970) carried out, they used both orthogonal and correlated dimensions in different parts of the same experiment. But when using the correlated dimensions, subjects were still asked to sort by one dimension and then also by the other. We were amazed to find that with separable dimensions they gave performance appropriate to the dimension by which they were told to sort, when in some circumstances they could have greatly improved their performance by using the correlated dimension. We suspected that the reason lay in the fact that they at some times also had to sort stimuli formed from orthogonal dimensions, and in these cases it would have been disastrous to attempt to use the alternative dimension. So in a later experiment (Felfoldy & Garner, 1971) we ran some subjects without their ever having to sort with orthogonal dimensions. In this case many of the subjects did in fact use the alternative correlated dimension when it was easier to do so. There is a moral here about the subject responding to the entire experimental context, but I will not pursue it further.

Structure and the Single Stimulus

One topic that always causes some difficulty in the matter of separating what is in the physically real part of critical realism and what is in the critical organism concerns the role of the single stimulus in perceived structure. I have pointed out that the concept of structure requires the existence of sets of stimuli, not single stimuli. But then I have also argued that any single stimulus leads to an inferred subset and total set of stimuli, and that the single stimulus then has structure by being a member of these different sets and subsets. But does such a process belie my argument that structure is a stimulus property? I think not, because we can still show that the stimulus implies what the subject infers. Thus we do not need to retreat to a subjectivist position on this matter; we simply accept the fact that the organism has more work to do when only a single stimulus must be dealt with.

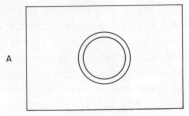

FIG. 8.1. Stimulus A.

I think I can illustrate this point, as well as elaborate on some of these concepts about structure, with the following illustration: Figure 8.1 shows a stimulus, labeled A. The rectangle is intended to represent the bounds of a card on which the stimulus is presented, so it really just frames the stimulus, rather than being part of it. What I would like each of you to do is describe the stimulus. I know, based on preliminary and casual testing, that most people describe it as a circle, perhaps as a double circle, or as a circle with two lines. Some are a bit more elaborate, and describe the stimulus as two concentric circles.

Now consider this same stimulus along with another one, stimulus B, both shown in Fig. 8.2. Once again I will ask you to describe stimulus A but keep in mind that stimulus B is also there. Is it clear that the size of the concentric circles now has to be mentioned to differentiate stimulus A from stimulus B? Few people bother to mention the size of the circle when they see just stimulus A. But it does have a size, as well as a form and a number of circles. The decision to describe the form and number of circles and not to describe the size is a decision to consider some properties of the stimulus as relevant and others as irrelevant. The addition of another stimulus producing variation in a property formerly considered irrelevant makes it become relevant.

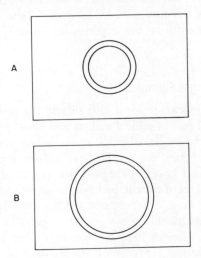

FIG. 8.2. Stimulus A in the context of stimulus B.

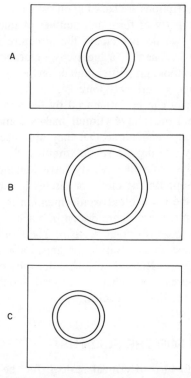

FIG. 8.3. Stimulus A in the context of stimuli B and C.

Now consider stimulus A along with stimulus B, but with stimulus C added, in Fig. 8.3. Please again describe stimulus A, but keep in mind that stimuli B and C are in the total picture. Few people, if any, bother to mention location of the concentric circles until it is deliberately varied, because the location somehow seems an irrelevant property of the stimulus. But even in Fig. 8.1 stimulus A did have a location within the rectangle, just as it had a size.

We could, of course, continue the process. Nobody, for example, thinks of mentioning the thickness of the lines, or the contrast of the lines against the background, or even the fact that the lines forming the circles are solid rather than broken. Some will mention that the lines are black, but not many will.

Perhaps the points I am trying to make are now clear. The single stimulus has no meaning except in a context of alternatives. When somebody uses the term circle, they infer that it could have been some other form, such as square or triangle. When somebody says there are two circles, or that the circle has two lines, they inferred the alternative of fewer or more lines. Each descriptive term used defines what the alternatives are, by defining what the stimulus is not. Thus the organism infers sets of stimulus alternatives, and without these inferred sets, no one can describe the single stimulus.

Nevertheless, the descriptions are based upon the stimulus properties. As I noted, the stimulus has the property of form and number of lines, but it has many other properties as well. So we do not create the structure that makes the stimulus meaningful—we select it. There is a hierarchy of properties or dimensions, and our descriptions use only those properties high up on the list of all possible properties, a list which is, incidentally, infinitely long.

But even this hierarchy can be influenced by the stimulus properties. We saw that the addition of real alternative stimuli makes some dimensional properties move up in the hierarchy, enough so that they are described. But the hierarchy can also be changed by altering the single stimulus. Suppose the circle had been drawn with a single line. Would anybody have bothered to mention that fact? I am quite sure not. Suppose the circle or circles had been drawn in red. Now I am sure that all but the color blind would mention the color, even though few mention the color when the circles are drawn in black.

So the perceptual process is critical realism. The world is real, and this reality includes things such as structure. But the organism also interacts with this reality to seek and select structure. Rarely, however, does the organism create structure. There is no need. Structure is everywhere to be found, and the information-processing organism need only look, find, and select.

CRITICAL REALISM FOR THE SCIENTIST

Now I would like to turn to critical realism for the scientist. How does he come to know that which he is seeking? If there is a difference between the ordinary perceiver as knower and the scientist as knower, I think it is in the greater role played by the critical aspect of critical realism for the scientist. I accept realism on the grounds that I do not know how to function as a scientist unless I accept it. Thus the epistemological position of realism is required for the scientist on pragmatic grounds if not on other grounds. Unless there is something real for us to know, I cannot justify all of the time, effort, and cost we put into knowing. Furthermore, I assume that the world we are trying to know is a structured world, an orderly one, and that my function as a scientist is to discover this structure.

The special skill of the scientist in knowing may to some extent be in the devices available to him to increase observational accuracy—devices such as microscopes and cathode ray tubes. But the greater skill is primarily a matter of his having better rational and critical processes to aid in the seeking and selection of structure. These are the things I want to talk about.

Converging Operations

The concept of converging operations (Garner, 1954; Garner, Hake, & Eriksen, 1956) is the key concept to me, and it is actually the specification of a critical realist's position in science. The basic idea is that we come to know things, usually described as concepts, by carrying out two or more experimental operations that converge on the single concept. A concept that is synonymous with a single operation is nothing more than a restatement of an experimental result. But a concept that arises as a consequence of converging operations has a reality that is independent of any single experimental observation. With sufficient ingenuity in developing observational procedures that provide convergence, we can come to know things that we cannot know from direct observation, because they are inaccessible to us. Memory, encoding, and perception itself are all such unobservable processes, things that occur in the organism, and that we can come to know by observing only inputs and outputs of the organism. However, we must have a variety of inputs and outputs, differing in their nature, to allow convergence to meaningful concepts that are in fact independent of any single observation or experimental result.

The best example of the formal use of converging operations in research that I have reported is the experiments Garner and Felfoldy (1970) carried out, experiments that clarified and provided definition to the concept of dimensional integrality. To remind you, in these experiments we used pairs of dimensions, but rather than using a single pair of dimensions, we used four different pairs, pairs that we hoped would give different results. Then we also used three different tasks with each pair of dimensions. The control task required speeded classification of stimuli varying only in one dimension; a second task required classification of stimuli generated from correlated (redundant) dimensions; and a third task required classification of stimuli generated from orthogonal dimensions. Facilitation could occur with correlated dimensions, and interference could occur with orthogonal dimensions. This joint converging result occurred with some stimulus dimensions and not with others. However, interference and facilitation always went together. Either both occurred or neither occurred.

Of course, if you remember the fifth lecture, you realize that we can also add convergence from direct similarity scaling and free-classification experiments to this list of results indicating that there is a relational property of pairs of dimensions, a property I have called integrality.

I would like to clarify the role of the converging operations further. I consider this set of converging operations to provide the basic definition of dimensional integrality. But these various experimental operations are all different types of psychophysical and information-processing experiments. Does this mean that the concept of dimensional integrality is an organismic concept? I have stated that I think it is a stimulus concept, not an organismic concept, although there are organismic concepts related to it. The fact that we are psychologists and thus use people in our experiments does not mean that we can only learn about people and nothing at all about the stimulus world to which people react. I think that dimensional integrality is a stimulus concept, and a large reason for this is that there seems to be little option on the part of the organism in dealing with integral dimensions. If, however, it is a stimulus concept, then sooner or later shouldn't we be able to specify whether a pair of dimensions is integral or separable without having to run through the set of converging operations? My answer is, yes, sooner or later, even though not now.

A similar problem existed in the research on visual patterns (Garner & Clement, 1963). Our original research simply showed that good patterns were those that subjects also classified into small sets. In fact, we had two experimental results based on two behavioral techniques—goodness ratings and classification—and showed that they were correlated. Such correlational techniques provide a form of convergence themselves. But then having established the concept that good patterns have few alternatives, we sought a physical basis for establishing number of alternatives and found one in rotations and reflections. So pattern goodness and number of alternatives does have a physical basis, a reality in the stimulus world. This process of establishing the existence and nature of a concept based upon psychophysical research and then seeking the physical basis for the concept is actually quite common in the research I have reported.

Variations in Procedures

The importance I feel for converging operations has some general consequences concerning what should be emphasized in the scientific endeavor. If convergence is so important, then our experimental procedures must allow convergence to occur. But before we can get convergence, we must introduce variation in our experimental procedures. There is a fairly common alternative view of science which emphasizes stabilizing on a few techniques, and thus seeking highly reliable concepts based upon the use of a single technique for a single concept. This is the attitude that states that intelligence is what the Stanford-Binet measures. I consider this point of view to be utterly self-defeating in the acquisition of knowledge, because it completely drops the critical part from critical realism.

Since convergence is the central idea, rather than precision of a single technique, then we should feel free to use techniques that are not as precise and reliable as we would otherwise like. The ultimate validity of a concept does not depend on any single procedure, but on a convergent result, so the importance of any one procedure is greatly diminished. We have used some procedures that have not been in the good graces of psychologists in the past few decades, and they have turned out to be extremely beneficial. Two of these which we have used more and more are subjective report and free classification.

To illustrate the use of subjective report, and also to illustrate how much each of us is a product of our times and scientific upbringing, I will describe the background of some of the research I and my co-workers have done on temporal patterns. When Royer and I (1966) first began to investigate the perception of temporal patterns, we naturally built some equipment with which to generate the patterns—many of them, in fact. We weren't quite sure what we were looking for, so we then simply listened to many of the patterns. The nature of the perceptual phenomenon was obvious to us from this listening: The stimulus was first heard as an unrelated sequence of elements but then, often quite suddenly, it became an organized temporal percept. But the number of alternative percepts or perceived structures was rather small.

Then we tried to figure out how to do an experiment on the matter, and we first thought of having subjects track the patterns by tapping them out in synchrony on two keys. After all, you cannot do psychological research without having a response, so we were seeking one; and even more, there should be one response per stimulus element, just as in all those learning experiments. What happened is that the attempt to track the stimuli completely disrupted the perceptual process. We were in a real quandary. After a year of intermittent listening on our part, the flash of insight occurred. Why not let the subject just listen, as we ourselves did, and when he heard the pattern as organized, then tell us about it? And that's what we did. We had him tell us about it by tracking the pattern out on the same two keys we were so rigidly fixated on. It turned out to be very easy to track the pattern once you heard it as an organized pattern, even though it was very difficult before that time. We simply assumed that the subject began tracking at the beginning of the pattern as he heard it, and that therefore the trackings did give us a description. We felt very pleased with ourselves for having rediscovered how to understand perception: Use descriptions, even if done with the hands rather than the mouth.

Garner and Gottwald (1967) later studied the learning of temporal patterns. We used quite a slow rate of presentation so that we could expect the subject to give a response in anticipation of each element, in the usual fashion of learning experiments. We, of course, were then going to analyze the locations of errors in learning to try to understand something about the perception of the patterns that were being learned. Shortly after the data collection began, Gottwald, who was then my research assistant, came to my office and suggested that we simply ask the subjects, after learning was complete, to describe what they learned—to tell us, in other words, what it was they had learned. After feeling foolish for not having thought of that myself, I agreed. That verbal description gave us more information than any other measure we took in the experiment. I am a slow learner on these things, but since then we have used some form of description by the subject in every experiment on temporal patterns. The profit has been great.

The other technique that my co-workers and I have used with valuable consequences is free classification. I will not describe any experiments here because they are described in the fifth lecture. But I will remark that they differentiate types of relation between dimensions at least as well, and I believe better, than do experiments using direct similarity scaling. More patterns of results can emerge with the free-classification technique.

Basically what we are doing with the use of techniques such as verbal description and free classification is to put less constraint on the subject. In order to use the more traditional constrained techniques, such as we use in our speeded classification tasks, we need to know quite a lot before setting up the experiment. We need to know enough to use the right constraints, and if we are wrong, then we can end up learning remarkably little from our experiments, or even worse, learning something that later turns out to be wrong. Furthermore, in our experience, it really turns out not to be that difficult to use the less constrained techniques. They can be used along with other techniques, in such a way as to provide effective convergence, often by simply adding a small amount to the experiment. When we added the verbal description in the Garner and Gottwald research, it took less than half a minute to have the subject describe what he had learned after he had taken perhaps half an hour to learn it. But we gained enormously.

Just a last comment on this topic. I am all for these freer techniques. But please remember that I am arguing for them as additional techniques rather than as substitute techniques. The key idea is variety of technique, and these freer techniques provide additional variety. To use only them would be as costly as to use only the more constrained techniques.

Scope of Investigation

Another consequence of the emphasis on converging operations concerns the scope of the investigation. If convergence is crucial in the scientific process, then we should not only increase the variety of our experimental procedures, but we should also increase the scope of our investigations. Let me try to be more explicit about this point. Note that the entire idea of converging operations decreases the importance of hypothesis testing as the main scientific procedure, while increasing the importance of having a large number of operations converging on the single concept. Parsimony of concept is, in this way of thinking, more important than the precise tying of concept to experimental operation. And particularly unimportant is having a very exact hypothesis before undertaking the experimental observations. What does become important is having some assurance that the concept resulting from the research is truly applicable to all instances that reasonably belong in the same population of instances.

Systematic variation of the realm of observation may further delimit and clarify the emergent concept. Such was the case when Felfoldy and I (Garner & Felfoldy, 1970) used several different pairs of dimensions in our experiments. I will not attempt a history of the research that has asked the question of whether irrelevant dimensions increase the time required for classification or discrimination. Almost every single experiment has used one set of dimensions, I presume arbitrarily selected. But the proper question was not whether such interference occurs, but rather under what circumstances it occurs. You can only answer a question of this sort by increasing the number of circumstances (in this case, pairs of dimensions) you investigate. When we did this, the concept of stimulus integrality became very clear.

I think I would argue that it is almost impossible for such a concept to have arisen in the tradition of psychology that assumes, as I once remarked (Garner, 1970), that a "stimulus is a stimulus is a stimulus, whose only function is to elicit behavior [p. 357]." As much as I generally like the information-processing approach to the study of perception, I do at times worry that the stimulus, that which provides the information part of information processing, is being neglected too much. We must understand the nature of information if we are to understand its processing.

Another consequence of expanding the realm of observation is to increase the generality of the concept and therefore our confidence that we are on the right track in understanding the object of study. This principle is best illustrated in our studies of pattern perception, both spatial and temporal. In the different studies in which we used spatial patterns, we always used all patterns of a defined population of patterns. For example, initially we generated and used all patterns of five dots in the nine cells of the matrix, although at the very beginning we unnecessarily omitted those in which a row or column of the matrix was empty. In later stages of the research, as we gained confidence that our concepts were general, we then selected a smaller number of patterns to work with.

In our studies of temporal pattern perception we did the same thing. In the first experiment we used every single pattern of eight dichotomous elements that could be generated, and in a later experiment we used all nine-event patterns. What is the advantage of such an approach to research? Primarily its advantage is in preventing our making the wrong selection of patterns, patterns that might inadvertently fit in with our preconceived notions about the nature of the process we are studying. And, of course, with the broad-spectrum approach, whatever concepts emerge from the research have greater generality.

Consider, for example, our evidence that the difficulty of perceiving a temporal pattern is related to the number of perceived alternative organizations, and that this number can be understood as the consequence of factors related to the fact that each element can be considered as a one-element temporal pattern. These principles emerged from a series of experiments all using large populations of patterns. What is the alternative approach? One alternative would be to generate an hypothesis, consider meaningful alternatives, select a few patterns to discriminate between them, and carry out the experiment. Suppose we hypothesize that pattern difficulty is related to the number of runs. We would have absolutely no difficulty selecting "crucial" patterns to test this hypothesis and finding confirmation of it. But we can also select another set of "crucial" patterns and find disconfirmation. The point is that the number of runs, while of some importance, is not a primary factor in pattern difficulty, but it can appear to be so with a restricted selection of patterns for testing.

Are there any obvious difficulties with this approach to research? There is one that has stood out in my experience. This approach, which emphasizes allowing concepts to emerge with large variation in technique and with a large scope of investigation, puts a great cognitive load on the experimenter. Hypothetical concepts are not accepted or rejected on the basis of a single t-test, a process that demands little of the researcher. Rather, they come from an examination of large amounts of data, with a constant search for a pattern of results that fits all of the data. I assure you that this procedure can be tiring and frustrating. Furthermore, frequently there are no statistical techniques appropriate to test whether the emergent concepts are statistically significant. In fact, the very idea of statistical tests itself is often quite inappropriate.

Still further, the methods of proof, the means by which you convey to the reader of your research papers that your concepts and explanations are correct, require that this same great cognitive load be put on the reader, and that is really not very nice. We have had problems with publication of much of this research, and I do not feel that the difficulty has been so much with a difference in research style, but is simply related to this problem of a heavy cognitive load on the reader. We have in some articles tried to decrease the cognitive load by pooling data and trying to make the presentation more in the traditional mode. We have then been asked for more data to justify what we are saying. Yet when we have given the large amounts of data, the request has come back for simplification. It is a difficult problem, and I do not see an obvious solution.

NORMATIVE AND DESCRIPTIVE MODELS IN SCIENCE

One last topic, and then my comments are over. Garner and Morton (1969) made a distinction between normative and descriptive models in the science of psychology, and I would like briefly to discuss this distinction because of its relation to the idea of critical realism as the epistemological approach that best typifies the scientific venture.

A descriptive model is, as the term implies, intended to provide a description of some psychological process. It is a model because it represents the process in some symbolic form, either mathematical symbols, little boxes in flow diagrams, or occasionally words, although we are less apt to call the description a model if it is done with words. The function of such models is to be right in correctly describing the processes they are intended to describe, even though we may accept wrongness as a temporary inadequacy, on the grounds that it is the best we can do at the moment.

In a more formal sense, models are often hypotheses about the processes we are studying, and as such are to be judged correct on the basis of experimental results obtained to test the models. It is not sensible to push this type of reasoning too far, because strictly speaking all models must be wrong to some degree since they cannot be completely isomorphic to process. Even though there is some limiting awkwardness in the use of descriptive models, they serve a very important function in psychology, and that is to represent reality. Thus descriptive models are designed to help us, as scientists, to deal with the realism part of critical realism.

Normative models, on the other hand, have a quite different function in the scientific process, and that is to deal with the critical part of critical realism. Normative models are those that are not intended to be an accurate representation of the reality we are trying to understand, but rather they are intended to aid in the rational process that we as scientists use in our search for knowledge. Since I have stated that I think the critical aspect of critical realism is of greater importance for the scientist than for the ordinary perceiver, naturally I feel that normative models have a very important role in science. I suppose if I had to choose, I would feel that they are more important than descriptive models.

What do normative models do, if they are not intended to describe the process we study? In talking about the role of mathematics in science (and to me mathematics is a model system) in 1962, I described what normative models can do this way: "Mathematics may, however, be used as a tool, sometimes a powerful tool, to examine theoretical problems without itself being a theory, nor yet becoming simply a technique for data processing. Mathematics may help us ask questions without presuming answers [p. 15]." This, to me, is the primary function of normative models: to help us ask questions. They may do this in a variety of ways.

Certainly one way is to provide a tool for analyzing the basic nature of the question. To illustrate, perceptual independence is not a unitary concept, and as we saw in the seventh lecture, it is necessary to distinguish between state and process correlation or nonindependence, as well as between several different kinds of process correlation. These distinctions were made with the help of both mathematical and diagrammatic models, but these distinctions were in no way made in order to assert that a particular kind of correlation did or did not exist for human organisms. The distinctions were made only to clarify the fact that the questions experimenters had been asking were not themselves clear, since a single construct was being used where several different constructs were required.

Another thing normative models can do is to provide the concepts themselves, a function even more basic than that of simply clarifying the nature of concepts. I think the concept of correlation is such a case. It can be defined mathematically and given a meaning in terms of the mathematical properties of a correlation coefficient. I hope I have chosen an example in which it is obvious that the concept is not intended to be a descriptive concept pertaining to human behavior, one that is right or wrong. It is a concept that is useful in asking many different kinds of psychological question.

Still another thing that normative models can do is set limits. The concept of a percent is one that may illustrate the point. Suppose I state that in this experiment the subjects made 113 errors. I should receive blank looks, because the number has no meaning without bounds. But if I state that there were 3139 total opportunities for errors, or better still that 3.6 percent errors were made, the number now has a meaning. Once again, however, the concept of a percent, of a normalized total, is not at all intended as a description of the processes we study. It just helps us come to know these processes.

Notice that in all of these examples an evaluation of the normative model would not be in terms of its accuracy in describing a process. Descriptive models are so evaluated, of course. Normative models can be right or wrong, but whether they are right or wrong depends on whether they help us get answers to a question, not on whether they correctly describe a process. Descriptive models must correspond to reality. Normative models must provide us with effective critical operations so that we can be successful critical realists.

Information Theory as Normative Model

Information theory has had an important part to play in information-processing approaches in psychology, and certainly in much of the research I have reported in these lectures. What has its role been? My answer is that it has been valuable primarily as a normative model. It is true that we use the measure of bits of information, but even that use is primarily as a normative model since it allows comparisons across experimental conditions that would be meaningless otherwise. But far more importantly, information theory has provided psychology with the basic concept of information itself, and it has clarified that information is a function not of what the stimulus is, but rather of what it might have been, of its alternatives. And it has made the concept of structure a far more meaningful and useful concept. This last has been its primary contribution to the subject matter of these lectures.

REFERENCES

Felfoldy, G. L., & Garner, W. R. The effects on speeded classification of implicit and explicit instructions regarding redundant dimensions. *Perception & Psychophysics,* 1971, **9**, 289–292.

Garner, W. R. Context effects and the validity of loudness scales. *Journal of Experimental Psychology,* 1954, **48**, 218–224.

Garner, W. R. *Uncertainty and structure as psychological concepts.* New York: Wiley, 1962.

Garner, W. R. The stimulus in information processing. *American Psychologist,* 1970, **25**, 350–358.

Garner, W. R., & Clement, D. E. Goodness of pattern and pattern uncertainty. *Journal of Verbal Learning and Verbal Behavior,* 1963, **2**, 446–452.

Garner, W. R., & Felfoldy, G. L. Integrality of stimulus dimensions in various types of information processing. *Cognitive Psychology,* 1970, **1**, 225–241.

Garner, W. R., & Gottwald, R. L. Some perceptual factors in the learning of sequential patterns of binary events. *Journal of Verbal Learning and Verbal Behavior,* 1967, **6**, 582–589.

Garner, W. R., Hake, H. W., & Eriksen, C. W. Operationism and the concept of perception. *Psychological Review,* 1956, **63**, 149–159.

Garner, W. R., & Morton, J. Perceptual independence: Definitions, models, and experimental paradigms. *Psychological Bulletin,* 1969, **72**, 233–259.

Gibson, J. J. *The senses considered as perceptual systems.* Boston: Houghton Mifflin, 1966.

Royer, F. L., & Garner, W. R. Response uncertainty and perceptual difficulty of auditory temporal patterns. *Perception & Psychophysics,* 1966,**1** , 41–47.

Whitman, J. R., & Garner, W. R. Concept learning as a function of form of internal structure. *Journal of Verbal Learning and Verbal Behavior,* 1963, **2**, 195–202.

THE PROCESSING OF
INFORMATION AND STRUCTURE

INDEXES

AUTHOR INDEX

SUBJECT INDEX

This book was set in Times Roman on a Mergenthaler VIP by David E. Seham Associates, New York.